OSCAR WILDE

HIS LIFE AND CONFESSIONS

VOLUME II

FRANK HARRIS

Oscar Wilde,
His Life and Confessions, Volume 2

Frank Harris

PO Box 2211
Fairfield, IA 52556
www.1stworldlibrary.com
First Edition

LCCN: 2007934128

Softcover ISBN: 978-1-4218-9641-0
Hardcover ISBN: 978-1-4218-9741-7
eBook ISBN: 978-1-4218-9541-3

1st World Library Literary Society

Giving Back to the World

"If you want to work on the core problem, it's early school literacy."

- James Barksdale, former CEO of Netscape

"No skill is more crucial to the future of a child, or to a democratic and prosperous society, than literacy."

- Los Angeles Times

"Literacy... means far more than learning how to read and write... The aim is to transmit... knowledge and promote social participation."

- UNESCO

"Literacy is not a luxury, it is a right and a responsibility. If our world is to meet the challenges of the twenty-first century we must harness the energy and creativity of all our citizens."

- President Bill Clinton

"Parents should be encouraged to read to their children, and teachers should be equipped with all available techniques for teaching literacy, so the varying needs and capacities of individual kids can be taken into account."

- Hugh Mackay

For he who sins a second time
Wakes a dead soul to pain,
And draws it from its spotted shroud,
And makes it bleed again,
And makes it bleed great gouts of blood,
And makes it bleed in vain.

—*The Ballad of Reading Gaol*

BOOK II

CHAPTER XVII

Prison for Oscar Wilde, an English prison with its insufficient bad food[1] and soul-degrading routine for that amiable, joyous, eloquent, pampered Sybarite. Here was a test indeed; an ordeal as by fire. What would he make of two years' hard labour in a lonely cell?

There are two ways of taking prison, as of taking most things, and all the myriad ways between these two extremes; would Oscar be conquered by it and allow remorse and hatred to corrupt his very heart, or would he conquer the prison and possess and use it? Hammer or anvil—which?

Victory has its virtue and is justified of itself like sunshine; defeat carries its own condemnation. Yet we have all tasted its bitter waters: only "infinite virtue" can pass through life victorious, Shakespeare tells us, and we mortals are not of infinite virtue. The myriad vicissitudes of the struggle search out all our weaknesses; test all our powers. Every victory shows a more difficult height to scale, a steeper pinnacle of god-like hardship—that's the reward of victory: it provides the hero with ever-new battle-fields: no rest for him this side the grave.

But what of defeat? What sweet is there in its bitter? This may be said for it; it is our great school: punishment teaches pity, just as suffering teaches sympathy. In defeat the brave soul learns kinship with other men, takes the rub to heart; seeks out the reason for the fall in his own weakness, and ever afterwards finds it impossible to judge, much less condemn his fellow. But after all no one can hurt us but ourselves; prison, hard labour, and the hate of men; what are these if they make you truer, wiser, kinder?

Have you come to grief through self-indulgence and good-living? Here are months in which men will take care that you shall eat badly and lie hard. Did you lack respect for others? Here are men who will show you no consideration. Were you careless of others' sufferings? Here now you shall agonize unheeded: gaolers and governors as well as black cells just to teach you. Thank your stars then for every day's experience, for, when you have learned the lesson of it and turned its discipline into service, the prison shall transform itself into a hermitage, the dungeon into a home; the burnt skilly shall be sweet in your mouth; and your rest on the plank-bed the dreamless slumber of a little child.

And if you are an artist, prison will be more to you than this; an astonishing vital and novel experience, accorded only to the chosen. What will you make of it? That's the question for you. It is a wonderful opportunity. Seen truly, a prison's more spacious than a palace; nay, richer, and for a loving soul, a far rarer experience. Thank then the spirit which steers men for the divine chance which has come to you; henceforth the prison shall be your domain; in future men will not think of it without thinking of you. Others may show them what the good things of life do for one; you will show them what suffering can do, cold and regretful sleepless hours and solitude, misery and distress. Others will teach the lessons of joy. The whole vast underworld of pity and pain, fear and horror and injustice is your kingdom. Men have drawn darkness about you as a curtain, shrouded you in blackest night; the light in you will shine the brighter. Always provided of course that the light is not put out altogether.

Hammer or anvil? How would Oscar Wilde take punishment?

* * * * *

We could not know for months. Yet he was an artist by nature—that gave one a glimmer of hope. We needed it. For outside at first there was an icy atmosphere of hatred and contempt. The mere mention of his name was met with expressions of disgust, or frozen silence.

One bare incident will paint the general feeling more clearly than pages of invective or description. The day after Oscar's sentence Mr. Charles Brookfield, who, it will be remembered, had raked together the witnesses that enabled Lord Queensberry to "justify" his accusation; assisted by Mr. Charles Hawtrey, the actor, gave a dinner to Lord Queensberry to celebrate their triumph. Some forty Englishmen of good position were present at the banquet—a feast to celebrate the ruin and degradation of a man of genius.

Yet there are true souls in England, noble, generous hearts. I remember a lunch at Mrs. Jeune's, where one declared that Wilde was at length enjoying his deserts; another regretted that his punishment was so slight, a third with precise knowledge intimated delicately and with quiet complacence that two years' imprisonment with hard labour usually resulted in idiocy or death: fifty per cent., it appeared, failed to win through. It was more to be dreaded on all accounts than five years' penal servitude. "You see it begins with starvation and solitary confinement, and that breaks up the strongest. I think it will be enough for our vainglorious talker." Miss Madeleine Stanley (now Lady Middleton) was sitting beside me, her fine, sensitive face clouded: I could not contain myself, I was being whipped on a sore.

"This must have been the way they talked in Jerusalem," I remarked, "after the world-tragedy."

"You were an intimate friend of his, were you not?" insinuated the delicate one gently.

"A friend and admirer," I replied, "and always shall be."

A glacial silence spread round the table, while the delicate one smiled with deprecating contempt, and offered some grapes to his neighbour; but help came. Lady Dorothy Nevill was a little further down the table: she had not heard all that was said, but had caught the tone of the conversation and divined the rest.

"Are you talking of Oscar Wilde?" she exclaimed. "I'm glad to hear you say you are a friend. I am, too, and shall always be proud of having known him, a most brilliant, charming man."

"I think of giving a dinner to him when he comes out, Lady Dorothy," I said.

"I hope you'll ask me," she answered bravely. "I should be glad to come. I always admired and liked him; I feel dreadfully sorry for him."

The delicate one adroitly changed the conversation and coffee came in, but Miss Stanley said to me:

"I wish I had known him, there must have been great good in him to win such friendship."

"Great charm in any case," I replied, "and that's rarer among men than even goodness."

The first news that came to us from prison was not altogether bad. He had broken down and was in the infirmary, but was getting better. The brave Stewart Headlam, who had gone bail for him, had visited him, the Stewart Headlam who was an English clergyman, and yet, wonder of wonders, a Christian. A little later one heard that Sherard had seen him, and brought about a reconciliation with his wife. Mrs. Wilde had been very good and had gone to the prison and had no doubt comforted him. Much to be hoped from all this....

For months and months the situation in South Africa took all my heart and mind.

In the first days of January, 1896, came the Jameson Raid, and I sailed for South Africa. I had work to do for *The Saturday Review*, absorbing work by day and night. In the summer I was back in England, but the task of defending the Boer farmers grew more and more arduous, and I only heard that Oscar was going on as well as could be expected.

Some time later, after he had been transferred to Reading Gaol, bad news leaked out, news that he was breaking up, was being punished, persecuted. His friends came to me, asking: could anything be done? As usual my only hope was in the supreme authority. Sir Evelyn Ruggles Brise was the head of the Prison Commission; after the Home Secretary, the most powerful person, the permanent official behind the Parliamentary figure-head; the man who knew and acted behind the man who talked. I sat down and wrote to him for an interview: by return came a courteous note giving me an appointment.

I told him what I had heard about Oscar, that his health was breaking down and his reason going, pointed out how monstrous it was to turn prison into a torture-chamber. To my utter astonishment he agreed with me, admitted, even, that an exceptional man ought to have exceptional treatment; showed not a trace of pedantry; good brains, good heart. He went so far as to say that Oscar Wilde should be treated with all possible consideration, that certain prison rules which pressed very hardly upon him should be interpreted as mildly as possible. He admitted that the punishment was much more severe to him than it would be to an ordinary criminal, and had nothing but admiration for his brilliant gifts.

"It was a great pity," he said, "that Wilde ever got into prison, a great pity."

I was pushing at an open door; besides the year or so which had elapsed since the condemnation had given time for reflection. Still, Sir Ruggles Brise's attitude was extra-ordinary, sympathetic at once and high-minded: another true Englishman at the head of affairs: infinite hope in that fact, and solace.

I had stuck to my text that something should be done at once to give Oscar courage and hope; he must not be murdered or left to despair.

Sir Ruggles Brise asked me finally if I would go to Reading and report on Oscar Wilde's condition and make any suggestion that might occur to me. He did not know if this could be arranged; but he would see the Home Secretary and would recommend it, if I were willing. Of course I was willing, more than willing. Two or three days later, I got another letter from him with another appointment, and again

I went to see him. He received me with charming kindness. The Home Secretary would be glad if I would go down to Reading and report on Oscar Wilde's state.

"Everyone," said Sir Ruggles Brise, "speaks with admiration and delight of his wonderful talents. The Home Secretary thinks it would be a great loss to English literature if he were really injured by the prison discipline. Here is your order to see him alone, and a word of introduction to the Governor, and a request to give you all information."

I could not speak. I could only shake hands with him in silence.

What a country of anomalies England is! A judge of the High Court a hard self-satisfied pernicious bigot, while the official in charge of the prisons is a man of wide culture and humane views, who has the courage of a noble humanity.

I went to Reading Gaol and sent in my letter. I was met by the Governor, who gave orders that Oscar Wilde should be conducted to a room where we could talk alone. I cannot give an account of my interviews with the Governor or the doctor; it would smack of a breach of confidence; besides all such conversations are peculiarly personal: some people call forth the best in us, others the worst. Without wishing to, I may have stirred up the lees. I can only say here that I then learned for the first time the full, incredible meaning of "Man's inhumanity to man."

In a quarter of an hour I was led into a bare room where Oscar Wilde was already standing by a plain deal table. The warder who had come with him then left us. We shook hands and sat down opposite to each other. He had changed greatly. He appeared much older; his dark brown hair was streaked with grey, particularly in front and over the ears. He was much thinner, had lost at least thirty-five pounds, probably forty or more. On the whole, however, he looked better physically than he had looked for years before his imprisonment: his eyes were clear and bright; the outlines of the face were no longer swamped in fat; the voice even was ringing and musical; he had improved bodily, I thought; though in repose his face wore a nervous, depressed and harassed air.

"You know how glad I am to see you, heart-glad to find you looking so well," I began, "but tell me quickly, for I may be able to help you, what have you to complain of; what do you want?"

For a long time he was too hopeless, too frightened to talk. "The list of my grievances," he said, "would be without end. The worst of it is I am perpetually being punished for nothing; this governor loves to punish, and he punishes by taking my books from me. It is perfectly awful to let the mind grind itself away between the upper and nether millstones of regret and remorse without respite; with books my life would be livable—any life," he added sadly.

"The life, then, is hard. Tell me about it."

"I don't like to," he said, "it is all so dreadful—and ugly and painful, I would rather not think of it," and he turned away despairingly.

"You must tell me, or I shall not be able to help you." Bit by bit I won the confession from him.

"At first it was a fiendish nightmare; more horrible than anything I had ever dreamt of; from the first evening when they made me undress before them and get into some filthy water they called a bath and dry myself with a damp, brown rag and put on this livery of shame. The cell was appalling: I could hardly breathe in it, and the food turned my stomach; the smell and sight of it were enough: I did not eat anything for days and days, I could not even swallow the bread; and the rest of the food was uneatable; I lay on the so-called bed and shivered all night long.... Don't ask me to speak of it, please. Words cannot convey the cumulative effect of a myriad discomforts, brutal handling and slow starvation. Surely like Dante I have written on my face the fact that I have been in hell. Only Dante never imagined any hell like an English prison; in his lowest circle people could move about; could see each other, and hear each other groan: there was some change, some human companionship in misery...."

"When did you begin to eat the food?" I asked.

"I can't tell, Frank," he replied. "After some days I got so hungry I had to eat a little, nibble at the outside of the bread, and drink some of the liquid; whether it was tea, coffee or gruel, I could not tell. As soon as I really ate anything it produced violent diarrhoea and I was ill all day and all night. From the beginning I could not sleep. I grew weak and had wild delusions.... You must not ask me to describe it. It is like asking a man who has gone through fever to describe one of the terrifying dreams. At Wandsworth I thought I should go mad; Wandsworth is the worst: no dungeon in hell can be worse; why is the food so bad? It even smelt bad. It was not fit for dogs."

"Was the food the worst of it?" I asked.

"The hunger made you weak, Frank; but the inhumanity was the worst of it; what devilish creatures men are. I had never known anything about them. I had never dreamt of such cruelties. A man spoke to me at exercise. You know you are not allowed to speak. He was in front of me, and he whispered, so that he could not be seen, how sorry he was for me, and how he hoped I would bear up. I stretched out my hands to him and cried, 'Oh, thank you, thank you.' The kindness of his voice brought tears into my eyes. Of course I was punished at once for speaking; a dreadful punishment. I won't think of it: I dare not. They are infinitely cunning in malice here, Frank; infinitely cunning in punishment.... Don't let us talk of it, it is too painful, too horrible that men should be so brutal."

"Give me an instance," I said, "of something less painful; something which may be bettered."

He smiled wanly. "All of it, Frank, all of it should be altered. There is no spirit in a prison but hate, hate masked in degrading formalism. They first break the will and rob you of hope, and then rule by fear. One day a warder came into my cell.

"'Take off your boots,' he said.

"Of course I began to obey him; then I asked:

"'What is it? Why must I take off my boots?'

"He would not answer me. As soon as he had my boots, he said:

"'Come out of your cell.'

"'Why?' I asked again. I was frightened, Frank. What had I done? I could not guess; but then I was often punished for nothing: what was it? No answer. As soon as we were in the corridor he ordered me to stand with my face to the wall, and went away. There I stood in my stocking feet waiting. The cold chilled me through; I began standing first on one foot and then on the other, racking my brains as to what they were going to do to me, wondering why I was being punished like this, and how long it would last; you know the thoughts fear-born that plague the mind.... After what seemed an eternity I heard him coming back. I did not dare to move or even look. He came up to me; stopped by me for a moment; my heart stopped; he threw down a pair of boots beside me, and said:

"'Go to your cell and put those on,' and I went into my cell shaking. That's the way they give you a new pair of boots in prison, Frank; that's the way they are kind to you."

"The first period was the worst?" I asked.

"Oh, yes, infinitely the worst! One gets accustomed to everything in time, to the food and the bed and the silence: one learns the rules, and knows what to expect and what to fear...."

"How did you win through the first period?" I asked.

"I died," he said quietly, "and came to life again, as a patient." I stared at him. "Quite true, Frank. What with the purgings and the semi-starvation and sleeplessness and, worst of all, the regret gnawing at my soul and the incessant torturing self-reproaches, I got weaker and weaker; my clothes hung on me; I could scarcely move. One Sunday morning after a very bad night I could not get out of bed. The warder came in and I told him I was ill."

"'You had better get up,' he said; but I couldn't take the good advice.

"'I can't,' I replied, 'you must do what you like with me.'

"Half an hour later the doctor came and looked in at the door. He never came near me; he simply called out:

"'Get up; no malingering; you're all right. You'll be punished if you don't get up,' and he went away.

"I had to get up. I was very weak; I fell off my bed while dressing, and bruised myself; but I got dressed somehow or other, and then I had to go with the rest to chapel, where they sing hymns, dreadful hymns all out of tune in praise of their pitiless God.

"I could hardly stand up; everything kept disappearing and coming back faintly: and suddenly I must have fallen...." He put his hand to his head. "I woke up feeling a pain in this ear. I was in the infirmary with a warder by me. My hand rested on a clean white sheet; it was like heaven. I could not help pushing my toes against the sheet to feel it, it was so smooth and cool and clean. The nurse with kind eyes said to me:

"'Do eat something,' and gave me some thin white bread and butter. Frank, I shall never forget it. The water came into my mouth in streams; I was so desperately hungry, and it was so delicious; I was so weak I cried," and he put his hands before his eyes and gulped down his tears.

"I shall never forget it: the warder was so kind. I did not like to tell him I was famished; but when he went away I picked the crumbs off the sheet and ate them, and when I could find no more I pulled myself to the edge of the bed, and picked up the crumbs from the floor and ate those as well; the white bread was so good and I was so hungry."

"And now?" I asked, not able to stand more.

"Oh, now," he said, with an attempt to be cheerful, "of

course it would be all right if they did not take my books away from me. If they would let me write. If only they would let me write as I wish, I should be quite content, but they punish me on every pretext. Why do they do it, Frank? Why do they want to make my life here one long misery?"

"Aren't you a little deaf still?" I asked, to ease the passion I felt of intolerable pity.

"Yes," he replied, "on this side, where I fell in the chapel. I fell on my ear, you know, and I must have burst the drum of it, or injured it in some way, for all through the winter it has ached and it often bleeds a little."

"But they could give you some cotton wool or something to put in it?" I said.

He smiled a poor wan smile:

"If you think one dare disturb a doctor or a warder for an earache, you don't know much about a prison; you would pay for it. Why, Frank, however ill I was now," and he lowered his voice to a whisper and glanced about him as if fearing to be overheard, "however ill I was I would not think of sending for the doctor. Not think of it," he said in an awestruck voice. "I have learned prison ways."

"I should rebel," I cried; "why do you let it break the spirit?"

"You would soon be broken, if you rebelled, here. Besides it is all incidental to the *System*. The *System*! No one outside knows what that means. It is an old story, I'm afraid, the story of man's cruelty to man."

"I think I can promise you," I said, "that the *System* will be altered a little. You shall have books and things to write with, and you shall not be harassed every moment by punishment."

"Take care," he cried in a spasm of dread, putting his hand on mine, "take care, they may punish me much worse. You don't know what they can do." I grew hot with indignation.

"Don't say anything, please, of what I have said to you. Promise me, you won't say anything. Promise me. I never complained, I didn't." His excitement was a revelation.

"All right," I replied, to soothe him.

"No, but promise me, seriously," he repeated. "You must promise me. Think, you have my confidence, it is private what I have said." He was evidently frightened out of self-control.

"All right," I said, "I will not tell; but I'll get the facts from the others and not from you."

"Oh, Frank," he said, "you don't know what they do. There is a punishment here more terrible than the rack." And he whispered to me with white sidelong eyes: "They can drive you mad in a week, Frank."[2]

"Mad!" I exclaimed, thinking I must have misunderstood him; though he was white and trembling.

"What about the warders?" I asked again, to change the subject, for I began to feel that I had supped full on horrors.

"Some of them are kind," he sighed. "The one that brought me in here is so kind to me. I should like to do something for him, when I get out. He's quite human. He does not mind talking to me and explaining things; but some of them at

Wandsworth were brutes.... I will not think of them again. I have sewn those pages up and you must never ask me to open them again: I dare not open them," he cried pitifully.

"But you ought to tell it all," I said, "that's perhaps the purpose you are here for: the ultimate reason."

"Oh, no, Frank, never. It would need a man of infinite strength to come here and give a truthful record of all that happened to him. I don't believe you could do it; I don't believe anybody would be strong enough. Starvation and purging alone would break down anyone's strength. Everybody knows that you are purged and starved to the edge of death. That's what two years' hard labour means. It's not the labour that's hard. It's the conditions of life that make it impossibly hard: they break you down body and soul. And if you resist, they drive you crazy.... But, please! don't say I said anything; you've promised, you know you have: you'll remember: won't you!"

I felt guilty: his insistence, his gasping fear showed me how terribly he must have suffered. He was beside himself with dread. I ought to have visited him sooner. I changed the subject.

"You shall have writing materials and your books, Oscar. Force yourself to write. You are looking better than you used to look; your eyes are brighter, your face clearer." The old smile came back into his eyes, the deathless humour.

"I've had a rest cure, Frank," he said, and smiled feebly.

"You should give record of this life as far as you can, and of all its influences on you. You have conquered, you know. Write the names of the inhuman brutes on their foreheads in vitriol, as Dante did for all time."

"No, no, I cannot: I will not: I want to live and forget. I could not, I dare not, I have not Dante's strength, nor his bitterness; I am a Greek born out of due time." He had said the true word at last.

"I will come again and see you," I replied. "Is there nothing else I can do? I hear your wife has seen you. I hope you have made it up with her?"

"She tried to be kind to me, Frank," he said in a dull voice, "she was kind, I suppose. She must have suffered; I'm sorry...." One felt he had no sorrow to spare for others.

"Is there nothing I can do?" I asked.

"Nothing, Frank, only if you could get me books and writing materials, if I could be allowed to use them really! But you won't say anything I have said to you, you promise me you won't?"

"I promise," I replied, "and I shall come back in a short time to see you again. I think you will be better then....

"Don't dread the coming out; you have friends who will work for you, great allies—" and I told him about Lady Dorothy Nevill at Mrs. Jeune's lunch.

"Isn't she a dear old lady?" he cried, "charming, brilliant, human creature! She might have stepped out of a page of Thackeray, only Thackeray never wrote a page quite dainty and charming enough. He came near it in his 'Esmond.' Oh, I remember you don't like the book, but it is beautifully written, Frank, in beautiful simple rhythmic English. It sings itself to the ear. Lady Dorothy" (how he loved the title!) "was always kind to me, but London is horrible. I could not live in London again. I must go away out of England. Do you remember talking to me, Frank, of France?" and he put both his hands on my shoulders, while tears ran down his face, and sighs broke from him. "Beautiful France, the one country in the world where they care for humane ideals and the humane life. Ah! if only I had gone with you to France," and the tears poured down his cheeks and our hands met convulsively.

"I'm glad to see you looking so well," I began again. "Books you shall have; for God's sake keep your heart up, and I will come back and see you, and don't forget you have good friends outside; lots of us!"

"Thank you, Frank; but take care, won't you, and remember your promise not to tell."

I nodded in assent and went to the door. The warder came in.

"The interview is over," I said; "will you take me downstairs?"

"If you will not mind sitting here, sir," he said, "for a minute. I must take him back first."

"I have been telling my friend," said Oscar to the warder, "how good you have been to me," and he turned and went, leaving with me the memory of his eyes and unforgettable smile; but I noticed as he disappeared that he was thin, and looked hunched up and bowed, in the ugly ill-fitting prison livery. I took out a bank note and put it under the blotting paper that had been placed on the table for me. In two or three minutes the warder came back, and as I left the room I thanked him for being kind to my friend, and told him how kindly Oscar had spoken of him.

"He has no business here, sir," the warder said. "He's no

more like one of our reg'lars than a canary is like one of them cocky little spadgers. Prison ain't meant for such as him, and he ain't meant for prison. He's that soft, sir, you see, and affeckshunate. He's more like a woman, he is; you hurt 'em without meaning to. I don't care what they say, I likes him; and he do talk beautiful, sir, don't he?"

"Indeed he does," I said, "the best talker in the world. I want you to look in the pad on the table. I have left a note there for you."

"Not for me, sir, I could not take it; no, sir, please not," he cried in a hurried, fear-struck voice. "You've forgotten something, sir, come back and get it, sir, do, please. I daren't."

In spite of my remonstrance he took me back and I had to put the note in my pocket.

"I could not, you know, sir, I was not kind to him for that." His manner changed; he seemed hurt.

I told him I was sure of it, sure, and begged him to believe, that if I were able to do anything for him, at any time, I'd be glad, and gave him my address. He was not even listening—an honest, good man, full of the milk of human kindness. How kind deeds shine starlike in this prison of a world. That warder and Sir Ruggles Brise each in his own place: such men are the salt of the English world; better are not to be found on earth.

FOOTNOTES:

[1] Some years ago *The Daily Chronicle* proved that though the general standard of living is lower in Germany and in France than in England; yet the prison food in France and especially in Germany is far better than in England and the

treatment of the prisoners far more humane.

[2] He was referring, I suppose, to the solitary confinement in a dark cell, which English ingenuity has invented and according to all accounts is as terrible as any of the tortures of the past. For those tortures were all physical, whereas the modern Englishman addresses himself to the brain and nerves, and finds the fear of madness more terrifying than the fear of pain. What a pity it is that Mr. Justice Wills did not know twenty-four hours of it, just twenty-four hours to teach him what "adequate punishment" for sensual self-indulgence means, and adequate punishment, too, for inhuman cruelty.

CHAPTER XVIII

On my return to London I saw Sir Ruggles Brise. No one could have shown me warmer sympathy, or more discriminating comprehension. I made my report to him and left the matter in his hands with perfect confidence. I took care to describe Oscar's condition to his friends while assuring them that his circumstances would soon be bettered. A little later I heard that the governor of the prison had been changed, that Oscar had got books and writing materials, and was allowed to have the gas burning in his cell to a late hour when it was turned down but not out. In fact, from that time on he was treated with all the kindness possible, and soon we heard that he was bearing the confinement and discipline better than could have been expected. Sir Evelyn Ruggles Brise had evidently settled the difficulty in the most humane spirit.

Later still I was told that Oscar had begun to write "De Profundis" in prison, and I was very hopeful about that too: no news could have given me greater pleasure. It seemed to me certain that he would justify himself to men by turning the punishment into a stepping-stone. And in this belief when the time came I ventured to call on Sir Ruggles Brise with another petition.

"Surely," I said, "Oscar will not be imprisoned for the full term; surely four or five months for good conduct will be remitted?"

Sir Ruggles Brise listened sympathetically, but warned me at once that any remission was exceptional; however, he would let me know what could be done, if I would call again in a week. Much to my surprise, he did not seem certain even about the good conduct.

I returned at the end of the week, and had another long talk with him. He told me that good conduct meant, in prison parlance, absence of punishment, and Oscar had been punished pretty often. Of course his offenses were minor offenses; nothing serious; childish faults indeed for the most part: he was often talking, and he was often late in the morning; his cell was not kept so well as it might be, and so forth; peccadilloes, all; yet a certificate of "good conduct" depended on such trifling observances. In face of Oscar's record Sir Ruggles Brise did not think that the sentence would be easily lessened. I was thunder-struck. But then no rules to me are sacrosanct; indeed, they are only tolerable because of the exceptions. I had such a high opinion of Ruggles Brise—his kindness and sense of fair play—that I ventured to show him my whole mind on the matter.

"Oscar Wilde," I said to him, "is just about to face life again: he is more than half reconciled to his wife; he has begun a book, is shouldering the burden. A little encouragement now and I believe he will do better things than he has ever done. I am convinced that he has far bigger things in him than we have seen yet. But he is extraordinarily sensitive and extraordinarily vain. The danger is that he may be frightened and blighted by the harshness and hatred of the world. He may shrink into himself and do nothing if the wind be not tempered a little for him. A hint of encouragement now, the feeling that men like yourself think him worthful and deserving of special kindly treatment, and I feel certain he will do great things. I really believe it is in your hands to save a man of extraordinary talent, and get the best out of him, if you care to do it."

"Of course I care to do it," he cried. "You cannot doubt that, and I see exactly what you mean; but it will not be easy."

"Won't you see what can be done?" I persisted. "Put your mind to discover how it should be done, how the Home Secretary may be induced to remit the last few months of Wilde's sentence."

After a little while he replied:

"You must believe that the authorities are quite willing to help in any good work, more than willing, and I am sure I speak for the Home Secretary as well as for myself; but it is for you to give us some reason for acting—a reason that could be avowed and defended."

I did not at first catch his drift; so I persevered:

"You admit that the reason exists, that it would be a good thing to favour Wilde, then why not do it?"

"We live," he said, "under parliamentary rule. Suppose the question were asked in the House, and I think it very likely in the present state of public opinion that the question would be asked: what should we answer? It would not be an avowable reason that we hoped Wilde would write new plays and books, would it? That reason ought to be sufficient, I grant you; but, you see yourself, it would not be so regarded."

"You are right, I suppose," I had to admit. "But if I got you a petition from men of letters, asking you to release Wilde for his health's sake: would that do?"

Sir Ruggles Brise jumped at the suggestion.

"Certainly," he exclaimed, "if some men of letters, men of position, wrote asking that Wilde's sentence should be diminished by three or four months on account of his health, I think it would have the best effect."

"I will see Meredith at once," I said, "and some others. How many names should I get?"

"If you have Meredith," he replied, "you don't need many others. A dozen would do, or fewer if you find a dozen too many."

"I don't think I shall meet with any difficulty," I replied, "but I will let you know."

"You will find it harder than you think," he concluded, "but if you get one or two great names the rest may follow. In any case one or two good names will make it easier for you."

Naturally I thanked him for his kindness and went away absolutely content. I had never set myself a task which seemed simpler. Meredith could not be more merciless than a Royal Commission. I returned to my office in *The Saturday Review* and got the Royal Commission report on this sentence of two years' imprisonment with hard labour. The Commission recommended that it should be wiped off the Statute Book as too severe. I drafted a little petition as colourless as possible:

"In view of the fact that the punishment of two years' imprisonment with hard labour has been condemned by a

Royal Commission as too severe, and inasmuch as Mr. Wilde has been distinguished by his work in letters and is now, we hear, suffering in health, we, your petitioners, pray—and so forth and so on."

I got this printed, and then sat down to write to Meredith asking when I could see him on the matter. I wanted his signature first to be printed underneath the petition, and then issue it. To my astonishment Meredith did not answer at once, and when I pressed him and set forth the facts he wrote to me that he could not do what I wished. I wrote again, begging him to let me see him on the matter. For the first time in my life he refused to see me: he wrote to me to say that nothing I could urge would move him, and it would therefore only be painful to both of us to find ourselves in conflict.

Nothing ever surprised me more than this attitude of Meredith's. I knew his poetry pretty well, and knew how severe he was on every sensual weakness perhaps because it was his own pitfall. I knew too what a fighter he was at heart and how he loved the virile virtues; but I thought I knew the man, knew his tender kindliness of heart, the founts of pity in him, and I felt certain I could count on him for any office of human charity or generosity. But no, he was impenetrable, hard. He told me long afterwards that he had rather a low opinion of Wilde's capacities, instinctive, deep-rooted contempt, too, for the showman in him, and an absolute abhorrence of his vice.

"That vile, sensual self-indulgence puts back the hands of the clock," he said, "and should not be forgiven."

For the life of me I could never forgive Meredith; never afterwards was he of any importance to me. He had always been to me a standard bearer in the eternal conflict, a leader in the Liberation War of Humanity, and here I found him pitiless to another who had been wounded on the same side in the great struggle: it seemed to me appalling. True, Wilde had not been wounded in fighting for us; true, he had fallen out and come to grief, as a drunkard might. But after all he had been fighting on the right side: had been a quickening intellectual influence: it was dreadful to pass him on the wayside and allow him callously to bleed to death. It was revoltingly cruel! The foremost Englishman of his time unable even to understand Christ's example, much less reach his height!

This refusal of Meredith's not only hurt me, but almost destroyed my hope, though it did not alter my purpose. I wanted a figurehead for my petition, and the figurehead I had chosen I could not get. I began to wonder and doubt. I next approached a very different man, the late Professor Churton Collins, a great friend of mine, who, in spite of an almost pedantic rigour of mind and character, had in him at bottom a curious spring of sympathy—a little pool of pure love for the poets and writers whom he admired. I got him to dinner and asked him to sign the petition; he refused, but on grounds other than those taken by Meredith.

"Of course Wilde ought to get out," he said, "the sentence was a savage one and showed bitter prejudice; but I have children, and my own way to make in the world, and if I did this I should be tarred with the Wilde brush. I cannot afford to do it. If he were really a great man I hope I should do it, but I don't agree with your estimate of him. I cannot think I am called upon to bell the British cat in his defence: it has many claws and all sharp."

As soon as he saw the position was unworthy of him, he shifted to new ground.

"If you were justified in coming to me, I should do it; but I am no one; why don't you go to Meredith, Swinburne or Hardy?"

I had to give up the Professor, as well as the poet. I knocked in turn at a great many doors, but all in vain. No one wished to take the odium on himself. One man, since become celebrated, said he had no position, his name was not good enough for the purpose. Others left my letters unanswered. Yet another sent a bare acknowledgment saying how sorry he was, but that public opinion was against Mr. Wilde; with one accord they all made excuses....

One day Professor Tyrrell of Trinity College, Dublin, happened to be in my office, while I was setting forth the difference between men of letters in France and England as exemplified by this conduct. In France among authors there is a recognised "*esprit de corps*," which constrains them to hold together. For instance when Zola was threatened with prosecution for "Nana," a dozen men like Cherbuliez, Feuillet, Dumas *fils*, who hated his work and regarded it as sensational, tawdry, immoral even, took up the cudgels for him at once; declared that the police were not judges of art, and should not interfere with a serious workman. All these Frenchmen, though they disliked Zola's work, and believed that his popularity was won by a low appeal, still admitted that he was a force in letters, and stood by him resolutely in spite of their own prepossessions and prejudices. But in England the feeling is altogether more selfish. Everyone consults his own sordid self-interest and is rather glad to see a social favourite come to grief: not a hand is stretched out to help him. Suddenly, Tyrrell broke in upon my exposition:

"I don't know whether my name is of any good to you," he said, "but I agree with all you have said, and my name might be classed with that of Churton Collins, though, of course,

I've no right to speak for literature," and without more ado he signed the petition, adding, "Regius Professor of Greek at Trinity College, Dublin."

"When you next see Oscar," he continued, "please tell him that my wife and I asked after him. We both hold him in grateful memory as a most brilliant talker and writer, and a charming fellow to boot. Confusion take all their English Puritanism."

Merely living in Ireland tends to make an Englishman more humane; but one name was not enough, and Tyrrell's was the only one I could get. In despair, and knowing that George Wyndham had had a great liking for Oscar, and admiration for his high talent, I asked him to lunch at the Savoy; laid the matter before him, and begged him to give me his name. He refused, and in face of my astonishment he excused himself by saying that, as soon as the rumour had reached him of Oscar's intimacy with Bosie Douglas, he had asked Oscar whether there was any truth in the scandalous report.

"You see," he went on, "Bosie is by way of being a relation of mine, and so I had the right to ask. Oscar gave me his word of honour that there was nothing but friendship between them. He lied to me, and that I can never forgive."

A politician unable to forgive a lie—surely one can hear the mocking laughter of the gods! I could say nothing to such paltry affected nonsense. Politician-like Wyndham showed me how the wind of popular feeling blew, and I recognised that my efforts were in vain.

There is no fellow-feeling among English men of letters; in fact they hold together less than any other class and, by himself, none of them wished to help a wounded member of the flock. I had to tell Sir Ruggles Brise that I had failed.

I have been informed since that if I had begun by asking Thomas Hardy, I might have succeeded. I knew Hardy; but never cared greatly for his talent. I daresay if I had had nothing else to do I might have succeeded in some half degree. But all these two years I was extremely busy and anxious; the storm clouds in South Africa were growing steadily darker and my attitude to South African affairs was exceedingly unpopular in London. It seemed to me vitally important to prevent England from making war on the Boers. I had to abandon the attempt to get Oscar's sentence shortened, and comfort myself with Sir Ruggles Brise's assurance that he would be treated with the greatest possible consideration.

Still, my advocacy had had a good effect.

Oscar himself has told us what the kindness shown to him in the last six months of his prison life really did for him. He writes in *De Profundis* that for the first part of his sentence he could only wring his hands in impotent despair and cry, "What an ending, what an appalling ending!" But when the new spirit of kindness came to him, he could say with sincerity: "What a beginning, what a wonderful beginning!" He sums it all up in these words:

"Had I been released after eighteen months, as I hoped to be, I would have left my prison loathing it and every official in it with a bitterness of hatred that would have poisoned my life. I have had six months more of imprisonment, but humanity has been in the prison with us all the time, and now when I go out I shall always remember great kindnesses that I have received here from almost everybody, and on the day of my release I shall give many thanks to many people, and ask to be remembered by them in turn."

This is the man whom Mr. Justice Wills addressed as

insensible to any high appeal.

Some time passed before I visited Oscar again. The change in him was extraordinary. He was light-hearted, gay, and looked better than I had ever seen him: clearly the austerity of prison life suited him. He met me with a jest:

"It is you, Frank!" he cried as if astonished, "always original! You come back to prison of your own free-will!"

He declared that the new governor—Major Nelson[3] was his name—had been as kind as possible to him. He had not had a punishment for months, and "Oh, Frank, the joy of reading when you like and writing as you please—the delight of living again!" He was so infinitely improved that his talk delighted me.

"What books have you?" I asked.

"I thought I should like the 'Oedipus Rex,'" he replied gravely; "but I could not read it. It all seemed unreal to me. Then I thought of St. Augustine, but he was worse still. The fathers of the Church were still further away from me; they all found it so easy to repent and change their lives: it does not seem to me easy. At last I got hold of Dante. Dante was what I wanted. I read the 'Purgatorio' all through, forced myself to read it in Italian to get the full savour and significance of it. Dante, too, had been in the depths and drunk the bitter lees of despair. I shall want a little library when I come out, a library of a score of books. I wonder if you will help me to get it. I want Flaubert, Stevenson, Baudelaire, Maeterlinck, Dumas *pere*, Keats, Marlowe, Chatterton, Anatole France, Theophile Gautier, Dante, Goethe, Meredith's poems, and his 'Egoist,' the Song of Solomon, too, Job, and, of course, the Gospels."

"I shall be delighted to get them for you," I said, "if you will send me the list. By the by, I hear that you have been reconciled to your wife; is that true? I should be glad to know it's true."

"I hope it will be all right," he said gravely, "she is very good and kind. I suppose you have heard," he went on, "that my mother died since I came here, and that leaves a great gap in my life.... I always had the greatest admiration and love for my mother. She was a great woman, Frank, a perfect idealist. My father got into trouble once in Dublin, perhaps you have heard about it?"

"Oh, yes," I said, "I have read the case." (It is narrated in the first chapter of this book.)

"Well, Frank, she stood up in court and bore witness for him with perfect serenity, with perfect trust and without a shadow of common womanly jealousy. She could not believe that the man she loved could be unworthy, and her conviction was so complete that it communicated itself to the jury: her trust was so noble that they became infected by it, and brought him in guiltless.[4] Extraordinary, was it not? She was quite sure too of the verdict. It is only noble souls who have that assurance and serenity....

"When my father was dying it was the same thing. I always see her sitting there by his bedside with a sort of dark veil over her head: quite silent, quite calm. Nothing ever troubled her optimism. She believed that only good can happen to us. When death came to the man she loved, she accepted it with the same serenity and when my sister died she bore it in the same high way. My sister was a wonderful creature, so gay and high-spirited, 'embodied sunshine,' I used to call her.

"When we lost her, my mother simply took it that it was best for the child. Women have infinitely more courage than men, don't you think? I have never known anyone with such perfect faith as my mother. She was one of the great figures of the world. What she must have suffered over my sentence I don't dare to think: I'm sure she endured agonies. She had great hopes of me. When she was told that she was going to die, and that she could not see me, for I was not allowed to go to her,[5] she said, 'May the prison help him,' and turned her face to the wall.

"She felt about the prison as you do, Frank, and really I think you are both right; it has helped me. There are things I see now that I never saw before. I see what pity means. I thought a work of art should be beautiful and joyous. But now I see that that ideal is insufficient, even shallow; a work of art must be founded on pity; a book or poem which has no pity in it, had better not be written....

"I shall be very lonely when I come out, and I can't stand loneliness and solitude; it is intolerable to me, hateful, I have had too much of it....

"You see, Frank, I am breaking with the past altogether. I am going to write the history of it. I am going to tell how I was tempted and fell, how I was pushed by the man I loved into that dreadful quarrel of his, driven forward to the fight with his father and then left to suffer alone....

"That is the story I am now going to tell. That is the book[6] of pity and of love which I am writing now—a terrible book....

"I wonder would you publish it, Frank? I should like it to appear in *The Saturday*."

"I'd be delighted to publish anything of yours," I replied,

"and happier still to publish something to show that you have at length chosen the better part and are beginning a new life. I'd pay you, too, whatever the work turns out to be worth to me; in any case much more than I pay Bernard Shaw or anyone else." I said this to encourage him.

"I'm sure of that," he answered. "I'll send you the book as soon as I've finished it. I think you'll like it"—and there for the moment the matter ended.

At length I felt sure that all would be well with him. How could I help feeling sure? His mind was richer and stronger than it had ever been; and he had broken with all the dark past. I was overjoyed to believe that he would yet do greater things than he had ever done, and this belief and determination were in him too, as anyone can see on reading what he wrote at this time in prison:

"There is before me so much to do that I would regard it as a terrible tragedy if I died before I was allowed to complete at any rate a little of it. I see new developments in art and life, each one of which is a fresh mode of perfection. I long to live so that I can explore what is no less than a new world to me. Do you want to know what this new world is? I think you can guess what it is. It is the world in which I have been living. Sorrow, then, and all that it teaches one, is my new world....

"I used to live entirely for pleasure. I shunned suffering and sorrow of every kind. I hated both...."

Through the prison bars Oscar had begun to see how mistaken he had been, how much greater, and more salutary to the soul, suffering is than pleasure.

"Out of sorrow have the worlds been built, and at the birth of a child or a star there is pain."

FOOTNOTES:

[3] Cfr. Appendix: "Criticisms by Robert Ross."

[4] I give Oscar's view of the trial just to show how his romantic imagination turned disagreeable facts into pleasant fiction. Oscar could only have heard of the trial, and perhaps his mother was his informant—which adds to the interest of the story.

[5] Permission to visit a dying mother is accorded in France, even to murderers. The English pretend to be more religious than the French; but are assuredly less humane.

[6] "De Profundis." What Oscar called "the terrible part" of the book—the indictment of Lord Alfred Douglas—has since been read out in Court and will be found in the Appendix to this volume.

CHAPTER XIX

Shortly before he came out of prison, one of Oscar's intimates told me he was destitute, and begged me to get him some clothes. I took the name of his tailor and ordered two suits. The tailor refused to take the order: he was not going to make clothes for Oscar Wilde. I could not trust myself to talk to the man and therefore sent my assistant editor and friend, Mr. Blanchamp, to have it out with him. The tradesman soul yielded to the persuasiveness of cash in advance. I sent Oscar the clothes and a cheque, and shortly after his release got a letter[7] thanking me.

A little later I heard on good authority a story which Oscar afterwards confirmed, that when he left Reading Gaol the correspondent of an American paper offered him L1,000 for an interview dealing with his prison life and experiences, but he felt it beneath his dignity to take his sufferings to market. He thought it better to borrow than to earn. He is partly to be excused, perhaps, when one remembers that he had still some pounds left of the large sums given him before his condemnation, by Miss S—, Ross, More Adey, and others. Still his refusal of such a sum as that offered by the New York paper shows how utterly contemptuous he was of money, even at a moment when one would have thought money would have been his chief preoccupation. He always lived in the day and rather heedlessly.

As soon as he left prison he crossed with some friends to France, and went to stay at the Hotel de la Plage at Berneval, a quiet little village near Dieppe. M. Andre Gide, who called on him there almost as soon as he arrived, gives a fair mental picture of him at this time. He tells how delighted he was to find in him the "Oscar Wilde of old," no longer the sensualist puffed out with pride and good living, but "the sweet Wilde" of the days before 1891. "I found myself taken back, not two years," he says, "but four or five. There was the same dreamy look, the same amused smile, the same voice."

He told M. Gide that prison had completely changed him, had taught him the meaning of pity. "You know," he went on, "how fond I used to be of 'Madame Bovary,' but Flaubert would not admit pity into his work, and that is why it has a petty and restrained character about it. It is the sense of pity by means of which a work gains in expanse, and by which it opens up a boundless horizon. Do you know, my dear fellow, it was pity which prevented my killing myself? During the first six months in prison I was dreadfully unhappy, so utterly miserable that I wanted to kill myself; but what kept me from doing so was looking at the others, and seeing that they were as unhappy as I was, and feeling sorry for them. Oh dear! what a wonderful thing pity is, and I never knew it."

He was speaking in a low voice without any excitement.

"Have you ever learned how wonderful a thing pity is? For my part I thank God every night, yes, on my knees I thank God for having taught it to me. I went into prison with a heart of stone, thinking only of my own pleasure; but now my heart is utterly broken—pity has entered into my heart. I have learned now that pity is the greatest and the most beautiful thing in the world. And that is why I cannot bear ill-will towards those who caused my suffering and those who condemned me; no, nor to anyone, because without them I should not have known all that. Alfred Douglas writes me terrible letters. He says he does not understand me, that he does not understand that I do not wish everyone ill, and that everyone has been horrid to me. No, he does not understand me. He cannot understand me any more. But I keep on telling him that in every letter: we cannot follow the same road. He has his and it is beautiful—I have mine. His is that of Alcibiades; mine is now that of St. Francis of Assisi."

How much of this is sincere and how much merely imagined and stated in order to incarnate the new ideal to perfection would be hard to say. The truth is not so saintly simple as the christianised Oscar would have us believe. The unpublished portions of "De Profundis" which were read out in the Douglas-Ransome trial prove, what all his friends know, that Oscar Wilde found it impossible to forgive or forget what seemed to him personal ill-treatment. There are beautiful pages in "De Profundis," pages of sweetest Christlike resignation and charity and no doubt in a certain mood Oscar was sincere in writing them. But there was another mood in him, more vital and more enduring, if not so engaging, a mood in which he saw himself as one betrayed and sacrificed and abandoned, and then he attributed his ruin wholly to his friend and did not hesitate to speak of him as the "Judas" whose shallow selfishness and imperious ill-temper and unfulfilled promises of monetary help had driven a great man to disaster.

That unpublished portion of "De Profundis" is in essence, from beginning to end, one long curse of Lord Alfred Douglas, an indictment apparently impartial, particularly at first; but in reality a bitter and merciless accusation, showing in Oscar Wilde a curious want of sympathy even with the man he said he loved. Those who would know Oscar Wilde as he really was will read that piece of rhetoric with care enough to notice that he reiterates the charge of shallow selfishness with such venom, that he discovers his own colossal egotism and essential hardness of heart. "Love," we are told, "suffereth long and is kind ... beareth all things, believeth all things, hopeth all things, endureth all things"—that sweet, generous, all-forgiving tenderness of love was not in the pagan, Oscar Wilde, and therefore even his deepest passion never won to complete reconciliation and ultimate redemption.

In this same talk with M. Gide, Oscar is reported to have said that he had known beforehand that a catastrophe was unavoidable; "there was but one end possible.... That state of things could not last; there had to be some end to it."

This view I believe is Gide's and not Oscar's. In any case I am sure that my description of him before the trials as full of insolent self-assurance is the truer truth. Of course he must have had forebodings; he was warned as I've related, again and again; but he took character-colour from his associates and he met Queensberry's first attempts at attack with utter disdain. He did not realise his danger at all. Gide reports him more correctly as adding:

"Prison has completely changed me. I was relying on it for that—Douglas is terrible. He cannot understand that—cannot understand that I am not taking up the same existence again. He accuses the others of having changed me."

I may publish here part of a letter of a prison warder which Mr. Stuart Mason reproduced in his excellent little book on Oscar Wilde. He says:

"No more beautiful life had any man lived, no more beautiful life could any man live than Oscar Wilde lived during the short period I knew him in prison. He wore upon his face an eternal smile; sunshine was on his face, sunshine of some sort must have been in his heart. People say he was not sincere: he was the very soul of sincerity when I knew him. If he did not continue that life after he left prison, then the forces of evil must have been too strong for him. But he tried, he honestly tried, and in prison he succeeded."

All this seems to me in the main, true. Oscar's gay vivacity would have astonished any stranger. Besides, the regular hours and scant plain food of prison had improved his health and the solitude and suffering had lent him a deeper emotional life. But there was an intense bitterness in him, a profound underlying sense of injury which came continually to passionate expression. Yet as soon as the miserable petty persecution of the prison was lifted from him, all the joyous gaiety and fun of his nature bubbled up irresistibly. There was no contradiction in this complexity. A man can hold in himself a hundred conflicting passions and impulses without confusion. At this time the dominant chord in Oscar was pity for others.

To my delight the world had evidence of this changed Oscar Wilde in a very short time. On May 28th, a few days after he left prison, there appeared in *The Daily Chronicle* a letter more than two columns in length, pleading for the kindlier treatment of little children in English prisons. The letter was written because Warder Martin[8] of Reading prison had been dismissed by the Commissioners for the dreadful crime of "having given some sweet biscuits to a little hungry child."...

I must quote a few paragraphs of this letter; because it shows how prison had deepened Oscar Wilde, how his own suffering had made him, as Shakespeare says, "pregnant to good pity," and also because it tells us what life was like in an English prison in our time. Oscar wrote:

"I saw the three children myself on the Monday preceding my release. They had just been convicted, and were standing in a row in the central hall in their prison dress carrying their sheets under their arms, previous to their being sent to the cells allotted to them.... They were quite small children, the youngest—the one to whom the warder gave the biscuits—being a tiny chap, for whom they had evidently been unable to find clothes small enough to fit. I had, of course, seen many children in prison during the two years during which I was myself confined. Wandsworth prison, especially, contained always a large number of children. But the little child I saw on the afternoon of Monday, the 17th, at Reading, was tinier than any one of them. I need not say how utterly distressed I was to see these children at Reading, for I knew the treatment in store for them. The cruelty that is practised by day and night on children in English prisons is incredible except to those that have witnessed it and are aware of the brutality of the system.

"People nowadays do not understand what cruelty is.... Ordinary cruelty is simply stupidity.

"The prison treatment of children is terrible, primarily from people not understanding the peculiar psychology of the child's nature. A child can understand a punishment inflicted by an individual, such as a parent, or guardian, and bear it with a certain amount of acquiescence. What it cannot understand is a punishment inflicted by society. It cannot realise what society is....

"The terror of a child in prison is quite limitless. I remember once in Reading, as I was going out to exercise, seeing in the dimly lit cell opposite mine a small boy. Two warders—not unkindly men—were talking to him, with some sternness apparently, or perhaps giving him some useful advice about his conduct. One was in the cell with him, the other was standing outside. The child's face was like a white wedge of sheer terror. There was in his eyes the terror of a hunted animal. The next morning I heard him at breakfast time crying, and calling to be let out. His cry was for his parents. From time to time I could hear the deep voice of the warder on duty telling him to keep quiet. Yet he was not even convicted of whatever little offence he had been charged with. He was simply on remand. That I knew by his wearing his own clothes, which seemed neat enough. He was, however, wearing prison socks and shoes. This showed that he was a very poor boy, whose own shoes, if he had any, were in a bad state. Justices and magistrates, an entirely ignorant class as a rule, often remand children for a week, and then perhaps remit whatever sentence they are entitled to pass. They call this 'not sending a child to prison.' It is of course a stupid view on their part. To a little child, whether he is in prison on remand or after conviction is not a subtlety of position he can comprehend. To him the horrible thing is to be there at all. In the eyes of humanity it should be a horrible thing for him to be there at all.

"This terror that seizes and dominates the child, as it seizes the grown man also, is of course intensified beyond power of expression by the solitary cellular system of our prisons. Every child is confined to its cell for twenty-three hours out of the twenty-four. This is the appalling thing. To shut up a child in a dimly lit cell for twenty-three hours out of the twenty-four is an example of the cruelty of stupidity. If an individual, parent or guardian, did this to a child, he would be severely punished....

"The second thing from which a child suffers in prison is hunger. The food that is given to it consists of a piece of usually badly baked prison bread and a tin of water for breakfast at half past seven. At twelve o'clock it gets dinner, composed of a tin of coarse Indian meal stirabout, and at half past five it gets a piece of dry bread and a tin of water for its supper. This diet in the case of a strong man is always productive of illness of some kind, chiefly, of course, diarrhoea, with its attendant weakness. In fact, in a big prison, astringent medicines are served out regularly by the warders as a matter of course. A child is as a rule incapable of eating the food at all. Anyone who knows anything about children knows how easily a child's digestion is upset by a fit of crying, or trouble and mental distress of any kind. A child who has been crying all day long and perhaps half the night, in a lonely, dimly lit cell, and is preyed upon by terror, simply cannot eat food of this coarse, horrible kind. In the case of the little child to whom Warder Martin gave the biscuits, the child was crying with hunger on Tuesday morning, and utterly unable to eat the bread and water served to it for breakfast.

"Martin went out after the breakfast had been served, and bought the few sweet biscuits for the child rather than see it starving. It was a beautiful action on his part, and was so recognised by the child, who, utterly unconscious of the regulation of the Prison Board, told one of the senior warders how kind this junior warder had been to him. The result was, of course, a report and a dismissal.[9]

"I know Martin extremely well, and I was under his charge for the last seven weeks of my imprisonment.... I was struck by the singular kindness and humanity of the way in which he spoke to me and to the other prisoners. Kind words are much in prison, and a pleasant 'good-morning' or 'good-evening' will make one as happy as one can be in prison. He was always gentle and considerate....

"A great deal has been talked and written lately about the contaminating influence of prison on young children. What is said is quite true. A child is utterly contaminated by prison life. But this contaminating influence is not that of the prisoners. It is that of the whole prison system—of the governor, the chaplain, the warders, the solitary cell, the isolation, the revolting food, the rules of the Prison Commissioners, the mode of discipline, as it is termed, of the life.

"Of course no child under fourteen years of age should be sent to prison at all. It is an absurdity, and, like many absurdities, of absolutely tragical results...."

This letter, I am informed, brought about some improvement in the treatment of young children in British prisons. But in regard to adults the British prison is still the torture chamber it was in Wilde's time; prisoners are still treated more brutally there than anywhere else in the civilised world; the food is the worst in Europe, insufficient indeed to maintain health; in many cases men are only saved from death by starvation through being sent to the infirmary. Though these facts are well known, *Punch*, the pet organ of the British middle-class, was not ashamed a little while ago to make a mock of some suggested reform, by publishing a picture of a British convict, with the villainous face of a Bill Sykes, lying on a sofa in his cell smoking a cigar with champagne at hand. This is not altogether due to stupidity, as Oscar tried to believe, but to reasoned selfishness. *Punch* and the class for which it caters would like to believe that many convicts are unfit to live, whereas the truth is that a good many of them are superior in humanity to the people who punish and slander them.

While waiting for his wife to join him, Oscar rented a little house, the Chalet Bourgeat, about two hundred yards away from the hotel at Berneval, and furnished it. Here he spent the whole of the summer writing, bathing, and talking to the few devoted friends who visited him from time to time.

Never had he been so happy: never in such perfect health. He was full of literary projects; indeed, no period of his whole life was so fruitful in good work. He was going to write some Biblical plays; one entitled "Pharaoh" first, and then one called "Ahab and Jezebel," which he pronounced Isabelle. Deeper problems, too, were much in his mind: he was already at work on "The Ballad of Reading Gaol," but before coming to that let me first show how happy the song-bird was and how divinely he sang when the dreadful cage was opened and he was allowed to use his wings in the heavenly sunshine.

Here is a letter from him shortly after his release which is one of the most delightful things he ever wrote. Fitly enough it was addressed to his friend of friends, Robert Ross, and I can only say that I am extremely obliged to Ross for allowing me to publish it:

> Hotel de la Plage. Berneval, near Dieppe, Monday night, May 31st (1897).

My dearest Robbie,

I have decided that the only way in which to get boots properly is to go to France to receive them. The Douane charged 3 francs. How could you frighten me as you did? The next time you order boots please come to Dieppe to get them sent to you. It is the only way and it will be an excuse for seeing you.

I am going to-morrow on a pilgrimage. I always wanted to be a pilgrim, and I have decided to start early to-morrow to the shrine of Notre Dame de Liesse. Do you know what Liesse is? It is an old word for joy. I suppose the same as Letizia, Laetitia. I just heard to-night of the shrine or chapel, by chance, as you would say, from the sweet woman of the auberge, who wants me to live always at Berneval. She says Notre Dame de Liesse is wonderful, and helps everyone to the secret of joy—I do not know how long it will take me to get to the shrine, as I must walk. But, from what she tells me, it will take at least six or seven minutes to get there, and as many to come back. In fact the chapel of Notre Dame de Liesse is just fifty yards from the Hotel. Isn't it extraordinary? I intend to start after I have had my coffee, and then to bathe. Need I say that this is a miracle? I wanted to go on a pilgrimage, and I find the little grey stone chapel of Our Lady of Joy is brought to me. It has probably been waiting for me all these purple years of pleasure, and now it comes to meet me with Liesse as its message. I simply don't know what to say. I wish you were not so hard to poor heretics,[10] and would admit that even for the sheep who has no shepherd there is a Stella Maris to guide it home. But you and More, especially More, treat me as a Dissenter. It is very painful and quite unjust.

Yesterday I attended Mass at 10 o'clock and afterwards bathed. So I went into the water without being a pagan. The consequence was that I was not tempted by either sirens or mermaidens, or any of the green-haired following of Glaucus. I really think that this is a remarkable thing. In my Pagan days the sea was always full of Tritons blowing conchs, and other unpleasant things. Now it is quite different. And yet you treat me as the President of Mansfield College; and after I had canonised you too.

Dear boy, I wish you would tell me if your religion makes you happy. You conceal your religion from me in a monstrous way. You treat it like writing in the *Saturday Review* for Pollock, or dining in Wardour Street off the fascinating dish that is served with tomatoes and makes men mad.[11] I know it is useless asking you, so don't tell me.

I felt an outcast in Chapel yesterday—not really, but a little in exile. I met a dear farmer in a corn field and he gave me a seat on his banc in church: so I was quite comfortable. He now visits me twice a day, and as he has no children, and is rich, I have made him promise to adopt *three*—two boys and a girl. I told him that if he wanted them, he would find them. He said he was afraid that they would turn out badly. I told him everyone did that. He really has promised to adopt three orphans. He is now filled with enthusiasm at the idea. He is to go to the *Cure* and talk to him. He told me that his own father had fallen down in a fit one day as they were talking together, and that he had caught him in his arms, and put him to bed, where he died, and that he himself had often thought how dreadful it was that if he had a fit there was no one to catch him in his arms. It is quite clear that he must adopt orphans, is it not?

I feel that Berneval is to be my home. I really do. Notre Dame de Liesse will be sweet to me, if I go on my knees to her, and she will advise me. It is extraordinary being brought here by a white horse that was a native of the place, and knew the road, and wanted to see its parents, now of advanced years. It is also extraordinary that I knew Berneval existed and was arranged for me.

M. Bonnet[12] wants to build me a Chalet, 1,000 metres of ground (I don't know how much that is—but I suppose about 100 miles) and a Chalet with a studio, a balcony, a salle-a-manger, a huge kitchen, and three bedrooms—a view of the sea, and trees—all for 12,000 francs—L480. If I can write a play I am going to have it begun. Fancy one's own lovely house and grounds in France for L480. No rent of any kind. Pray consider this, and approve, if you think well. Of course, not till I have done my play.

An old gentleman lives here in the hotel. He dines alone in

his room, and then sits in the sun. He came here for two days and has stayed two years. His sole sorrow is that there is no theatre. Monsieur Bonnet is a little heartless about this, and says that as the old gentleman goes to bed at 8 o'clock a theatre would be of no use to him. The old gentleman says he only goes to bed at 8 o'clock because there is no theatre. They argued the point yesterday for an hour. I sided with the old gentleman, but Logic sides with Monsieur Bonnet, I believe.

I had a sweet letter from the Sphinx.[13] She gives me a delightful account of Ernest[14] subscribing to Romeike while his divorce suit was running, and not being pleased with some of the notices. Considering the growing appreciation of Ibsen I must say that I am surprised the notices were not better, but nowadays everybody is jealous of everyone else, except, of course, husband and wife. I think I shall keep this last remark of mine for my play.

Have you got my silver spoon[15] from Reggie? You got my silver brushes out of Humphreys,[16] who is bald, so you might easily get my spoon out of Reggie, who has so many, or used to have. You know my crest is on it. It is a bit of Irish silver, and I don't want to lose it. There is an excellent substitute called Britannia metal, very much liked at the Adelphi and elsewhere. Wilson Barrett writes, "I prefer it to silver." It would suit dear Reggie admirably. Walter Besant writes, "I use none other." Mr. Beerbohm Tree also writes, "Since I have tried it I am a different actor; my friends hardly recognise me." So there is obviously a demand for it.

I am going to write a Political Economy in my heavier moments. The first law I lay down is, "Whenever there exists a demand, there is *no* supply." This is the only law that explains the extraordinary contrast between the soul of man and man's surroundings. Civilisations continue because people hate them. A modern city is the exact opposite of what everyone wants. Nineteenth-century dress is the result of our horror of the style. The tall hat will last as long as people dislike it.

Dear Robbie, I wish you would be a little more considerate, and not keep me up so late talking to you. It is very flattering to me and all that, but you should remember that I need rest. Good-night. You will find some cigarettes and some flowers by your bedside. Coffee is served below at 8 o'clock. Do you mind? If it is too early for you I don't at all mind lying in bed an extra hour. I hope you will sleep well. You should as Lloyd is not on the Verandah.[17]

TUESDAY MORNING, 9.30.

The sea and sky are opal—no horrid drawing master's line between them—just one fishing boat, going slowly, and drawing the wind after it. I am going to bathe.

6 O'CLOCK.

Bathed and have seen a Chalet here which I wish to take for the season—quite charming—a splendid view: a large writing room, a dining room, and three lovely bedrooms—besides servants' rooms and also a huge balcony.

[In this blank space he had roughly drawn a ground plan of the imagined Chalet.]

I don't know the scale the drawing, but the of rooms are larger than the plan is.

1. Salle-a-manger.
2. Salon.
3. Balcony.

All on ground floor
with steps from balcony
to ground.

The rent for the season or year is, what do you think?—L32.

Of course I must have it: I will take my meals here—separate and reserved table: it is within two minutes walk. Do tell me to take it. When you come again your room will be waiting for you. All I need is a domestique. The people here are most kind.

I made my pilgrimage—the interior of the Chapel is of course a modern horror—but there is a black image of Notre Dame de Liesse—the chapel is as tiny as an undergraduate's room at Oxford. I hope to get the Cure to celebrate Mass in it soon; as a rule the service is only held there in July and August; but I want to see a Mass quite close.

There is also another thing I must write to you about.

I adore this place. The whole country is lovely, and full of forest and deep meadow. It is simple and healthy. If I live in Paris I may be doomed to things I don't desire. I am afraid of big towns. Here I get up at 7.30. I am happy all day. I go to bed at 10. I am frightened of Paris. I want to live here.

I have seen the "terrain." It is the best here, and the only one left. I must build a house. If I could build a chalet for 12,000 francs—L500—and live in a home of my own, how happy I would be. I must raise the money somehow. It would give me a home, quiet, retired, healthy, and near England. If I live in Egypt I know what my life would be. If I live in the south of Italy I know I should be idle and worse. I want to live here. Do think over this and send me over the architect.[18] M. Bonnet is excellent and is ready to carry out any idea. I want a little chalet of wood and plaster walls, the wooden beams showing and the white square of plaster diapering the framework—like, I regret to say—Shakespeare's house—like old English sixteenth-century farmers' houses. So your architect has me waiting for him, as he is waiting for me.

Do you think the idea absurd?

I got the *Chronicle*, many thanks. I see the writer on Prince —A.2.11.—does not mention my name—foolish of her—it is a woman.

I, as you, the poem of my days, are away, am forced to write. I have begun something that I think will be very good.

I breakfast to-morrow with the Stannards: what a great passionate, splendid writer John Strange Winter is! How little people understand her work! *Bootle's Baby* is an "oeuvre symboliste"—it is really only the style and the subject that are wrong. Pray never speak lightly of *Bootle's Baby*—Indeed pray never speak of it at all—I never do.

Yours,

OSCAR.

Please send a *Chronicle* to my wife.

MRS. C.M. HOLLAND,
Maison Benguerel,
Bevaix,
Pres de Neuchatel,

just marking it—and if my second letter appears, mark that.

Also cut out the letter[19] and enclose it in an envelope to:

MR. ARTHUR CRUTHENDEN,
Poste Restante, G.P.O., Reading,

with just these lines:

Dear friend,

The enclosed will interest you. There is also another letter waiting in the post office for you from me with a little money. Ask for it if you have not got it.

Yours sincerely,

C.3.3.

I have no one but you, dear Robbie, to do anything. Of course the letter to Reading must go at once, as my friends come out on Wednesday morning early.

This letter displays almost every quality of Oscar Wilde's genius in perfect efflorescence—his gaiety, joyous merriment and exquisite sensibility. Who can read of the little Chapel to Notre Dame de Liesse without emotion quickly to be changed to mirth by the sunny humour of those delicious specimens of self-advertisement: "Mr. Beerbohm Tree also writes: 'Since I have tried it, I am a different actor, my friends hardly recognise me.'"

This letter is the most characteristic thing Oscar Wilde ever wrote, a thing produced in perfect health at the topmost height of happy hours, more characteristic even than "The Importance of Being Earnest," for it has not only the humour of that delightful farce-comedy, but also more than a hint of the deeper feeling which was even then forming itself into a master-work that will form part of the inheritance of men forever.

"The Ballad of Reading Gaol" belongs to this summer of

1897. A fortunate conjuncture of circumstances—the prison discipline excluding all sense-indulgence, the kindness shown him towards the end of his imprisonment and of course the delight of freedom—gave him perfect physical health and hope and joy in work, and so Oscar was enabled for a few brief months to do better than his best. He assured me and I believe that the conception of "The Ballad" came to him in prison and was due to the alleviation of his punishment and the permission accorded to him to write and read freely—a divine fruit born directly of his pity for others and the pity others felt for him.

"The Ballad of Reading Gaol"[20] was published in January, 1898, over the signature of C.3.3., Oscar's number in prison. In a few weeks it ran through dozens of editions in England and America and translations appeared in almost every European language, which is proof not so much of the excellence of the poem as the great place the author held in the curiosity of men. The enthusiasm with which it was accepted in England was astounding. One reviewer compared it with the best of Sophocles; another said that "nothing like it has appeared in our time." No word of criticism was heard: the most cautious called it a "simple poignant ballad, ... one of the greatest in the English language." This praise is assuredly not too generous. Yet even this was due to a revulsion of feeling in regard to Oscar himself rather than to any understanding of the greatness of his work. The best public felt that he had been dreadfully over-punished, and made a scapegoat for worse offenders and was glad to have the opportunity of repairing its own fault by over-emphasising Oscar's repentance and over-praising, as it imagined, the first fruits of the converted sinner.

"The Ballad of Reading Gaol" is far and away the best poem Oscar Wilde ever wrote; we should try to appreciate it as the future will appreciate it. We need not be afraid to trace it to its source and note what is borrowed in it and what is original. After all necessary qualifications are made, it will stand as a great and splendid achievement.

Shortly before "The Ballad" was written, a little book of poetry called "A Shropshire Lad" was published by A.E. Housman, now I believe professor of Latin at Cambridge. There are only a hundred odd pages in the booklet; but it is full of high poetry—sincere and passionate feeling set to varied music. His friend, Reginald Turner, sent Oscar a copy of the book and one poem in particular made a deep impression on him. It is said that "his actual model for 'The Ballad of Reading Gaol' was 'The Dream of Eugene Aram' with 'The Ancient Mariner' thrown in on technical grounds"; but I believe that Wilde owed most of his inspiration to "A Shropshire Lad."

Here are some verses from Housman's poem and some verses from "The Ballad":

> On moonlit heath and lonesome bank
> The sheep beside me graze;
> And yon the gallows used to clank
> Fast by the four cross ways.
>
> A careless shepherd once would keep
> The flocks by moonlight there,[21]
> And high amongst the glimmering sheep
> The dead men stood on air.
>
> They hang us now in Shrewsbury jail:
> The whistles blow forlorn,
> And trains all night groan on the rail
> To men that die at morn.
>
> There sleeps in Shrewsbury jail to-night,

Or wakes, as may betide,
A better lad, if things went right,
Than most that sleep outside.

And naked to the hangman's noose
The morning clocks will ring
A neck God made for other use
Than strangling in a string.

And sharp the link of life will snap,
And dead on air will stand
Heels that held up as straight a chap
As treads upon the land.

So here I'll watch the night and wait
To see the morning shine
When he will hear the stroke of eight
And not the stroke of nine;

And wish my friend as sound a sleep
As lads I did not know,
That shepherded the moonlit sheep
A hundred years ago.

THE BALLAD OF READING GAOL

It is sweet to dance to violins
When Love and Life are fair:
To dance to flutes, to dance to lutes,
Is delicate and rare:
But it is not sweet with nimble feet
To dance upon the air!

And as one sees most fearful things
In the crystal of a dream,
We saw the greasy hempen rope

Hooked to the blackened beam
And heard the prayer the hangman's snare
Strangled into a scream.

And all the woe that moved him so
That he gave that bitter cry,
And the wild regrets, and the bloody sweats,
None knew so well as I:
For he who lives more lives than one
More deaths than one must die.

There are better things in "The Ballad of Reading Gaol" than those inspired by Housman. In the last of the three verses I quote there is a distinction of thought which Housman hardly reached.

"For he who lives more lives than one
More deaths than one must die."

There are verses, too, wrung from the heart which have a diviner influence than any product of the intellect:

The Chaplain would not kneel to pray
By his dishonoured grave:
Nor mark it with that blessed Cross
That Christ for sinners gave,
Because the man was one of those
Whom Christ came down to save.

* * * * *

This too I know—and wise were it
If each could know the same—
That every prison that men build
Is built with bricks of shame,
And bound with bars lest Christ should see

How men their brothers maim.

With bars they blur the gracious moon,
And blind the goodly sun:
And they do well to hide their Hell,
For in it things are done
That Son of God nor son of man
Ever should look upon!

The vilest deeds like poison weeds
Bloom well in prison-air:
It is only what is good in Man
That wastes and withers there:
Pale Anguish keeps the heavy gate,
And the Warder is Despair.

* * * * *

And he of the swollen purple throat,
And the stark and staring eyes,
Waits for the holy hands that took
The Thief to Paradise;
And a broken and a contrite heart
The Lord will not despise.

"The Ballad of Reading Gaol" is beyond all comparison the greatest ballad in English: one of the noblest poems in the language. This is what prison did for Oscar Wilde.

When speaking to him later about this poem I remember assuming that his prison experiences must have helped him to realise the suffering of the condemned soldier and certainly lent passion to his verse. But he would not hear of it.

"Oh, no, Frank," he cried, "never; my experiences in prison were too horrible, too painful to be used. I simply blotted them out altogether and refused to recall them."

"What about the verse?" I asked:

> "We sewed the sacks, we broke the stones,
> We turned the dusty drill:
> We banged the tins, and bawled the hymns,
> And sweated on the mill:
> And in the heart of every man
> Terror was lying still."

"Characteristic details, Frank, merely the *decor* of prison life, not its reality; that no one could paint, not even Dante, who had to turn away his eyes from lesser suffering."

It may be worth while to notice here, as an example of the hatred with which Oscar Wilde's name and work were regarded, that even after he had paid the penalty for his crime the publisher and editor, alike in England and America, put anything but a high price on his best work. They would have bought a play readily enough because they would have known that it would make them money, but a ballad from his pen nobody seemed to want. The highest price offered in America for "The Ballad of Reading Gaol" was one hundred dollars. Oscar found difficulty in getting even L20 for the English rights from the friend who published it; yet it has sold since by hundreds of thousands and is certain always to sell.

I must insert here part of another letter from Oscar Wilde which appeared in *The Daily Chronicle*, 24th March, 1898, on the cruelties of the English prison system; it was headed, "Don't read this if you want to be happy to-day," and was signed by "The Author of 'The Ballad of Reading Gaol.'" It was manifestly a direct outcome of his prison experiences. The letter was simple and affecting; but it had little or no influence on the English conscience. The Home Secretary was about to reform (!) the prison system by appointing more inspectors. Oscar Wilde pointed out that inspectors could do nothing but see that the regulations were carried out. He took up the position that it was the regulations which needed reform. His plea was irrefutable in its moderation and simplicity: but it was beyond the comprehension of an English Home Secretary apparently, for all the abuses pointed out by Oscar Wilde still flourish. I can't help giving some extracts from this memorable indictment: memorable for its reserve and sanity and complete absence of any bitterness:

"... The prisoner who has been allowed the smallest privilege dreads the arrival of the inspectors. And on the day of any prison inspection the prison officials are more than usually brutal to the prisoners. Their object is, of course, to show the splendid discipline they maintain.

"The necessary reforms are very simple. They concern the needs of the body and the needs of the mind of each unfortunate prisoner.

"With regard to the first, there are three permanent punishments authorised by law in English prisons:

"1. Hunger.

"2. Insomnia.

"3. Disease.

"The food supplied to prisoners is entirely inadequate. Most of it is revolting in character. All of it is insufficient. Every prisoner suffers day and night from hunger....

"The result of the food—which in most cases consists of weak gruel, badly baked bread, suet and water—is disease in the form of incessant diarrhoea. This malady, which ultimately with most prisoners becomes a permanent disease, is a recognised institution in every prison. At Wandsworth Prison, for instance—where I was confined for two months, till I had to be carried into hospital, where I remained for another two months—the warders go round twice or three times a day with astringent medicine, which they serve out to the prisoners as a matter of course. After about a week of such treatment it is unnecessary to say that the medicine produces no effect at all.

"The wretched prisoner is thus left a prey to the most weakening, depressing and humiliating malady that can be conceived, and if, as often happens, he fails from physical weakness to complete his required evolutions at the crank, or the mill, he is reported for idleness and punished with the greatest severity and brutality. Nor is this all.

"Nothing can be worse than the sanitary arrangements of English prisons.... The foul air of the prison cells, increased by a system of ventilation that is utterly ineffective, is so sickening and unwholesome that it is not uncommon for warders, when they come into the room out of the fresh air, and open and inspect each cell, to be violently sick....

"With regard to the punishment of insomnia, it only exists in Chinese and English prisons. In China it is inflicted by placing the prisoner in a small bamboo cage; in England by means of the plank bed. The object of the plank bed is to produce insomnia. There is no other object in it, and it invariably succeeds. And even when one is subsequently allowed a hard mattress, as happens in the course of imprisonment, one still suffers from insomnia. It is a revolting and ignorant punishment.

"With regard to the needs of the mind, I beg that you will allow me to say something.

"The present prison system seems almost to have for its aim the wrecking and the destruction of the mental faculties. The production of insanity is, if not its object, certainly its result. That is a well-ascertained fact. Its causes are obvious. Deprived of books, of all human intercourse, isolated from every humane and humanising influence, condemned to eternal silence, robbed of all intercourse with the external world, treated like an unintelligent animal, brutalised below the level of any of the brute-creation, the wretched man who is confined in an English prison can hardly escape becoming insane."

This letter ended by saying that if all the reforms suggested were carried out much would still remain to be done. It would still be advisable to "humanise the governors of prisons, to civilise the warders, and to Christianise the Chaplains."

This letter was the last effort of the new Oscar, the Oscar who had manfully tried to put the prison under his feet and to learn the significance of sorrow and the lesson of love which Christ brought into the world.

In the beautiful pages about Jesus which form the greater part of *De Profundis*, also written in those last hopeful months in Reading Gaol, Oscar shows, I think, that he might have done much higher work than Tolstoi or Renan had he set himself resolutely to transmute his new insight into some form of art. Now and then he divined the very secret of Jesus:

"When he says 'Forgive your enemies' it is not for the sake of the enemy, but for one's own sake that he says so, and because love is more beautiful than hate. In his own entreaty to the young man, 'Sell all that thou hast and give to the poor,' it is not of the state of the poor that he is thinking but of the soul of the young man, the soul that wealth was marring."

In many of these pages Oscar Wilde really came close to the divine Master; "the image of the Man of Sorrows," he says, "has fascinated and dominated art as no Greek god succeeded in doing."... And again:

"Out of the carpenter's shop at Nazareth had come a personality infinitely greater than any made by myth and legend, and one, strangely enough, destined to reveal to the world the mystical meaning of wine and the real beauties of the lilies of the field as none, either on Cithaeron or Enna, has ever done. The song of Isaiah, 'He is despised and rejected of men, a man of sorrows and acquainted with grief: and we hid as it were our faces from him,' had seemed to him to prefigure himself, and in him the prophecy was fulfilled."

In this spirit Oscar made up his mind that he would write about "Christ as the precursor of the romantic movement in life" and about "The artistic life considered in its relation to conduct."

By bitter suffering he had been brought to see that the moment of repentance is the moment of absolution and self-realisation, that tears can wash out even blood. In "The Ballad of Reading Gaol" he wrote:

> And with tears of blood he cleansed the hand,
> The hand that held the steel:
> For only blood can wipe out blood,
> And only tears can heal:
> And the crimson stain that was of Cain

Became Christ's snow-white seal.

This is the highest height Oscar Wilde ever reached, and alas! he only trod the summit for a moment. But as he says himself: "One has perhaps to go to prison to understand that. And, if so, it may be worth while going to prison." He was by nature a pagan who for a few months became a Christian, but to live as a lover of Jesus was impossible to this "Greek born out of due time," and he never even dreamed of a reconciling synthesis....

The arrest of his development makes him a better representative of his time: he was an artistic expression of the best English mind: a Pagan and Epicurean, his rule of conduct was a selfish Individualism:—"Am I my brother's keeper?" This attitude must entail a dreadful Nemesis, for it condemns one Briton in every four to a pauper's grave. The result will convince the most hardened that such selfishness is not a creed by which human beings can live in society.

* * * * *

This summer of 1897 was the harvest time in Oscar Wilde's Life; and his golden Indian summer. We owe it "De Profundis," the best pages of prose he ever wrote, and "The Ballad of Reading Gaol," his only original poem; yet one that will live as long as the language: we owe it also that sweet and charming letter to Bobbie Ross which shows him in his habit as he lived. I must still say a word or two about him in this summer in order to show the ordinary working of his mind.

On his release, and, indeed, for a year or two later, he called himself Sebastian Melmoth. But one had hardly spoken a half a dozen words to him, when he used to beg to be called Oscar Wilde. I remember how he pulled up someone who had just been introduced to him, who persisted in addressing him as Mr. Melmoth.

"Call me Oscar Wilde," he pleaded, "Mr. Melmoth is unknown, you see."

"I thought you preferred it," said the stranger excusing himself.

"Oh, dear, no," interrupted Oscar smiling, "I only use the name Melmoth to spare the blushes of the postman, to preserve his modesty," and he laughed in the old delightful way.

It was always significant to me the eager delight with which he shuffled off the new name and took up the old one which he had made famous.

An anecdote from his life in the Chalet at this time showed that the old witty pagan in Oscar was not yet extinct.

An English lady who had written a great many novels and happened to be staying in Dieppe heard of him, and out of kindness or curiosity, or perhaps a mixture of both motives, wrote and invited him to luncheon. He accepted the invitation. The good lady did not know how to talk to Mr. Sebastian Melmoth, and time went heavily. At length she began to expatiate on the cheapness of things in France; did Mr. Melmoth know how wonderfully cheap and good the living was?

"Only fancy," she went on, "you would not believe what that claret you are drinking costs."

"Really?" questioned Oscar, with a polite smile.

"Of course I get it wholesale," she explained, "but it only costs me sixpence a quart."

"Oh, my dear lady, I'm afraid you have been cheated," he exclaimed, "ladies should never buy wine. I'm afraid you have been sadly overcharged."

The humour may excuse the discourtesy, but Oscar was so uniformly polite to everyone that the incident simply shows how ineffably he had been bored.

This summer of 1897 was the decisive period and final turning-point in Oscar Wilde's career. So long as the sunny weather lasted and friends came to visit him from time to time Oscar was content to live in the Chalet Bourgeat; but when the days began to draw in and the weather became unsettled, the dreariness of a life passed in solitude, indoors, and without a library became insupportable. He was being drawn in two opposite directions. I did not know it at the time; indeed he only told me about it months later when the matter had been decided irrevocably; but this was the moment when his soul was at stake between good and evil. The question was whether his wife would come to him again or whether he would yield to the solicitations of Lord Alfred Douglas and go to live with him.

Mr. Sherard has told in his book how he brought about the first reconciliation between Oscar and his wife; and how immediately afterwards he received a letter from Lord Alfred Douglas threatening to shoot him like a dog, if, by any words of his, Wilde's friendship was lost to him, Douglas.

Unluckily Mrs. Wilde's family were against her going back to her husband; they begged her not to go; talked to her of her duty to her children and herself, and the poor woman hesitated. Finally her advisers decided for her, and Mrs.

Wilde wrote this decision to Oscar's solicitors shortly before his release: Oscar's probation was to last at least a year. I do not know enough about Mrs. Wilde and her relations with her family and with her husband even to discuss her inaction: I dare not criticise her: but she did not go to her husband when if she had gone boldly she might have saved him. She knew Lord Alfred Douglas' influence over him; knew that it had already brought him to grief. Gide says, and Oscar himself told me afterwards, that he had come out of prison determined not to go back to Alfred Douglas and the old life. It seems a pity that his wife did not act promptly; she allowed herself to believe that a time of probation was necessary. The delay wounded Oscar, and all the while, as he told me a little later, he was resisting an influence which had dominated his life in the past.

"I got a letter almost every day, Frank, begging me to come to Posilippo, to the villa which Lord Alfred Douglas had rented. Every day I heard his voice calling, 'Come, come, to sunshine and to me. Come to Naples with its wonderful museum of bronzes and Pompeii and Paestum, the city of Poseidon: I am waiting to welcome you. Come.'

"Who could resist it, Frank? love calling, calling with outstretched arms; who could stay in bleak Berneval and watch the sheets of rain falling, falling—and the grey mist shrouding the grey sea, and think of Naples and love and sunshine; who could resist it all? I could not, Frank, I was so lonely and I hated solitude. I resisted as long as I could, but when chill October came and Bosie came to Rouen for me, I gave up the struggle and yielded."

Could Oscar Wilde have won and made for himself a new and greater life? The majority of men are content to think that such a victory was impossible to him. Everyone knows that he lost; but I at least believe that he might have won. His wife was on the point of yielding, I have since been told; on the point of complete reconciliation when she heard that he had gone to Naples and returned to his old habit of living; a few days made all the difference.

It was at the instigation of Lord Alfred Douglas that Oscar began the insane action against Lord Queensberry, in which he put to hazard his success, his position, his good name and liberty, and lost them all. Two years later at the same tempting, he committed soul-suicide.

He was not only better in health than he had ever been; but he was talking and writing better than ever before and full of literary projects which would certainly have given him money and position and a measure of happiness besides increasing his reputation. From the moment he went to Naples he was lost, and he knew it himself; he never afterwards wrote anything: as he used to say, he could never afterwards face his own soul.

He could never have won up again, the world says, and shrugs careless shoulders. It is a cheap, unworthy conclusion. Some of us still persist in believing that Oscar Wilde might easily have won and never again been caught in that dreadful wind which whips the victims of sensual desire about unceasingly, driving them hither and thither without rest in that awful place where: "Nulla speranza gli conforta mai." (No hope ever comforts!)

FOOTNOTES:

[7] Reproduced in the Appendix.

[8] Fac-simile copies of some of the notes Oscar wrote to Warder Martin about these children are reproduced in the Appendix. The notes were written on scraps of paper and

pushed under his cell-door; they are among the most convincing evidences of Oscar's essential humanity and kindness of heart.

[9] The Home Secretary, Sir Matthew White Ridley, when questioned by Mr. Michael Davitt in the House of Commons, May 25, 1897, declared that this dismissal of a warder for feeding a little hungry child at his own expense was "fully justified" and a "proper step." This same Home Secretary appointed his utterly incompetent brother to be a judge of the High Court.

[10] The correspondent to whom Wilde writes and the other friend referred to are Roman Catholics.

[11] This refers to a story which Wilde was much interested in at the time.

[12] The proprietor of the hotel.

[13] The Sphinx is a nickname for Mrs. Leverson, author of "The Eleventh Hour," and other witty novels.

[14] Ernest was her husband.

[15] The silver spoon is a proposed line for a play given by Ross to Turner (Reggie).

[16] Wilde's solicitor in Regina v. Wilde.

[17] A reference to the "Vailima Letters" of Stevenson which Wilde read when he was in prison.

[18] An architect who sent Wilde books on his release from prison.

[19] His letter to *The Daily Chronicle* about Warder Martin and the little children.

[20] The Ballad was finished in Naples and Alfred Douglas has since declared that he helped Oscar Wilde to write it. I have no wish to dispute this: Alfred Douglas' poetic gift was extraordinary, far greater than Oscar Wilde's. The poem was conceived in prison and a good deal of it was printed before Oscar went near Alfred Douglas and some of the best stanzas in it are to be found in this earlier portion: no part of the credit of it, in my opinion, belongs to Alfred Douglas. See Appendix for Ross's opinion.

[21] Hanging in chains was called keeping sheep by moonlight.

CHAPTER XX

"Non dispetto, ma doglia."
—*Dante.*

Oscar Wilde did not stay long in Naples, a few brief months; the forbidden fruit quickly turned to ashes in his mouth.

I give the following extracts from a letter he wrote to Robert Ross in December, 1897, shortly after leaving Naples, because it describes the second great crisis in his life and is besides the bitterest thing he ever wrote and therefore of peculiar value:

> "The facts of Naples are very bald. Bosie for four months, by endless lies, offered me a home. He offered me love, affection, and care, and promised that I should never want for anything. After four months I accepted his offer, but when we met on our way to Naples, I found he had no money, no plans, and had forgotten all his promises. His one idea was that I should raise the money for us both; I did so to the extent of L120. On this Bosie lived quite happy. When it came to his having to pay his own share he became terribly unkind and penurious, except where his own pleasures were concerned, and when my allowance ceased, he left.

"With regard to the L500[22] which he said was a debt of honour, he has written to me to say that he admits the debt of honour, but as lots of gentlemen don't pay their debts of honour, it is quite a common thing and no one thinks any the worse of them.

> "I don't know what you said to Constance, but the bald fact is that I accepted the offer of the home, and found that I was expected to provide the money, and when I could no longer do so I was left to my own devices. It is the most bitter experience of a bitter life. It is a blow quite awful. It had to come, but I know it is better I should never see him again, I don't want to, it fills me with horror."

A word of explanation will explain his reference to his wife, Constance, in this letter: by a deed of separation made at the end of his imprisonment, Mrs. Wilde undertook to allow Oscar L150 a year for life, under the condition that the allowance was to be forfeited if Oscar ever lived under the same roof with Lord Alfred Douglas. Having forfeited the allowance Oscar got Robert Ross to ask his wife to continue it and in spite of the forfeiture Mrs. Wilde continually sent Oscar money through Robert Ross, merely stipulating that her husband should not be told whence the money came. Ross, too, who had also sent him L150 a year, resumed his monthly payments as soon as he left Douglas.

My friendship with Oscar Wilde, which had been interrupted after he left prison by a silly gibe directed rather against the go-between he had sent to me than against him, was renewed in Paris early in 1898. I have related the little misunder-standing in the Appendix. I had never felt anything but the most cordial affection for Oscar and as soon as I went to Paris and met him I explained what had seemed to him unkind. When I asked him about his life since his release he told me simply that he had quarrelled with Bosie Douglas.

I did not attribute much importance to this; but I could not help noticing the extraordinary change that had taken place in him since he had been in Naples. His health was almost as good as ever; in fact, the prison discipline with its two years of hard living had done him so much good that his health continued excellent almost to the end.

But his whole manner and attitude to life had again changed: he now resembled the successful Oscar of the early nineties: I caught echoes, too, in his speech of a harder, smaller nature; "that talk about reformation, Frank, is all nonsense; no one ever really reforms or changes. I am what I always was."

He was mistaken: he took up again the old pagan standpoint; but he was not the same; he was reckless now, not thoughtless, and, as soon as one probed a little beneath the surface, depressed almost to despairing. He had learnt the meaning of suffering and pity, had sensed their value; he had turned his back upon them all, it is true, but he could not return to pagan carelessness, and the light-hearted enjoyment of pleasure. He did his best and almost succeeded; but the effort was there. His creed now was what it used to be about 1892: "Let us get what pleasure we may in the fleeting days; for the night cometh, and the silence that can never be broken."

The old doctrine of original sin, we now call reversion to type; the most lovely garden rose, if allowed to go without discipline and tendance, will in a few generations become again the common scentless dog-rose of our hedges. Such a reversion to type had taken place in Oscar Wilde. It must be inferred perhaps that the old pagan Greek in him was stronger than the Christian virtues which had been called into being by the discipline and suffering of prison. Little by little, as he began to live his old life again, the lessons learned in prison seemed to drop from him and be forgotten. But in reality the high thoughts he had lived with, were not lost; his lips had been touched by the divine fire; his eyes had seen the world-wonder of sympathy, pity and love and, strangely enough, this higher vision helped, as we shall soon see, to shake his individuality from its centre, and thus destroyed his power of work and completed his soul-ruin. Oscar's second fall—this time from a height—was fatal and made writing impossible to him. It is all clear enough now in retrospect though I did not understand it at the time. When he went to live with Bosie Douglas he threw off the Christian attitude, but afterwards had to recognise that "De Profundis" and "The Ballad of Reading Gaol" were deeper and better work than any of his earlier writings. He resumed the pagan position; outwardly and for the time being he was the old Oscar again, with his Greek love of beauty and hatred of disease, deformity and ugliness, and whenever he met a kindred spirit, he absolutely revelled in gay paradoxes and brilliant flashes of humour. But he was at war with himself, like Milton's Satan always conscious of his fall, always regretful of his lost estate and by reason of this division of spirit unable to write. Perhaps because of this he threw himself more than ever into talk.

He was beyond all comparison the most interesting companion I have ever known: the most brilliant talker, I cannot but think, that ever lived. No one surely ever gave himself more entirely in speech. Again and again he declared that he had only put his talent into his books and plays, but his genius into his life. If he had said into his talk, it would have been the exact truth.

People have differed a great deal about his mental and physical condition after he came out of prison. All who knew him really, Ross, Turner, More Adey, Lord Alfred Douglas and myself, are agreed that in spite of a slight deafness he was never better in health, never indeed so well. But some French friends were determined to make him out a martyr.

In his picture of Wilde's last years, Gide tells us that "he had suffered too grievously from his imprisonment.... His will had been broken ... nothing remained in his shattered life but a mouldy ruin,[23] painful to contemplate, of his former self. At times he seemed to wish to show that his brain was still active. Humour there was; but it was far-fetched, forced and threadbare."

These touches may be necessary in order to complete a French picture of the social outcast. They are not only untrue when applied to Oscar Wilde, but the reverse of the truth; he never talked so well, was never so charming a companion as in the last years of his life.

In the very last year his talk was more genial, more humorous, more vivid than ever, with a wider range of thought and intenser stimulus than before. He was a born *improvisatore*. At the moment he always dazzled one out of judgment. A phonograph would have discovered the truth; a great part of his charm was physical; much of his talk mere topsy-turvy paradox, the very froth of thought carried off by gleaming, dancing eyes, smiling, happy lips, and a melodious voice.

The entertainment usually started with some humorous play on words. One of the company would say something obvious or trivial, repeat a proverb or commonplace tag such as, "Genius is born, not made," and Oscar would flash in smiling, "not 'paid,' my dear fellow, not 'paid.'"

An interesting comment would follow on some doing of the day, a skit on some accepted belief or a parody of some pretentious solemnity, a winged word on a new book or a new author, and when everyone was smiling with amused enjoyment, the fine eyes would become introspective, the beautiful voice would take on a grave music and Oscar would begin a story, a story with symbolic second meaning or a glimpse of new thought, and when all were listening enthralled, of a sudden the eyes would dance, the smile break forth again like sunshine and some sparkling witticism would set everyone laughing.

The spell was broken, but only for a moment. A new clue would soon be given and at once Oscar was off again with renewed brio to finer effects.

The talking itself warmed and quickened him extraordinarily: he loved to show off and astonish his audience, and usually talked better after an hour or two than at the beginning. His verve was inexhaustible. But always a great part of the fascination lay in the quick changes from grave to gay, from pathos to mockery, from philosophy to fun.

There was but little of the actor in him. When telling a story he never mimicked his personages; his drama seldom lay in clash of character, but in thought; it was the sheer beauty of the words, the melody of the cadenced voice, the glowing eyes which fascinated you and always and above all the scintillating, coruscating humour that lifted his monologues into works of art.

Curiously enough he seldom talked of himself or of the incidents of his past life. After the prison he always regarded himself as a sort of Prometheus and his life as symbolic; but his earlier experiences never suggested themselves to him as specially significant; the happenings of his life after his fall seemed predestined and fateful to him; yet of those he spoke but seldom. Even when carried away by his own eloquence, he kept the tone of good society.

When you came afterwards to think over one of those wonderful evenings when he had talked for hours, almost without interruption, you hardly found more than an epigram, a fugitive flash of critical insight, an apologue or pretty story charmingly told. Over all this he had cast the glittering, sparkling robe of his Celtic gaiety, verbal humour, and sensual enjoyment of living. It was all like champagne; meant to be drunk quickly; if you let it stand, you soon realised that some still wines had rarer virtues. But there was always about him the magic of a rich and *puissant* personality; like some great actor he could take a poor part and fill it with the passion and vivacity of his own nature, till it became a living and memorable creation.

He gave the impression of wide intellectual range, yet in reality he was not broad; life was not his study nor the world-drama his field. His talk was all of literature and art and the vanities; the light drawing-room comedy on the edge of farce was his kingdom; there he ruled as a sovereign.

Anyone who has read Oscar Wilde's plays at all carefully, especially "The Importance of Being Earnest," must, I think, see that in kindly, happy humour he is without a peer in literature. Who can ever forget the scene between the town and country girl in that delightful farce-comedy. As soon as the London girl realises that the country girl has hardly any opportunity of making new friends or meeting new men, she exclaims:

"Ah! now I know what they mean when they talk of agricultural depression."

This sunny humour is Wilde's especial contribution to literature: he calls forth a smile whereas others try to provoke laughter. Yet he was as witty as anyone of whom we have record, and some of the best epigrams in English are his. "The cynic knows the price of everything and the value of nothing" is better than the best of La Rochefoucauld, as good as the best of Vauvenargues or Joubert. He was as wittily urbane as Congreve. But all the witty things that one man can say may be numbered on one's fingers. It was through his humour that Wilde reigned supreme. It was his humour that lent his talk its singular attraction. He was the only man I have ever met or heard of who could keep one smiling with amusement hour after hour. True, much of the humour was merely verbal, but it was always gay and genial: summer-lightning humour, I used to call it, unexpected, dazzling, full of colour yet harmless.

Let me try and catch here some of the fleeting iridescence of that radiant spirit. Some years before I had been introduced to Mdlle. Marie Anne de Bovet by Sir Charles Dilke. Mdlle. de Bovet was a writer of talent and knew English uncommonly well; but in spite of masses of fair hair and vivacious eyes she was certainly very plain. As soon as she heard I was in Paris, she asked me to present Oscar Wilde to her. He had no objection, and so I made a meeting between them. When he caught sight of her, he stopped short: seeing his astonishment, she cried to him in her quick, abrupt way:

"N'est-ce pas, M. Wilde, que je suis la femme la plus laide de France?" (Come, confess, Mr. Wilde, that I am the ugliest woman in France.)

Bowing low, Oscar replied with smiling courtesy:

"Du monde, Madame, du monde." (In the world, madame, in the world.)

No one could help laughing; the retort was irresistible. He

should have said: "Au monde, madame, au monde," but the meaning was clear.

Sometimes this thought-quickness and happy dexterity had to be used in self-defence. Jean Lorrain was the wittiest talker I have ever heard in France, and a most brilliant journalist. His life was as abandoned as it could well be; in fact, he made a parade of strange vices. In the days of Oscar's supremacy he always pretended to be a friend and admirer. About this time Oscar wanted me to know Stephane Mallarme. He took me to his rooms one afternoon when there was a reception. There were a great many people present. Mallarme was standing at the other end of the room leaning against the chimney piece. Near the door was Lorrain, and we both went towards him, Oscar with outstretched hands:

"Delighted to see you, Jean."

For some reason or other, most probably out of tawdry vanity, Lorrain folded his arms theatrically and replied:

"I regret I cannot say as much: I can no longer be one of your friends, M. Wilde."

The insult was stupid, brutal; yet everyone was on tiptoe to see how Oscar would answer it.

"How true that is," he said quietly, as quickly as if he had expected the traitor-thrust, "how true and how sad! At a certain time in life all of us who have done anything like you and me, Lorrain, must realise that we no longer have any friends in this world; but only lovers." (Plus d'amis, seulement des amants.)

A smile of approval lighted up every face.

"Well said, well said," was the general exclamation. His humour was almost invariably generous, kind.

One day in a Paris studio the conversation turned on the character of Marat: one Frenchman would have it that he was a fiend, another saw in him the incarnation of the revolution, a third insisted that he was merely the gamin of the Paris streets grown up. Suddenly one turned to Oscar, who was sitting silent, and asked his opinion: he took the ball at once, gravely.

"*Ce malheureux! Il n'avait pas de veine—pour une fois qu'il a pris un bain....*" (Poor devil, he was unlucky! To come to such grief for once taking a bath.)

For a little while Oscar was interested in the Dreyfus case, and especially in the Commandant Esterhazy, who played such a prominent part in it with the infamous *bordereau* which brought about the conviction of Dreyfus. Most Frenchmen now know that the *bordereau* was a forgery and without any real value.

I was curious to see Esterhazy, and Oscar brought him to lunch one day at Durand's. He was a little below middle height, extremely thin and as dark as any Italian, with an enormous hook nose and heavy jaw. He looked to me like some foul bird of prey: greed and cunning in the restless brown eyes set close together, quick resolution in the out-thrust, bony jaws and hard chin; but manifestly he had no capacity, no mind: he was meagre in all ways. For a long time he bored us by insisting that Dreyfus was a traitor, a Jew, and a German; to him a trinity of faults, whereas he, Esterhazy, was perfectly innocent and had been very badly treated. At length Oscar leant across the table and said to him in French with, strange to say, a slight Irish accent, not noticeable when he spoke English:

"The innocent," he said, "always suffer, M. le Commandant; it is their *metier*. Besides, we are all innocent till we are found out; it is a poor, common part to play and within the compass of the meanest. The interesting thing surely is to be guilty and so wear as a halo the seduction of sin."

Esterhazy appeared put out for a moment, and then he caught the genial gaiety of the reproof and the hint contained in it. His vanity would not allow him to remain long in a secondary *role*, and so, to our amazement, he suddenly broke out:

"Why should I not make my confession to you? I will. It is I, Esterhazy, who alone am guilty. I wrote the *bordereau*. I put Dreyfus in prison, and all France can not liberate him. I am the maker of the plot, and the chief part in it is mine."

To his surprise we both roared with laughter. The influence of the larger nature on the smaller to such an extraordinary issue was irresistibly comic. At the time no one even suspected Esterhazy in connection with the *bordereau*.

Another example, this time of Oscar's wit, may find a place here. Sir Lewis Morris was a voluminous poetaster with a common mind. He once bored Oscar by complaining that his books were boycotted by the press; after giving several instances of unfair treatment he burst out: "There's a conspiracy against me, a conspiracy of silence; but what can one do? What should I do?"

"Join it," replied Oscar smiling.

Oscar's humour was for the most part intellectual, and something like it can be found in others, though the happy fecundity and lightsome gaiety of it belonged to the individual temperament and perished with him. I remember once trying to give an idea of the different sides of his humour, just to see how far it could be imitated.

I made believe to have met him at Paddington, after his release from Reading, though he was brought to Pentonville in private clothes by a warder on May 18th, and was released early the next morning, two years to the hour from the commencement of the Sessions at which he was convicted on May 25th. The Act says that you must be released from the prison in which you are first confined. I pretended, however, that I had met him. The train, I said, ran into Paddington Station early in the morning. I went across to him as he got out of the carriage: grey dawn filled the vast echoing space; a few porters could be seen scattered about; it was all chill and depressing.

"Welcome, welcome, Oscar!" I cried holding out my hands. "I am sorry I'm alone. You ought to have been met by troops of boys and girls flower-crowned, but alas! you will have to content yourself with one middle-aged admirer."

"Yes, it's really terrible, Frank," he replied gravely. "If England persists in treating her criminals like this, she does not deserve to have any...."

"Ah," said an old lady to him one day at lunch, "I know you people who pretend to be a great deal worse than you are, I know you. I shouldn't be afraid of you."

"Naturally we pretend to be bad, dear lady," he replied; "it is the only way to make ourselves interesting to you. Everyone believes a man who pretends to be good, he is such a bore; but no one believes a man who says he is evil. That makes him interesting."

"Oh, you are too clever for me," replied the old lady nodding her head. "You see in my day none of us went to Girton and Newnham. There were no schools then for the higher education of women."

"How absurd such schools are, are they not?" cried Oscar. "Were I a despot, I should immediately establish schools for the lower education of women. That's what they need. It usually takes ten years living with a man to complete a woman's education."

"Then what would you do," asked someone, "about the lower education of man?"

"That's already provided for, my dear fellow, amply provided for; we have our public schools and universities to see to that. What we want are schools for the higher education of men, and schools for the lower education of women."

Genial persiflage of this sort was his particular *forte* whether my imitation of it is good or bad.

His kindliness was ingrained. I never heard him say a gross or even a vulgar word, hardly even a sharp or unkind thing. Whether in company or with one person, his mind was all dedicated to genial, kindly, flattering thoughts. He hated rudeness or discussion or insistence as he hated ugliness or deformity.

One evening of this summer a trivial incident showed me that he was sinking deeper in the mud-honey of life.

A new play was about to be given at the Francais and because he expressed a wish to see it I bought a couple of tickets. We went in and he made me change places with him in order to be able to talk to me; he was growing nearly deaf in the bad ear. After the first act we went outside to smoke a cigarette.

"It's stupid," Oscar began, "fancy us two going in there to listen to what that foolish Frenchman says about love; he knows nothing about it; either of us could write much better on the theme. Let's walk up and down here under the columns and talk."

The people began to go into the theatre again and, as they were disappearing, I said:

"It seems rather a pity to waste our tickets; so many wish to see the play."

"We shall find someone to give them to," he said indifferently, stopping by one of the pillars.

At that very moment as if under his hand appeared a boy of about fifteen or sixteen, one of the gutter-snipe of Paris. To my amazement, he said:

"Bon soir, Monsieur Wilde."

Oscar turned to him smiling.

"Vous etes Jules, n'est-ce pas?" (you are Jules, aren't you?) he questioned.

"Oui, M. Wilde."

"Here is the very boy you want," Oscar cried; "let's give him the tickets, and he'll sell them, and make something out of them," and Oscar turned and began to explain to the boy how I had given two hundred francs for the tickets, and how, even now, they should be worth a louis or two.

"Des jaunets" (yellow boys), cried the youth, his sharp face lighting up, and in a flash he had vanished with the tickets.

"You see he knows me, Frank," said Oscar, with the childish pleasure of gratified vanity.

"Yes," I replied drily, "not an acquaintance to be proud of, I should think."

"I don't agree with you, Frank," he said, resenting my tone, "did you notice his eyes? He is one of the most beautiful boys I have ever seen; an exact replica of Emilienne D'Alencon,[24] I call him Jules D'Alencon, and I tell her he must be her brother. I had them both dining with me once and the boy is finer than the girl, his skin far more beautiful.

"By the way," he went on, as we were walking up the Avenue de l'Opera, "why should we not see Emilienne; why should she not sup with us, and you could compare them? She is playing at Olympia, near the Grand Hotel. Let's go and compare Aspasia and Agathon, and for once I shall be Alcibiades, and you the moralist, Socrates."

"I would rather talk to you," I replied.

"We can talk afterwards, Frank, when all the stars come out to listen; now is the time to live and enjoy."

"As you will," I said, and we went to the Music Hall and got a box, and he wrote a little note to Emilienne D'Alencon, and she came afterwards to supper with us. Though her face was pretty she was pre-eminently dull and uninteresting without two ideas in her bird's head. She was all greed and vanity, and could talk of nothing but the hope of getting an engagement in London: could he help her, or would Monsieur, referring to me, as a journalist get her some good puffs in advance? Oscar promised everything gravely.

While we were supping inside, Oscar caught sight of the boy passing along the Boulevard. At once he tapped on the window, loud enough to attract his attention. Nothing loth, the boy came in, and the four of us had supper together—a strange quartette.

"Now, Frank," said Oscar, "compare the two faces and you will see the likeness," and indeed there was in both the same Greek beauty—the same regularity of feature, the same low brow and large eyes, the same perfect oval.

"I am telling my friend," said Oscar to Emilienne in French, "how alike you two are, true brother and sister in beauty and in the finest of arts, the art of living," and they both laughed.

"The boy is better looking," he went on to me in English. "Her mouth is coarse and hard; her hands common, while the boy is quite perfect."

"Rather dirty, don't you think?" I could not help remarking.

"Dirty, of course, but that's nothing; nothing is so immaterial as colouring; form is everything, and his form is perfect, as exquisite as the David of Donatello. That's what he's like, Frank, the David of Donatello," and he pulled his jowl, delighted to have found the painting word.

As soon as Emilienne saw that we were talking of the boy, her interest in the conversation vanished, even more quickly than her appetite. She had to go, she said suddenly; she was so sorry, and the discontented curiosity of her look gave place again to the smirk of affected politeness.

"*Au revoir, n'est-ce pas? a Charing Cross, n'est-ce-pas,*

Monsieur? Vous ne m'oublierez pas?..."

As we turned to walk along the boulevard I noticed that the boy, too, had disappeared. The moonlight was playing with the leaves and boughs of the plane trees and throwing them in Japanese shadow-pictures on the pavement: I was given over to thought; evidently Oscar imagined I was offended, for he launched out into a panegyric on Paris.

"The most wonderful city in the world, the only civilised capital; the only place on earth where you find absolute toleration for all human frailties, with passionate admiration for all human virtues and capacities.

"Do you remember Verlaine, Frank? His life was nameless and terrible, he did everything to excess, was drunken, dirty and debauched, and yet there he would sit in a cafe on the Boul' Mich', and everybody who came in would bow to him, and call him *maitre* and be proud of any sign of recognition from him because he was a great poet.

"In England they would have murdered Verlaine, and men who call themselves gentlemen would have gone out of their way to insult him in public. England is still only half-civilised; Englishmen touch life at one or two points without suspecting its complexity. They are rude and harsh."

All the while I could not help thinking of Dante and his condemnation of Florence, and its "hard, malignant people," the people who still had something in them of "the mountain and rock" of their birthplace:—"*E tiene ancor del monte e del macigno.*"

"You are not offended, Frank, are you, with me, for making you meet two caryatides of the Parisian temple of pleasure?"

"No, no," I cried, "I was thinking how Dante condemned Florence and its people, its ungrateful malignant people, and how when his teacher, Brunetto Latini, and his companions came to him in the underworld, he felt as if he, too, must throw himself into the pit with them. Nothing prevented him from carrying out his good intention (*buona voglia*) except the fear of being himself burned and baked as they were. I was just thinking that it was his great love for Latini which gave him the deathless words:

... "Non dispetto, ma doglia
La vostra condizion dentro mi fisse.

"Not contempt but sorrow...."

"Oh, Frank," cried Oscar, "what a beautiful incident! I remember it all. I read it this last winter in Naples.... Of course Dante was full of pity as are all great poets, for they know the weakness of human nature."

But even "the sorrow" of which Dante spoke seemed to carry with it some hint of condemnation; for after a pause he went on:

"You must not judge me, Frank: you don't know what I have suffered. No wonder I snatch now at enjoyment with both hands. They did terrible things to me. Did you know that when I was arrested the police let the reporters come to the cell and stare at me. Think of it—the degradation and the shame—as if I had been a monster on show. Oh! you knew! Then you know, too, how I was really condemned before I was tried; and what a farce my trial was. That terrible judge with his insults to those he was sorry he could not send to the scaffold.

"I never told you the worst thing that befell me. When they

took me from Wandsworth to Reading, we had to stop at Clapham Junction. We were nearly an hour waiting for the train. There we sat on the platform. I was in the hideous prison clothes, handcuffed between two warders. You know how the trains come in every minute. Almost at once I was recognised, and there passed before me a continual stream of men and boys, and one after the other offered some foul sneer or gibe or scoff. They stood before me, Frank, calling me names and spitting on the ground—an eternity of torture."

My heart bled for him.

"I wonder if any punishment will teach humanity to such people, or understanding of their own baseness?"

After walking a few paces he turned to me:

"Don't reproach me, Frank, even in thought. You have no right to. You don't know me yet. Some day you will know more and then you will be sorry, so sorry that there will be no room for any reproach of me. If I could tell you what I suffered this winter!"

"This winter!" I cried. "In Naples?"

"Yes, in gay, happy Naples. It was last autumn that I really fell to ruin. I had come out of prison filled with good intentions, with all good resolutions. My wife had promised to come back to me. I hoped she would come very soon. If she had come at once, if she only had, it might all have been different. But she did not come. I have no doubt she was right from her point of view. She has always been right.

"But I was alone there in Berneval, and Bosie kept on calling me, calling, and as you know I went to him. At first it was all wonderful. The bruised leaves began to unfold in the light and warmth of affection; the sore feeling began to die out of me.

"But at once my allowance from my wife was stopped. Yes, Frank," he said, with a touch of the old humour, "they took it away when they should have doubled it. I did not care. When I had money I gave it to him without counting, so when I could not pay I thought Bosie would pay, and I was content. But at once I discovered that he expected me to find the money. I did what I could; but when my means were exhausted, the evil days began. He expected me to write plays and get money for us both as in the past; but I couldn't; I simply could not. When we were dunned his temper went to pieces. He has never known what it is to want really. You have no conception of the wretchedness of it all. He has a terrible, imperious, irritable temper."

"He's the son of his father," I interjected.

"Yes," said Oscar, "I am afraid that's the truth, Frank; he is the son of his father; violent, and irritable, with a tongue like a lash. As soon as the means of life were straitened, he became sullen and began reproaching me; why didn't I write? Why didn't I earn money? What was the good of me? As if I could write under such conditions. No man, Frank, has ever suffered worse shame and humiliation.

"At last there was a washing bill to be paid; Bosie was dunned for it, and when I came in, he raged and whipped me with his tongue. It was appalling; I had done everything for him, given him everything, lost everything, and now I could only stand and see love turned to hate: the strength of love's wine making the bitter more venomous. Then he left me, Frank, and now there is no hope for me. I am lost, finished, a derelict floating at the mercy of the stream, without plan or purpose.... And the worst of it is, I know, if men have treated me badly, I have treated myself worse; it is our sins against ourselves we can never forgive.... Do you wonder that I snatch at any pleasure?"

He turned and looked at me all shaken; I saw the tears pouring down his cheeks.

"I cannot talk any more, Frank," he said in a broken voice, "I must go."

I called a cab. My heart was so heavy within me, so sore, that I said nothing to stop him. He lifted his hand to me in sign of farewell, and I turned again to walk home alone, understanding, for the first time in my life, the full significance of the marvellous line in which Shakespeare summed up his impeachment of the world and his own justification: the only justification of any of us mortals:

> "A man more sinn'd against than sinning."

FOOTNOTES:

[22] This was the sum promised by the whole Queensberry family and by Lord Alfred Douglas in particular to Oscar to defray the costs of that first action for libel which they persuaded him to bring against Lord Queensberry. Ross has since stated in court that it was never paid. The history of the monies promised and supplied to Oscar at that time is so extraordinary and so characteristic of the age that it might well furnish a chapter to itself. Here it is enough just to say that those who ought to have supplied him with money evaded the obligation, while others upon whom he had no claim, helped him liberally; but even large sums slipped through his careless fingers like water.

[23] Cfr. Appendix: "Criticisms by Robert Ross."

[24] One of the prettiest daughters of the game to be found in Paris at the time.

CHAPTER XXI

The more I considered the matter, the more clearly I saw, or thought I saw, that the only chance of salvation for Oscar was to get him to work, to give him some purpose in life, and the reader should remember here that at this time I had not read "De Profundis" and did not know that Oscar in prison had himself recognised this necessity. After all, I said to myself, nothing is lost if he will only begin to write. A man should be able to whistle happiness and hope down the wind and take despair to his bed and heart, and win courage from his harsh companion. Happiness is not essential to the artist: happiness never creates anything but memories. If Oscar would work and not brood over the past and study himself like an Indian Fakir, he might yet come to soul-health and achievement. He could win back everything; his own respect, and the respect of his fellows, if indeed that were worth winning. An artist, I knew, must have at least the self-abnegation of the hero, and heroic resolution to strive and strive, or he will never bring it far even in his art. If I could only get Oscar to work, it seemed to me everything might yet come right. I spent a week with him, lunching and dining and putting all this before him, in every way.

I noticed that he enjoyed the good eating and the good drinking as intensely as ever. He was even drinking too much I thought, was beginning to get stout and flabby again, but the good living was a necessity to him, and it certainly did not prevent him from talking charmingly. But as soon as I pressed him to write he would shake his head:

"Oh, Frank, I cannot, you know my rooms; how could I write there? A horrid bedroom like a closet, and a little sitting room without any outlook. Books everywhere; and no place to write; to tell you the truth I cannot even read in it. I can do nothing in such miserable poverty."

Again and again he came back to this. He harped upon his destitution, so that I could not but see purpose in it. He was already cunning in the art of getting money without asking for it. My heart ached for him; one goes down hill with such fatal speed and ease, and the mire at the bottom is so loathsome. I hastened to say:

"I can let you have a little money; but you ought to work, Oscar. After all why should anyone help you, if you will not help yourself? If I cannot aid you to save yourself, I am only doing you harm."

"A base sophism, Frank, mere sophistry, as you know: a good lunch is better than a bad one for any living man."

I smiled, "Don't do yourself injustice: you could easily gain thousands and live like a prince again. Why not make the effort?"

"If I had pleasant, sunny rooms I'd try.... It's harder than you think."

"Nonsense, it's easy for you. Your punishment has made your name known in every country in the world. A book of yours would sell like wildfire; a play of yours would draw in any capital. You might live here like a prince. Shakespeare lost love and friendship, hope and health to boot—everything, and yet forced himself to write 'The Tempest.' Why can't you?"

"I'll try, Frank, I'll try."

I may just mention here that any praise of another man, even of Shakespeare, was sure to move Oscar to emulation. He acknowledged no superior. In some articles in *The Saturday Review* I had said that no one had ever given completer record of himself than Shakespeare. "We know him better than we know any of our contemporaries," I went on, "and he is better worth knowing." At once Oscar wrote to me objecting to this phrase. "Surely, Frank, you have forgotten me. Surely, I am better worth knowing than Shakespeare?"

The question astonished me so that I could not make up my mind at once; but when he pressed me later I had to tell him that Shakespeare had reached higher heights of thought and feeling than any modern, though I was probably wrong in saying that I knew him better than I knew a living man.

I had to go back to England and some little time elapsed before I could return to Paris; but I crossed again early in the summer, and found he had written nothing.

I often talked with him about it; but now he changed his ground a little.

"I can't write, Frank. When I take up my pen all the past comes back: I cannot bear the thoughts ... regret and remorse, like twin dogs, wait to seize me at any idle moment. I must go out and watch life, amuse, interest myself, or I should go mad. You don't know how sore it is about my heart, as soon as I am alone. I am face to face with my own soul; the Oscar of four years ago, with his beautiful secure life, and his glorious easy triumphs, comes up before me, and I cannot stand the contrast.... My eyes burn with tears. If you care for me, Frank, you will not ask me to write."

"You promised to try," I said somewhat harshly, "and I want you to try. You haven't suffered more than Dante suffered in exile and poverty; yet you know if he had suffered ten times as much, he would have written it all down. Tears, indeed! the fire in his eyes would have dried the tears."

"True enough, Frank, but Dante was all of one piece whereas I am drawn in two different directions. I was born to sing the joy and pride of life, the pleasure of living, the delight in everything beautiful in this most beautiful world, and they took me and tortured me till I learned pity and sorrow. Now I cannot sing the joy, heartily, because I know the suffering, and I was never made to sing of suffering. I hate it, and I want to sing the love songs of joy and pleasure. It is joy alone which appeals to my soul; the joy of life and beauty and love—I could sing the song of Apollo the Sun-God, and they try to force me to sing the song of the tortured Marsyas."

This to me was his true and final confession. His second fall after leaving prison had put him "at war with himself." This is, I think, the very heart of truth about his soul; the song of sorrow, of pity and renunciation was not his song, and the experience of suffering prevented him from singing the delight of life and the joy he took in beauty. It never seemed to occur to him that he could reach a faith which should include both self-indulgence and renunciation in a larger acceptance of life.

In spite of his sunny nature he had a certain amount of jealousy and envy in him which was always brought to light by the popular success of those whom he had known and measured. I remember his telling me once that he wrote his first play because he was annoyed at the way Pinero was being praised—"Pinero, who can't write at all: he is a stage-carpenter and nothing else. His characters are made of dough; and never was there such a worthless style, or rather such a complete absence of style: he writes like a grocer's assistant."

I noticed now that this trait of jealousy was stronger in him than ever. One day I showed him an English illustrated paper which I had bought on my way to lunch. It contained a picture of George Curzon (I beg his pardon, Lord Curzon) as Viceroy of India. He was photographed in a carriage with his wife by his side: the gorgeous state carriage drawn by four horses, with outriders, and escorted by cavalry and cheering crowds—all the paraphernalia and pomp of imperial power.

"Do you see that?" cried Oscar angrily; "fancy George Curzon being treated like that. I know him well; a more perfect example of plodding mediocrity was never seen in the world. He had never a thought or phrase above the common."

"I know him pretty well, too," I replied. "His incurable commonness is the secret of his success. He 'voices,' as he would say himself, the opinion of the average man on every subject. He might be a leader-writer on the *Mail* or *Times*. What do you know of the average man or of his opinions? But the man in the street, as he is called to-day, can only learn from the man who is just one step above himself, and so the George Curzons come to success in life. That, too, is the secret of the popularity of this or that writer. Hall Caine is an even larger George Curzon, a better endowed mediocrity."

"But why should he have fame and state and power?" Oscar

cried indignantly.

"State and power, because he is George Curzon, but fame he never will have, and I suspect if the truth were known, in the moments when he too comes face to face with his own soul, as you say, he would give a good deal of his state and power for a very little of your fame."

"That is probably true, Frank," cried Oscar, "that is almost certainly the crumpled rose-leaf of his couch, but how grossly he is over-estimated and over-rewarded.... Do you know Wilfred Blunt?"

"I have met him," I replied, "but don't know him. We met once and he bragged preposterously about his Arab ponies. I was at that time editor of *The Evening News*: and Mr. Blunt tried hard to talk down to my level."

"He is by way of being a poet, and he has a very real love of literature."

"I know," I said; "I really know his work and a good deal about him and have nothing but praise for the way he championed the Egyptians, and for his poetry when he has anything to say."

"Well, Frank, he had a sort of club at Crabbett Park, a club for poets, to which only poets were invited, and he was a most admirable and perfect host. Lady Blunt could never make out what he was up to. He used to get us all down to Crabbett, and the poet who was received last had to make a speech about the new poet—a speech in which he was supposed to tell the truth about the new-comer. Blunt took the idea, no doubt, from the custom of the French Academy. Well, he asked me down to Crabbett Park, and George Curzon, if you please, was the poet picked to make the speech about me."

"Good God," I cried, "Curzon a poet. It's like Kitchener being taken for a great captain, or Salisbury for a statesman."

"He writes verses, Frank, but of course there is not a line of poetry in him: his verses are good enough though, well-turned, I mean, and sharp, if not witty. Well, Curzon had to make this speech about me after dinner. We had a delightful dinner, quite perfect, and then Curzon got up. He had evidently prepared his speech carefully, it was bristling with innuendoes; sneering side-hits at strange sins. Everyone looked at his fellow and thought the speech the height of bad taste.

"Mediocrity always detests ability, and loathes genius; Curzon wanted to prove to himself that at any rate in the moralities he was my superior.

"When he sat down I had to answer him. That was the programme. Of course I had not prepared a speech, had not thought about Curzon, or what he might say, but I got up, Frank, and told the kindliest truth about him, and everyone took it for the bitterest sarcasm, and cheered and cheered me, though what I said was merely the truth. I told how difficult it was for Curzon to work and study at Oxford. Everyone wanted to know him because of his position, because he was going into Parliament, and certain to make a great figure there; and everyone tried to make up to him, but he knew that he must not yield to such seduction, so he sat in his room with a wet towel about his head, and worked and worked without ceasing.

"In the earlier examinations, which demand only memory, he won first honours. But even success could not induce him to relax his efforts; he lived laborious days and took every college examination seriously; he made out dates in red ink, and hung them on his wall, and learnt pages of uninteresting events and put them in blue ink in his memory, and at last came out of the 'Final Schools' with second honours. And now, I concluded, 'this model youth is going into life, and he is certain to treat it seriously, certain to win at any rate second honours in it, and have a great and praiseworthy career.'

"Frank, they roared with laughter, and, to do Curzon justice, at the end he came up to me and apologised, and was charming. Indeed, they all made much of me and we had a great night.

"I remember we talked all the night through, or rather I talked and everyone else listened, for the great principle of the division of labour is beginning to be understood in English Society. The host gives excellent food, excellent wine, excellent cigarettes, and super-excellent coffee, that's his part, and all the men listen, that's theirs: while I talk and the stars twinkle their delight.

"Wyndham was there, too; you know George Wyndham, with his beautiful face and fine figure: he is infinitely cleverer than Curzon but he has not Curzon's push and force, or perhaps, as you say, he is not in such close touch with the average man as Curzon; he was charming to me.

"In the morning we all trooped out to see the dawn, and some of the young ones, wild with youth and high spirits, Curzon of course among the number, stripped off their clothes and rushed down to the lake and began swimming and diving about like a lot of schoolboys. There is a great deal of the schoolboy in all Englishmen, that is what makes them so lovable. When they came out they ran over the grass to dry themselves, and then began playing lawn tennis, just as they were, stark naked, the future rulers of England. I shall never forget the scene. Wilfred Blunt had gone up to his wife's apartments and had changed into some fantastic pyjamas; suddenly he opened an upper window and came out and perched himself, cross-legged, on the balcony, looking down at the mad game of lawn tennis, for all the world like a sort of pink and green Buddha, while I strolled about with someone, and ordered fresh coffee and talked till the dawn came with silent silver feet lighting up the beautiful greenery of the park....

"Now George Curzon plays king in India: Wyndham is on the way to power, and I'm hiding in shame and poverty here in Paris, an exile and outcast. Do you wonder that I cannot write, Frank? The awful injustice of life maddens me. After all, what have they done in comparison with what I have done?

"Close the eyes of all of us now and fifty years hence, or a hundred years hence, no one will know anything about Curzon or Wyndham or Blunt: whether they lived or died will be a matter of indifference to everyone; but my comedies and my stories and 'The Ballad of Reading Gaol' will be known and read by millions, and even my unhappy fate will call forth world-wide sympathy."

It was all true enough, and good to keep in mind; but even when Oscar spoke of greater men than himself, he took the same attitude: his self-esteem was extraordinary. He did not compare his work with that of others; was not anxious to find his true place, as even Shakespeare was. From the beginning, from youth on, he was convinced that he was a great man and going to do great things. Many of us have the same belief and are just as persuaded, but the belief is not ever present with us as it was with Oscar, moulding all his actions. For instance, I remarked once that his handwriting was unforgettable and characteristic. "I worked at it," he said, "as a boy; I wanted a distinctive handwriting; it had to be clear and beautiful and peculiar to me. At length I got it but it took time and patience. I always wanted everything about me to be distinctive," he added, smiling.

He was proud of his physical appearance, inordinately pleased with his great height, vain of it even. "Height gives distinction," he declared, and once even went so far as to say, "One can't picture Napoleon as small; one thinks only of his magnificent head and forgets the little podgy figure; it must have been a great nuisance to him: small men have no dignity."

All this utterly unconscious of the fact that most tall men have no ever present-sense of their height as an advantage. Yet on the whole one agrees with Montaigne that height is the chief beauty of a man: it gives presence.

Oscar never learned anything from criticism; he had a good deal of personal dignity in spite of his amiability, and when one found fault with his work, he would smile vaguely or change the subject as if it didn't interest him.

Again and again I played on his self-esteem to get him to write; but always met the same answer.

"Oh, Frank, it's impossible, impossible for me to work under these disgraceful conditions."

"But you can have better conditions now and lots of money if you'll begin to work."

He shook his head despairingly. Again and again I tried, but failed to move him, even when I dangled money before him. I didn't then know that he was receiving regularly more than

L300 a year. I thought he was completely destitute, dependent on such casual help as friends could give him. I have a letter from him about this time asking me for even L5[25] as if he were in extremest need.

On one of my visits to Paris after discussing his position, I could not help saying to him:

"The only thing that will make you write, Oscar, is absolute, blank poverty. That's the sharpest spur after all—necessity."

"You don't know me," he replied sharply. "I would kill myself. I can endure to the end; but to be absolutely destitute would show me suicide as the open door."

Suddenly his depressed manner changed and his whole face lighted up.

"Isn't it comic, Frank, the way the English talk of the 'open door,' while their doors are always locked, and barred, and bolted, even their church doors? Yet it is not hypocrisy in them; they simply cannot see themselves as they are; they have no imagination."

A long pause, and he went on gravely:

"Suicide, Frank, is always the temptation of the unfortunate, a great temptation."

"Suicide is the natural end of the world-weary," I replied; "but you enjoy life intensely. For you to talk of suicide is ridiculous."

"Do you know that my wife is dead, Frank?"[26]

"I had heard it," I said.

"My way back to hope and a new life ends in her grave," he went on. "Everything I do, Frank, is irrevocable."

He spoke with a certain grave sincerity.

"The great tragedies of the world are all final and complete; Socrates would not escape death, though Crito opened the prison door for him. I could not avoid prison, though you showed me the way to safety. We are fated to suffer, don't you think? as an example to humanity—'an echo and a light unto eternity.'"

"I think it would be finer, instead of taking the punishment lying down, to trample it under your feet, and make it a rung of the ladder."

"Oh, Frank, you would turn all the tragedies into triumphs, you are a fighter. My life is done."

"You love life," I cried, "as much as ever you did; more than anyone I have ever seen."

"It is true," he cried, his face lighting up quickly, "more than anyone, Frank. Life delights me. The people passing on the Boulevards, the play of the sunshine in the trees; the noise, the quick movement of the cabs, the costumes of the *cochers* and *sergents-de-ville*; workers and beggars, pimps and prostitutes—all please me to the soul, charm me, and if you would only let me talk instead of bothering me to write I should be quite happy. Why should I write any more? I have done enough for fame.

"I will tell you a story, Frank," he broke off, and he told me a slight thing about Judas. The little tale was told delightfully, with eloquent inflections of voice and still more eloquent pauses....

"The end of all this is," I said before going back to London, "that you will not write?"

"No, no, Frank," he said, "that I cannot write under these conditions. If I had money enough; if I could shake off Paris, and forget those awful rooms of mine and get to the Riviera for the winter and live in some seaside village of the Latins with the blue sea at my feet, and the blue sky above, and God's sunlight about me and no care for money, then I would write as naturally as a bird sings, because I should be happy and could not help it....

"You write stories taken from the fight of life; you are careless of surroundings, I am a poet and can only sing in the sunshine when I am happy."

"All right," I said, snatching at the half-promise. "It is just possible that I may get hold of some money during the next few months, and, if I do, you shall go and winter in the South, and live as you please without care of money. If you can only sing when the cage is beautiful and sunlight floods it, I know the very place for you."

With this sort of vague understanding we parted for some months.

FOOTNOTES:

[25] *Cfr.* Appendix.

[26] See Appendix.

CHAPTER XXII

"A GREAT ROMANTIC PASSION"

There is no more difficult problem for the writer, no harder task than to decide how far he should allow himself to go in picturing human weakness. We have all come from the animal and can all without any assistance from books imagine easily enough the effects of unrestrained self-indulgence. Yet it is instructive and pregnant with warning to remark that, as soon as the sheet anchor of high resolve is gone, the frailties of man tend to become master-vices. All our civilisation is artificially built up by effort; all high humanity is the reward of constant striving against natural desires.

In the fall of this year, 1898, I sold *The Saturday Review* to Lord Hardwicke and his friends, and as soon as the purchase was completed, I think in November, I wired to Oscar that I should be in Paris in a short time, and ready to take him to the South for his holiday. I sent him some money to pave the way.

A few days later I crossed and wired to him from Calais to dine with me at Durand's, and to begin dinner if I happened to be late.

While waiting for dinner, I said:

"I want to stay two or three days in Paris to see some pictures. Would you be ready to start South on Thursday next?" It was then Monday, I think.

"On Thursday?" he repeated. "Yes, Frank, I think so."

"There is some money for anything you may want to buy," I said and handed him a cheque I had made payable to self and signed, for he knew where he could cash it.

"How good of you, Frank, I cannot thank you enough. You start on Thursday," he added, as if considering it.

"If you would rather wait a little," I said, "say so: I'm quite willing."

"No, Frank, I think Thursday will do. We are really going to the South for the whole winter. How wonderful; how gorgeous it will be."

We had a great dinner and talked and talked. He spoke of some of the new Frenchmen, and at great length of Pierre Louys, whom he described as a disciple:

"It was I, Frank, who induced him to write his 'Aphrodite' in prose." He spoke, too, of the Grand Guignol Theatre.

"Le Grand Guignol is the first theatre in Paris. It looks like a nonconformist chapel, a barn of a room with a gallery at the back and a little wooden stage. There you see the primitive tragedies of real life. They are as ugly and as fascinating as life itself. You must see it and we will go to Antoine's as well: you must see Antoine's new piece; he is doing great work."

We kept dinner up to an unconscionable hour. I had much to tell of London and much to hear of Paris, and we talked and drank coffee till one o'clock, and when I proposed supper Oscar accepted the idea with enthusiasm.

"I have often lunched with you from two o'clock till nine, Frank, and now I am going to dine with you from nine o'clock till breakfast to-morrow morning."

"What shall we drink?" I asked.

"The same champagne, Frank, don't you think?" he said, pulling his jowl; "there is no wine so inspiring as that dry champagne with the exquisite *bouquet*. You were the first to say my plays were the champagne of literature."

When we came out it was three o'clock and I was tired and sleepy with my journey, and Oscar had drunk perhaps more than was good for him. Knowing how he hated walking I got a *voiture de cercle* and told him to take it, and I would walk to my hotel. He thanked me and seemed to hesitate.

"What is it now?" I asked, wanting to get to bed.

"Just a word with you," he said, and drew me away from the carriage where the *chasseur* was waiting with the rug. When he got me three or four paces away he said, hesitatingly:

"Frank, could you ... can you let me have a few pounds? I'm very hard up."

I stared at him; I had given him a cheque at the beginning of the dinner: had he forgotten? Or did he perchance want to keep the hundred pounds intact for some reason? Suddenly it occurred to me that he might be without even enough for the carriage. I took out a hundred franc note and gave it to him.

"Thank you, so much," he said, thrusting it into his waistcoat pocket, "it's very kind of you."

"You will turn up to-morrow at lunch at one?" I said, as I put him into the little brougham.

"Yes, of course, yes," he cried, and I turned away.

Next day at lunch he seemed to meet me with some embarrassment:

"Frank, I want to ask you something. I'm really confused about last night; we dined most wisely, if too well. This morning I found you had given me a cheque, and I found besides in my waistcoat pocket a note for a hundred francs. Did I ask you for it at the end? 'Tap' you, the French call it," he added, trying to laugh.

I nodded.

"How dreadful!" he cried. "How dreadful poverty is! I had forgotten that you had given me a cheque, and I was so hard up, so afraid you might go away without giving me anything, that I asked you for it. Isn't poverty dreadful?"

I nodded; I could not say a word: the fact told so much.

The chastened mood of self-condemnation did not last long with him or go deep; soon he was talking as merrily and gaily as ever.

Before parting I said to him:

"You won't forget that you are going on Thursday night?"

"Oh, really!" he cried, to my surprise, "Thursday is very

near; I don't know whether I shall be able to come."

"What on earth do you mean?" I asked.

"The truth is, you know, I have debts to pay, and I have not enough."

"But I will give you more," I cried, "what will clear you?"

"Fifty more I think will do. How good you are!"

"I will bring it with me to-morrow morning."

"In notes please, will you? French money. I find I shall want it to pay some little things at once, and the time is short."

I thought nothing of the matter. The next day at lunch I gave him the money in French notes. That night I said to him:

"You know we are going away to-morrow evening: I hope you'll be ready? I have got the tickets for the *Train de Luxe*."

"Oh, I'm so sorry!" he cried, "I can't be ready."

"What is it now?" I asked.

"Well, it's money. Some more debts have come in."

"Why will you not be frank with me, and tell me what you owe? I will give you a cheque for it. I don't want to drag it out of you bit by bit. Tell me a sum that will make you free, and I will give it to you. I want you to have a perfect six months, and how can you if you are bothered with debts?"

"How kind you are to me! Do you really mean it?"

"Of course I do."

"Really?" he said.

"Yes," I said, "tell me what it is."

"I think, I believe ... would another fifty be too much?"

"I will give it you to-morrow. Are you sure that will be enough?"

"Oh, yes, Frank; but let's go on Sunday. Sunday is such a good day for travelling, and it's always so dull everywhere, we might just as well spend it on the train. Besides, no one travels on Sunday in France, so we are sure to be able to take our ease in our train. Won't Sunday do, Frank?"

"Of course it will," I replied laughing; but a day or two later he was again embarrassed, and again told me it was money, and then he confessed to me that he was afraid at first I should not have paid all his debts, if I had known how much they were, and so he thought by telling me of them little by little, he would make sure at least of something. This pitiful, pitiable confession depressed me on his account. It showed practice in such petty tricks and all too little pride. Of course it did not alter my admiration of his qualities; nor weaken in any degree my resolve to give him a fair chance. If he could be saved, I was determined to save him.

We met at the Gare de Lyons on Sunday evening. I found he had dined at the buffet: there was a surprising number of empty bottles on the table; he seemed terribly depressed.

"Someone was dining with me, Frank, a friend," he offered by way of explanation.

"Why did he not wait? I should like to have seen him."

"Oh, he was no one you would have cared about, Frank," he replied.

I sat with him and took a cup of coffee, whilst waiting for the train. He was wretchedly gloomy; scarcely spoke indeed; I could not make it out. From time to time he sighed heavily, and I noticed that his eyes were red, as if he had been crying.

"What is the matter?" I asked.

"I will tell you later, perhaps. It is very hard; parting is like dying," and his eyes filled with tears.

We were soon in the train running out into the night. I was as light-hearted as could be. At length I was free of journalism, I thought, and I was going to the South to write my Shakespeare book, and Oscar would work, too, when the conditions were pleasant. But I could not win a single smile from him; he sat downcast, sighing hopelessly from time to time.

"What on earth's the matter?" I cried. "Here you are going to the sunshine, to blue skies, and the wine-tinted Mediterranean, and you're not content. We shall stop in a hotel near a little sun-baked valley running down to the sea. You walk from the hotel over a carpet of pine needles, and when you get into the open, violets and anemones bloom about your feet, and the scent of rosemary and myrtle will be in your nostrils; yet instead of singing for joy the bird droops his feathers and hangs his head as if he had the 'pip.'"

"Oh, don't," he cried, "don't," and he looked at me with tears filling his eyes; "you don't know, Frank, what a great romantic passion is."

"Is that what you are suffering from?"

"Yes, a great romantic passion."

"Good God!" I laughed; "who has inspired this new devotion?"

"Don't make fun of me, Frank, or I will not tell you; but if you will listen I will try to tell you all about it, for I think you should know, besides, I think telling it may ease my pain, so come into the cabin and listen.

"Do you remember once in the summer you wired me from Calais to meet you at Maire's restaurant, meaning to go afterwards to Antoine's Theatre, and I was very late? You remember, the evening Rostand was dining at the next table. Well, it was that evening. I drove up to Maire's in time, and I was just getting out of the victoria when a little soldier passed, and our eyes met. My heart stood still; he had great dark eyes and an exquisite olive-dark face—a Florentine bronze, Frank, by a great master. He looked like Napoleon when he was first Consul, only—less imperious, more beautiful....

"I got out hypnotised, and followed him down the Boulevard as in a dream; the *cocher* came running after me, I remember, and I gave him a five franc piece, and waved him off; I had no idea what I owed him; I did not want to hear his voice; it might break the spell; mutely I followed my fate. I overtook the boy in a short time and asked him to come and have a drink, and he said to me in his quaint French way:

"'*Ce n'est pas de refus!*' (Too good to refuse.)"

"We went into a cafe, and I ordered something, I forget what, and we began to talk. I told him I liked his face; I had had a friend once like him; and I wanted to know all about him. I was in a hurry to meet you, but I had to make friends with him first. He began by telling me all about his mother, Frank, yes, his mother." Oscar smiled here in spite of himself.

"But at last I got from him that he was always free on Thursdays, and he would be very glad to see me then, though he did not know what I could see in him to like. I found out that the thing he desired most in the world was a bicycle; he talked of nickel-plated handle bars, and chains—and finally I told him it might be arranged. He was very grateful and so we made a rendezvous for the next Thursday, and I came on at once to dine with you."

"Goodness!" I cried laughing. "A soldier, a nickel-plated bicycle and a great romantic passion!"

"If I had said a brooch, or a necklace, some trinket which would have cost ten times as much, you would have found it quite natural."

"Yes," I admitted, "but I don't think I'd have introduced the necklace the first evening if there had been any romance in the affair, and the nickel-plated bicycle to me seems irresistibly comic."

"Frank," he cried reprovingly, "I cannot talk to you if you laugh; I am quite serious. I don't believe you know what a great romantic passion is; I am going to convince you that you don't know the meaning of it."

"Fire away," I replied, "I am here to be convinced. But I don't think you will teach me that there is any romance except where there is another sex."

"Don't talk to me of the other sex," he cried with distaste in voice and manner. "First of all in beauty there is no comparison between a boy and a girl. Think of the enormous, fat hips which every sculptor has to tone down, and make lighter, and the great udder breasts which the artist has to make small and round and firm, and then picture the exquisite slim lines of a boy's figure. No one who loves beauty can hesitate for a moment. The Greeks knew that; they had the sense of plastic beauty, and they understood that there is no comparison."

"You must not say that," I replied; "you are going too far; the Venus of Milo is as fine as any Apollo, in sheer beauty; the flowing curves appeal to me more than your weedy lines."

"Perhaps they do, Frank," he retorted, "but you must see that the boy is far more beautiful. It is your sex-instinct, your sinful sex-instinct which prevents you worshipping the higher form of beauty. Height and length of limb give distinction; slightness gives grace; women are squat! You must admit that the boy's figure is more beautiful; the appeal it makes far higher, more spiritual."

"Six of one and half-a-dozen of the other," I barked. "Your sculptor knows it is just as hard to find an ideal boy's figure as an ideal girl's; and if he has to modify the most perfect girl's figure, he has to modify the most perfect boy's figure as well. If he refines the girl's breasts and hips he has to pad the boy's ribs and tone down the great staring knee-bones and the unlovely large ankles; but please go on, I enjoy your special pleading and your romantic passion interests me; though you have not yet come to the romance, let alone the passion."

"Oh, Frank," he cried, "the story is full of romance; every meeting was an event in my life. You have no idea how intelligent he is; every evening we spent together he was different; he had grown, developed. I lent him books and he read them, and his mind opened from week to week like a flower, till in a short time, a few months, he became an exquisite companion and disciple. Frank, no girl grows like that; they have no minds, and what intelligence they have is all given to wretched vanities, and personal jealousies. There is no intellectual companionship possible with them. They want to talk of dress, and not of ideas, and how persons look and not of what they are. How can you have the flower of romance without a brotherhood of soul?"

"Sisterhood of soul seems to me infinitely finer," I said, "but go on."

"I shall convince you," he declared; "I must be able to, because all reason is on my side. Let me give you one instance. Of course my boy had his bicycle; he used to come to me on it and go to and fro from the barracks on it. When you came to Paris in September, you invited me to dine one night, one Thursday night, when he was to come to me. I told him I had to go and dine with you. He didn't mind; but was glad when I said I had an English editor for a friend, glad that I should have someone to talk to about London and the people I used to know. If it had been a woman I loved, I should have been forced to tell lies: she would have been jealous of my past. I told him the truth, and when I spoke about you he grew interested and excited, and at last he put a wish before me. He wanted to know if he might come and leave his bicycle outside and look through the window of the restaurant, just to see us at dinner. I told him there might possibly be women-guests. He replied that he would be delighted to see me in dress-clothes talking to gentlemen and ladies.

"Might he come?" he persisted.

"Of course I said he could come, and he came, but I never saw him.

"The next time we met he told me all about it; how he had picked you out from my description of you, and how he knew Baueer from his likeness to Dumas *pere*, and he was delightful about it all.

"Now, Frank, would any girl have come to see you enjoying yourself with other people? Would any girl have stared through the window and been glad to see you inside amusing yourself with other men and women? You know there's not a girl on earth with such unselfish devotion. There is no comparison, I tell you, between the boy and the girl; I say again deliberately, you don't know what a great romantic passion is or the high unselfishness of true love."

"You have put it with extraordinary ability," I said, "as of course I knew you would. I think I can understand the charm of such companionship; but only from the young boy's point of view, not from yours. I can understand how you have opened to him a new heaven and a new earth, but what has he given you? Nothing. On the other hand any finely gifted girl would have given you something. If you had really touched her heart, you would have found in her some instinctive tenderness, some proof of unselfish, exquisite devotion that would have made your eyes prickle with a sense of inferiority.

"After all, the essence of love, the finest spirit of that companionship you speak about, of the sisterhood of soul, is that the other person should quicken you, too; open to you new horizons, discover new possibilities; and how could your soldier boy help you in any way? He brought you no new ideas, no new feelings, could reveal no new thoughts to you. I can see no romance, no growth of soul in such a connection. But the girl is different from the man in all ways. You have as much to learn from her as she has from you, and neither of you can come to ideal growth in any other way: you are both half-parts of humanity—complements, and in need of each other."

"You have put it very cunningly, Frank, as I expected you would, to return your compliment, but you must admit that with the boy, at any rate, you have no jealousy, no mean envyings, no silly inanities. There it is, Frank, some of us hate 'cats.' I can give reasons for my dislike, which to me are conclusive."

"The boy who would beg for a bicycle is not likely to be without mean envyings," I replied. "Now you have talked about romance and companionship," I went on, "but can you really feel passion?"

"Frank, what a silly question! Do you remember how Socrates says he felt when the chlamys blew aside and showed him the limbs of Charmides? Don't you remember how the blood throbbed in his veins and how he grew blind with desire, a scene more magical than the passionate love-lines of Sappho?

"There is no other passion to be compared with it. A woman's passion is degrading. She is continually tempting you. She wants your desire as a satisfaction for her vanity more than anything else, and her vanity is insatiable if her desire is weak, and so she continually tempts you to excess, and then blames you for the physical satiety and disgust which she herself has created. With a boy there is no vanity in the matter, no jealousy, and therefore none of the tempting, not a tenth part of the coarseness; and consequently desire is always fresh and keen. Oh, Frank, believe me, you don't know what a great romantic passion is."

"What you say only shows how little you know women," I replied. "If you explained all this to the girl who loves you, she would see it at once, and her tenderness would grow with her self-abnegation; we all grow by giving. If the woman cares more than the man for caresses and kindness, it is because she feels more tenderness, and is capable of intenser devotion."

"You don't know what you are talking about, Frank," he retorted. "You repeat the old accepted commonplaces. The boy came to the station with me to-night. He knew I was going away for six months. His heart was like lead, tears gathered in his eyes again and again in spite of himself, and yet he tried to be gay and bright for my sake; he wanted to show me how glad he was that I should be happy, how thankful he was for all I had done for him, and the new mental life I had created in him. He did his best to keep my courage up. I cried, but he shook his tears away. 'Six months will soon be over,' he said, 'and perhaps you will come back to me, and I shall be glad again.' Meantime he will write charming letters to me, I'm sure.

"Would any girl take a parting like that? No; she would be jealous and envious, and wonder why you were enjoying yourself in the South while she was condemned to live in the rainy, cold North. Would she ask you to tell her of all the beautiful girls you met, and whether they were charming and bright, as the boy asked me to tell him of all the interesting people I should meet, so that he, too, might take an interest in them? A girl in his place would have been ill with envy and malice and jealousy. Again I repeat, you don't know what a high romantic passion is."

"Your argument is illogical," I cried, "if the girl is jealous, it is because she has given herself more completely: her exclusiveness is the other side of her devotion and tenderness; she wants to do everything for you, to be with you and help you in every way, and in case of illness or poverty or danger, you would find how much more she had to give than your red-breeched soldier."

"That's merely a rude gibe and not an argument, Frank."

"As good an argument as your 'cats,'" I replied; "your little soldier boy with his nickel-plated bicycle only makes me grin," and I grinned.

"You are unpardonable," he cried, "unpardonable, and in your soul you know that all the weight of argument is on my side. In your soul you must know it. What is the food of passion, Frank, but beauty, beauty alone, beauty always, and in beauty of form and vigour of life there is no comparison. If you loved beauty as intensely as I do, you would feel as I feel. It is beauty which gives me joy, makes me drunk as with wine, blind with insatiable desire...."

CHAPTER XXIII

He was an incomparable companion, perfectly amiable, yet vivid, and eager as a child, always interested and interesting. We awoke at Avignon and went out in pyjamas and overcoats to stretch our legs and get a bowl of coffee on the platform in the pearly grey light of early morning. After coffee and cigarettes he led the way to the other end of the platform, that we might catch a glimpse of the town wall which, though terribly restored, yet, when seen from a distance, transports one back five hundred years to the age of chivalry.

"How I should have loved to be a troubadour, or a *trouvere*, Frank; that was my true *metier*, to travel from castle to castle singing love songs and telling romantic stories to while away the tedium of the lives of the great. Fancy the reception they would have given me for bringing a new joy into their castled isolation, new ideas, new passions—a breath of gossip and scandal from the outside world to relieve the intolerable boredom of the middle ages. I should have been kept at the Court of Aix: I think they would have bound me with flower-chains, and my fame would have spread all through the sunny vineyards and grey olive-clad hills of Provence."

When we got into the train again he began:

"We stop next at Marseilles, don't we, Frank? A great historic town for nearly three thousand years. One really feels a barbarian in comparison, and yet all I know of Marseilles is that it is famous for *bouillabaisse*. Suppose we stop and get some?"

"*Bouillabaisse*," I replied, "is not peculiar to Marseilles or the *Rue Cannebiere*. You can get it all along this coast. There is only one thing necessary to it and that is *rascasse*, a fish caught only among the rocks: you will get excellent *bouillabaisse* at lunch where we are going."

"Where are we going? You have not told me yet."

"It is for you to decide," I answered. "If you want perfect quiet there are two places in the Esterel mountains, Agay and La Napoule. Agay is in the middle of the Esterel. You would be absolutely alone there except for the visit of an occasional French painter. La Napoule is eight or ten miles from Cannes, so that you are within reach of a town and its amusements. There is still another place I had thought of, quieter than either, in the mountains behind Nice."

"Nice sounds wonderful, Frank, but I should meet too many English people there who would know me, and they are horribly rude. I think we will choose La Napoule."

About ten o'clock we got out at La Napoule and installed ourselves in the little hotel, taking up three of the best rooms on the second or top floor, much to the delight of the landlord. At twelve we had breakfast under a big umbrella in the open air, looking over the sea. I had put the landlord on his mettle, and he gave us a fry of little red mullet, which made us understand how tasteless whitebait are: then a plain beefsteak *aux pommes*, a morsel of cheese, and a sweet omelette. We both agreed that we had had a most excellent breakfast. The coffee left a good deal to be desired, and there was no champagne on the list fit to drink; but both these faults could be remedied by the morrow, and were remedied.

We spent the rest of the day wandering between the seashore and the pine-clad hills. The next morning I put in some work, but in the afternoon I was free to walk and explore. On one of my first tramps I discovered a monastery among the hills hundreds of feet above the sea, built and governed by an Italian monk. I got to know the Pere Vergile[27] and had a great talk with him. He was both wise and strong, with ingratiating, gentle manners. Had he gone as a boy from his little Italian fishing village to New York or Paris, he would have certainly come to greatness and honour. One afternoon I took Oscar to see him: the monastery was not more than three-quarters of an hour's stroll from our hotel; but Oscar grumbled at the walk as a nuisance, said it was miles and miles; the road, too, was rough, and the sun hot. The truth was, he was abnormally lazy. But he fascinated the Italian with his courteous manner and vivid speech, and as soon as we were alone the Abbe asked me who he was.

"He must be a great man," he said, "he has the stamp of a great man, and he must have lived in courts: he has the charming, graceful, smiling courtesy of the great."

"Yes," I nodded mysteriously, "a great man—incognito."

The Abbe kept us to dinner, made us taste of his oldest wines, and a special liqueur of his own distilling; told us how he had built the monastery with no money, and when we exclaimed with wonder, reproved us gently:

"All great things are built with faith, and not with money; why wonder that this little building stands firmly on that everlasting foundation?"

When we came out of the monastery it was already night, and the moonlight was throwing fantastic leafy shadows on the path, as we walked down through the avenue of forest to the sea shore.

"You remember those words of Vergil, Frank—*per amica silentia lunae*—they always seem to me indescribably beautiful; the most magic line about the moon ever written, except Browning's in the poem in which he mentioned Keats—'him even.' I love that 'amica silentia.' What a beautiful nature the man had who could feel 'the *friendly* silences of the moon.'"

When we got down the hill he declared himself tired.

"Tired after a mile?" I asked.

"Tired to death, worn out," he said, laughing at his own laziness.

"Shall we get a boat and row across the bay?"

"How splendid! of course, let's do it," and we went down to the landing stage. I had never seen the water so calm; half the bay was veiled by the mountain, and opaque like unpolished steel; a little further out, the water was a purple shield, emblazoned with shimmering silver. We called a fisherman and explained what we wanted. When we got into the boat, to my astonishment, Oscar began calling the fisher boy by his name; evidently he knew him quite well. When we landed I went up from the boat to the hotel, leaving Oscar and the boy together....

A fortnight taught me a good deal about Oscar at this time; he was intensely indolent: quite content to kill time by the hour talking to the fisher lads, or he would take a little carriage and drive to Cannes and amuse himself at some wayside cafe.

He never cared to walk and I walked for miles daily, so that we spent only one or at most two afternoons a week together, meeting so seldom that nearly all our talks were significant. Several times contemporary names came up and I was compelled to notice for the first time that really he was contemptuous of almost everyone, and had a sharp word to say about many who were supposed to be his friends. One day we spoke of Ricketts and Shannon; I was saying that had Ricketts lived in Paris he would have had a great reputation: many of his designs I thought extraordinary, and his intellect was peculiarly French—*mordant* even. Oscar did not like to hear praise of anyone.

"Do you know my word for them, Frank? I like it. I call them 'Temper and Temperament.'"

Was his punishment making him a little spiteful or was it the temptation of the witty phrase?

"What do you think of Arthur Symons?" I asked.

"Oh, Frank, I said of him long ago that he was a sad example of an Egoist who had no Ego."

"And what of your compatriot, George Moore? He's popular enough," I continued.

"Popular, Frank, as if that counted. George Moore has conducted his whole education in public. He had written two or three books before he found out there was such a thing as English grammar. He at once announced his discovery and so won the admiration of the illiterate. A few years later he discovered that there was something architectural in style, that sentences had to be built up into a paragraph, and paragraphs into chapters and so on. Naturally he cried this revelation, too, from the housetops, and thus won the admiration of the journalists who had been making rubble-heaps all their lives without knowing it. I'm much afraid, Frank, in spite of all his efforts, he will die before he reaches the level from which writers start. It's a pity because he has certainly a little real talent. He differs from Symons in that he has an Ego, but his Ego has five senses and no soul."

"What about Bernard Shaw?" I probed further, "after all he's going to count."

"Yes, Frank, a man of real ability but with a bleak mind. Humorous gleams as of wintry sunlight on a bare, harsh landscape. He has no passion, no feeling, and without passionate feeling how can one be an artist? He believes in nothing, loves nothing, not even Bernard Shaw, and really, on the whole, I don't wonder at his indifference," and he laughed mischievously.

"And Wells?" I asked.

"A scientific Jules Verne," he replied with a shrug.

"Did you ever care for Hardy?" I continued.

"Not greatly. He has just found out that women have legs underneath their dresses, and this discovery has almost wrecked his life. He writes poetry, I believe, in his leisure moments, and I am afraid it will be very hard reading. He knows nothing of love; passion to him is a childish illness like measles—poor unhappy spirit!"

"You might be describing Mrs. Humphry Ward," I cried.

"God forbid, Frank," he exclaimed with such mock horror I had to laugh. "After all, Hardy is a writer and a great landscape painter."

"I don't know why it is," he went on, "but I am always match-making when I think of English celebrities. I should so much like to have introduced Mrs. Humphry Ward blushing at eighteen or twenty to Swinburne, who would of course have bitten her neck in a furious kiss, and she would have run away and exposed him in court, or else have suffered agonies of mingled delight and shame in silence.

"And if one could only marry Thomas Hardy to Victoria Cross he might have gained some inkling of real passion with which to animate his little keepsake pictures of starched ladies. A great many writers, I think, might be saved in this way, but there would still be left the Corellis and Hall Caines that one could do nothing with except bind them back to back, which would not even tantalise them, and throw them into the river, a new *noyade*: the Thames at Barking, I think, would be about the place for them...."

"Where do you go every afternoon?" I asked him once casually.

"I go to Cannes, Frank, and sit in a cafe and look across the sea to Capri, where Tiberius used to sit like a spider watching, and I think of myself as an exile, the victim of one of his inscrutable suspicions, or else I am in Rome looking at the people dancing naked, but with gilded lips, through the streets at the *Floralia*. I sup with the *arbiter elegantiarum* and come back to La Napoule, Frank," and he pulled his jowl, "to the simple life and the charm of restful friendship."

More and more clearly I saw that the effort, the hard work, of writing was altogether beyond him: he was now one of those men of genius, talkers merely, half artists, half dreamers, whom Balzac describes contemptuously as wasting their lives, "talking to hear themselves talk"; capable indeed of fine conceptions and of occasional fine phrases, but incapable of the punishing toil of execution; charming companions, fated in the long run to fall to misery and destitution.

Constant creation is the first condition of art as it is the first condition of life.

I asked him one day if he remembered the terrible passage about those "eunuchs of art" in "La Cousine Bette."

"Yes, Frank," he replied; "but Balzac was probably envious of the artist-talker; at any rate, we who talk should not be condemned by those to whom we dedicate our talents. It is for posterity to blame us; but after all I have written a good deal. Do you remember how Browning's Sarto defends himself?

> "Some good son
> Paint my two hundred pictures—let him try."

He did not see that Balzac, one of the greatest talkers that ever lived according to Theophile Gautier, was condemning the temptation to which he himself had no doubt yielded too often. To my surprise, Oscar did not even read much now. He was not eager to hear new thoughts, a little rebellious to any new mental influence. He had reached his zenith, I suppose: had begun to fossilise, as men do when they cease to grow.

One day at lunch I questioned him:

"You told me once that you always imagined yourself in the

place of every historic personage. Suppose you had been Jesus, what religion would you have preached?"

"What a wonderful question!" he cried. "What religion is mine? What belief have I?

"I believe most of all in personal liberty for every human soul. Each man ought to do what he likes, to develop as he will. England, or rather London, for I know little of England outside London, was an ideal place to me, till they punished me because I did not share their tastes. What an absurdity it all was, Frank: how dared they punish me for what is good in my eyes? How dared they?" and he fell into moody thought.... The idea of a new gospel did not really interest him.

It was about this time he first told me of a new play he had in mind.

"It has a great scene, Frank," he said. "Imagine a *roue* of forty-five who is married; incorrigible, of course, Frank, a great noble who gets the person he is in love with to come and stay with him in the country. One evening his wife, who has gone upstairs to lie down with a headache, is behind a screen in a room half asleep; she is awakened by her husband's courting. She cannot move, she is bound breathless to her couch; she hears everything. Then, Frank, the husband comes to the door and finds it locked, and knowing that his wife is inside with the host, beats upon the door and will have entrance, and while the guilty ones whisper together—the woman blaming the man, the man trying to think of some excuse, some way out of the net—the wife gets up very quietly and turns on the lights while the two cowards stare at her with wild surmise. She passes to the door and opens it and the husband rushes in to find his hostess as well as the host and his wife. I think it is a great scene, Frank, a great stage picture."

"It is," I said, "a great scene; why don't you write it?"

"Perhaps I shall, Frank, one of these days, but now I am thinking of some poetry, a 'Ballad of a Fisher Boy,' a sort of companion to 'The Ballad of Reading Gaol,' in which I sing of liberty instead of prison, joy instead of sorrow, a kiss instead of an execution. I shall do this joy-song much better than I did the song of sorrow and despair."

"Like Davidson's 'Ballad of a Nun,'" I said, for the sake of saying something.

"Naturally Davidson would write the 'Ballad of a Nun,' Frank; his talent is Scotch and severe; but I should like to write 'The Ballad of a Fisher Boy,'" and he fell to dreaming.

The thought of his punishment was oft with him. It seemed to him hideously wrong and unjust. But he never questioned the right of society to punish. He did not see that, if you once grant that, the wrong done to him could be defended.

"I used to think myself a lord of life," he said. "How dared those little wretches condemn me and punish me? Everyone of them tainted with a sensuality which I loathe."

To call him out of this bitter way of regret I quoted Shakespeare's sonnet:

> "For why should others' false adulterate eyes
> Give salutation to my sportive blood?
> Or on my frailties why are frailer spies,
> Which in their wills count bad what I think good?"

"His complaint is exactly yours, Oscar."

"It's astonishing, Frank, how well you know him, and yet you deny his intimacy with Pembroke. To you he is a living man; you always talk of him as if he had just gone out of the room, and yet you persist in believing in his innocence."

"You misapprehend me," I said, "the passion of his life was for Mary Fitton, to give her a name; I mean the 'dark lady' of the sonnets, who was Beatrice, Cressida and Cleopatra, and you yourself admit that a man who has a mad passion for a woman is immune, I think the doctors call it, to other influences."

"Oh, yes, Frank, of course; but how could Shakespeare with his beautiful nature love a woman to that mad excess?"

"Shakespeare hadn't your overwhelming love of plastic beauty," I replied; "he fell in love with a dominant personality, the complement of his own yielding, amiable disposition."

"That's it," he broke in, "our opposites attract us irresistibly—the charm of the unknown!"

"You often talk now," I went on, "as if you had never loved a woman; yet you must have loved—more than one."

"My salad days, Frank," he quoted, smiling, "when I was green in judgment, cold of blood."

"No, no," I persisted, "it is not a great while since you praised Lady So and So and the Terrys enthusiastically."

"Lady—," he began gravely (and I could not but notice that the mere title seduced him to conventional, poetic language), "moves like a lily in water; I always think of her as a lily; just as I used to think of Lily Langtry as a tulip, with a figure like a Greek vase carved in ivory. But I always adored the Terrys: Marion is a great actress with subtle charm and enigmatic fascination: she was my 'Woman of no importance,' artificial and enthralling; she belongs to my theatre—"

As he seemed to have lost the thread, I questioned again.

"And Ellen?"

"Oh, Ellen's a perfect wonder," he broke out, "a great character. Do you know her history?" And then, without waiting for an answer, he continued:

"She began as a model for Watts, the painter, when she was only some fifteen or sixteen years of age. In a week she read him as easily as if he had been a printed book. He treated her with condescending courtesy, *en grand seigneur*, and, naturally, she had her revenge on him.

"One day her mother came in and asked Watts what he was going to do about Ellen. Watts said he didn't understand. 'You have made Ellen in love with you,' said the mother, and it is impossible that could have happened unless you had been attentive to her.'

"Poor Watts protested and protested, but the mother broke down and sobbed, and said the girl's heart would be broken, and at length, in despair, Watts asked what he was to do, and the mother could only suggest marriage.

"Finally they were married."

"You don't mean that," I cried, "I never knew that Watts had married Ellen Terry."

"Oh, yes," said Oscar, "they were married all right. The

mother saw to that, and to do him justice, Watts kept the whole family like a gentleman. But like an idealist, or, as a man of the world would say, a fool, he was ashamed of his wife; he showed great reserve to her, and when he gave his usual dinners or receptions, he invited only men and so, carefully, left her out.

"One evening he had a dinner; a great many well-known people were present and a bishop was on his right hand, when, suddenly, between the cheese and the pear, as the French would say, Ellen came dancing into the room in pink tights with a basket of roses around her waist with which she began pelting the guests. Watts was horrified, but everyone else delighted, the bishop in especial, it is said, declared he had never seen anything so romantically beautiful. Watts nearly had a fit, but Ellen danced out of the room with all their hearts in her basket instead of her roses.

"To me that's the true story of Ellen Terry's life. It may be true or false in reality, but I believe it to be true in fact as in symbol; it is not only an image of her life, but of her art. No one knows how she met Irving or learned to act, though, as you know, she was one of the best actresses that ever graced the English stage. A great personality. Her children even have inherited some of her talent."

It was only famous actresses such as Ellen Terry and Sarah Bernhardt and great ladies that Oscar ever praised. He was a snob by nature; indeed this was the chief link between him and English society. Besides, he had a rooted contempt for women and especially for their brains. He said once, of some one: "he is like a woman, sure to remember the trivial and forget the important."

It was this disdain of the sex which led him, later, to take up our whole dispute again.

"I have been thinking over our argument in the train," he began; "really it was preposterous of me to let you off with a drawn battle; you should have been beaten and forced to haul down your flag. We talked of love and I let you place the girl against the boy: it is all nonsense. A girl is not made for love; she is not even a good instrument of love."

"Some of us care more for the person than the pleasure," I replied, "and others—. You remember Browning:

Nearer we hold of God Who gives, than of His tribes that take, I must believe."

"Yes, yes," he replied impatiently, "but that's not the point. I mean that a woman is not made for passion and love; but to be a mother.

"When I married, my wife was a beautiful girl, white and slim as a lily, with dancing eyes and gay rippling laughter like music. In a year or so the flower-like grace had all vanished; she became heavy, shapeless, deformed: she dragged herself about the house in uncouth misery with drawn blotched face and hideous body, sick at heart because of our love. It was dreadful. I tried to be kind to her; forced myself to touch and kiss her; but she was sick always, and—oh! I cannot recall it, it is all loathsome.... I used to wash my mouth and open the window to cleanse my lips in the pure air. Oh, nature is disgusting; it takes beauty and defiles it: it defaces the ivory-white body we have adored, with the vile cicatrices of maternity: it befouls the altar of the soul.

"How can you talk of such intimacy as love? How can you idealise it? Love is not possible to the artist unless it is sterile."

"All her suffering did not endear her to you?" I asked in

amazement; "did not call forth that pity in you which you used to speak of as divine?"

"Pity, Frank," he exclaimed impatiently; "pity has nothing to do with love. How can one desire what is shapeless, deformed, ugly? Desire is killed by maternity; passion buried in conception," and he flung away from the table.

At length I understood his dominant motive: *trahit sua quemque voluptas*, his Greek love of form, his intolerant cult of physical beauty, could take no heed of the happiness or well-being of the beloved.

"I will not talk to you about it, Frank; I am like a Persian, who lives by warmth and worships the sun, talking to some Esquimau, who answers me with praise of blubber and nights spent in ice houses and baths of foul vapour. Let's talk of something else."

FOOTNOTES:

[27] He lived till November, 1910.

CHAPTER XXIV

A little later I was called to Monte Carlo and went for a few days, leaving Oscar, as he said, perfectly happy, with good food, excellent champagne, absinthe and coffee, and his simple fisher friends.

When I came back to La Napoule, I found everything altered and altered for the worse. There was an Englishman of a good class named M—staying at the hotel. He was accompanied by a youth of seventeen or eighteen whom he called his servant. Oscar wanted to know if I minded meeting him.

"He is charming, Frank, and well read, and he admires me very much: you won't mind his dining with us, will you?"

"Of course not," I replied. But when I saw M—I thought him an insignificant, foolish creature, who put to show a great admiration for Oscar, and drank in his words with parted lips; and well he might, for he had hardly any brains of his own. He had, however, a certain liking for the poetry and literature of passion.[28]

To my astonishment Oscar was charming to him, chiefly I think because he was well off, and was pressing Oscar to spend the summer with him at some place he had in

Switzerland. This support made Oscar recalcitrant to any influence I might have had over him. When I asked him if he had written anything whilst I was away, he replied casually:

"No, Frank, I don't think I shall be able to write any more. What is the good of it? I cannot force myself to write."

"And your 'Ballad of a Fisher Boy'?" I asked.

"I have composed three or four verses of it," he said, smiling at me, "I have got them in my head," and he recited two or three, one of which was quite good, but none of them startling.

Not having seen him for some days, I noticed that he was growing stout again: the good living and constant drinking seemed to ooze out of him; he began to look as he looked in the old days in London just before the catastrophe.

One morning I asked him to put the verses on paper which he had recited to me, but he would not; and when I pressed him, cried:

"Let me live, Frank; tasks remind me of prison. You do not know how I abhor even the memory of it: it was degrading, inhuman!"

"Prison was the making of you," I could not help retorting, irritated by what seemed to me a mere excuse. "You came out of it better in health and stronger than I have ever known you. The hard living, regular hours and compulsory chastity did you all the good in the world. That is why you wrote those superb letters to the 'Daily Chronicle,' and the 'Ballad of Reading Gaol'; the State ought really to put you in prison and keep you there."

For the first time in my life I saw angry dislike in his eyes.

"You talk poisonous nonsense, Frank," he retorted. "Bad food is bad for everyone, and abstinence from tobacco is mere torture to me. Chastity is just as unnatural and devilish as hunger; I hate both. Self-denial is the shining sore on the leprous body of Christianity."

To all this M—giggled applause, which naturally excited the combative instincts in me—always too alert.

"All great artists," I replied, "have had to practise chastity; it is chastity alone which gives vigour and tone to mind and body, while building up a reserve of extraordinary strength. Your favourite Greeks never allowed an athlete to go into the palaestra unless he had previously lived a life of complete chastity for a whole year. Balzac, too, practised it and extolled its virtues, and goodness knows he loved all the mud-honey of Paris."

"You are hopelessly wrong, Frank, what madness will you preach next! You are always bothering one to write, and now forsooth you recommend chastity and 'skilly,' though I admit," he added laughing, "that your 'skilly' includes all the indelicacies of the season, with champagne, Mocha coffee, and absinthe to boot. But surely you are getting too puritanical. It's absurd of you; the other day you defended conventional love against my ideal passion."

He provoked me: his tone was that of rather contemptuous superiority. I kept silent: I did not wish to retort as I might have done if M—had not been present.

But Oscar was determined to assert his peculiar view. One or two days afterwards he came in very red and excited and more angry than I had ever seen him.

"What do you think has happened, Frank?"

"I do not know. Nothing serious, I hope."

"I was sitting by the roadside on the way to Cannes. I had taken out a Vergil with me and had begun reading it. As I sat there reading, I happened to raise my eyes, and who should I see but George Alexander—George Alexander on a bicycle. I had known him intimately in the old days, and naturally I got up delighted to see him, and went towards him. But he turned his head aside and pedalled past me deliberately. He meant to cut me. Of course I know that just before my trial in London he took my name off the bill of my comedy, though he went on playing it. But I was not angry with him for that, though he might have behaved as well as Wyndham,[29] who owed me nothing, don't you think?

"Here there was nobody to see him, yet he cut me. What brutes men are! They not only punish me as a society, but now they are trying as individuals to punish me, and after all I have not done worse than they do. What difference is there between one form of sexual indulgence and another? I hate hypocrisy and hypocrites! Think of Alexander, who made all his money out of my works, cutting me, Alexander! It is too ignoble. Wouldn't you be angry, Frank?"

"I daresay I should be," I replied coolly, hoping the incident would be a spur to him.

"I've always wondered why you gave Alexander a play? Surely you didn't think him an actor?"

"No, no!" he exclaimed, a sudden smile lighting up his face; "Alexander doesn't act on the stage; he behaves. But wasn't it mean of him?"

I couldn't help smiling, the dart was so deserved.

"Begin another play," I said, "and the Alexanders will immediately go on their knees to you again. On the other hand, if you do nothing you may expect worse than discourtesy. Men love to condemn their neighbours' pet vice. You ought to know the world by this time."

He did not even notice the hint to work, but broke out angrily:

"What you call vice, Frank, is not vice: it is as good to me as it was to Caesar, Alexander, Michelangelo and Shakespeare. It was first of all made a sin by monasticism, and it has been made a crime in recent times, by the Goths—the Germans and English—who have done little or nothing since to refine or exalt the ideals of humanity. They all damn the sins they have no mind to, and that's their morality. A brutal race; they overeat and overdrink and condemn the lusts of the flesh, while revelling in all the vilest sins of the spirit. If they would read the 23rd chapter of St. Matthew and apply it to themselves, they would learn more than by condemning a pleasure they don't understand. Why, even Bentham refused to put what you call a 'vice' in his penal code, and you yourself admitted that it should not be punished as a crime; for it carries no temptation with it. It may be a malady; but, if so, it appears only to attack the highest natures. It is disgraceful to punish it. The wit of man can find no argument which justifies its punishment."

"Don't be too sure of that," I retorted.

"I have never heard a convincing argument which condemns it, Frank; I do not believe such a reason exists."

"Don't forget," I said, "that this practice which you defend is condemned by a hundred generations of the most civilised races of mankind."

"Mere prejudice of the unlettered, Frank."

"And what is such a prejudice?" I asked. "It is the reason of a thousand generations of men, a reason so sanctified by secular experience that it has passed into flesh and blood and become an emotion and is no longer merely an argument. I would rather have one such prejudice held by men of a dozen different races than a myriad reasons. Such a prejudice is incarnate reason approved by immemorial experience.

"What argument have you against cannibalism; what reason is there why we should not fatten babies for the spit and eat their flesh? The flesh is sweeter, African travellers tell us, than any other meat, tenderer at once and more sustaining; all reasons are in favour of it. What hinders us from indulging in this appetite but prejudice, sacred prejudice, an instinctive loathing at the bare idea?

"Humanity, it seems to me, is toiling up a long slope leading from the brute to the god: again and again whole generations, sometimes whole races, have fallen back and disappeared in the abyss. Every slip fills the survivors with fear and horror which with ages have become instinctive, and now you appear and laugh at their fears and tell them that human flesh is excellent food, and that sterile kisses are the noblest form of passion. They shudder from you and hate and punish you, and if you persist they will kill you. Who shall say they are wrong? Who shall sneer at their instinctive repulsion hallowed by ages of successful endeavour?"

"Fine rhetoric, I concede," he replied, "but mere rhetoric. I never heard such a defence of prejudice before. I should not have expected it from you. You admit you don't share the prejudice; you don't feel the horror, the instinctive loathing you describe. Why? Because you are educated, Frank, because you know that the passion Socrates felt was not a low passion, because you know that Caesar's weakness, let us say, or the weakness of Michelangelo or of Shakespeare, is not despicable. If the desire is not a characteristic of the highest humanity, at least it is consistent with it."[30]

"I cannot admit that," I answered. "First of all, let us leave Shakespeare out of the question, or I should have to ask you for proofs of his guilt, and there are none. About the others there is this to be said, it is not by imitating the vices and weaknesses of great men that we shall get to their level. And suppose we are fated to climb above them, then their weaknesses are to be dreaded.

"I have not even tried to put the strongest reasons before you; I should have thought your own mind would have supplied them; but surely you see that the historical argument is against you. This vice of yours is dropping out of life, like cannibalism: it is no longer a practice of the highest races. It may have seemed natural enough to the Greeks, to us it is unnatural. Even the best Athenians condemned it; Socrates took pride in never having yielded to it; all moderns denounce it disdainfully. You must see that the whole progress of the world, the current of educated opinion, is against you, that you are now a 'sport,' a peculiarity, an abnormality, a man with six fingers: not a 'sport' that is, full of promise for the future, but a 'sport' of the dim backward and abysm of time, an arrested development."

"You are bitter, Frank, almost rude."

"Forgive me, Oscar, forgive me, please; it is because I want you at long last to open your eyes, and see things as they are."

"But I thought you were with us, Frank, I thought at least you condemned the punishment, did not believe in the barbarous penalties."

"I disbelieve in all punishment," I said; "it is by love and not by hate that men must be redeemed. I believe, too, that the time is already come when the better law might be put in force, and above all, I condemn punishment which strikes a man, an artist like you, who has done beautiful and charming things as if he had done nothing. At least the good you have accomplished should be set against the evil. It has always seemed monstrous to me that you should have been punished like a Taylor. The French were right in their treatment of Verlaine: they condemned the sin, while forgiving the sinner because of his genius. The rigour in England is mere puritanic hypocrisy, shortsightedness and racial self-esteem."

"All I can say, Frank, is, I would not limit individual desire in any way. What right has society to punish us unless it can prove we have hurt or injured someone else against his will? Besides, if you limit passion you impoverish life, you weaken the mainspring of art, and narrow the realm of beauty."

"All societies," I replied, "and most individuals, too, punish what they dislike, right or wrong. There are bad smells which do not injure anyone; yet the manufacturers of them would be indicted for committing a nuisance. Nor does your plea that by limiting the choice of passion you impoverish life, appeal to me. On the contrary, I think I could prove that passion, the desire of the man for the woman and the woman for the man, has been enormously strengthened in modern times. Christianity has created, or at least cultivated, modesty, and modesty has sharpened desire. Christianity has helped to lift woman to an equality with man, and this modern intellectual development has again intensified passion out of all knowledge. The woman who is not a slave but an equal, who gives herself according to her own feeling, is infinitely more desirable to a man than any submissive serf who is always waiting on his will. And this movement intensifying passion is every day gaining force.

"We have a far higher love in us than the Greeks, infinitely higher and more intense than the Romans knew; our sensuality is like a river banked in with stone parapets, the current flows higher and more vehemently in the narrower bed."

"You may talk as you please, Frank, but you will never get me to believe that what I know is good to me, is evil. Suppose I like a food that is poison to other people, and yet quickens me; how dare they punish me for eating of it?"

"They would say," I replied, "that they only punish you for inducing others to eat it."

He broke in: "It is all ignorant prejudice, Frank; the world is slowly growing more tolerant and one day men will be ashamed of their barbarous treatment of me, as they are now ashamed of the torturings of the Middle Ages. The current of opinion is making in our favour and not against us."

"You don't believe what you say," I cried; "if you really thought humanity was going your way, you would have been delighted to play Galileo. Instead of writing a book in prison condemning your companion who pushed you to discovery and disgrace, you would have written a book vindicating your actions. 'I am a martyr,' you would have cried, 'and not a criminal, and everyone who holds the contrary is wrong.'

"You would have said to the jury:

"'In spite of your beliefs, and your cherished dogmas; in spite of your religion and prejudice and fanatical hatred of me, you are wrong and I am right: the world does move.'"

"But you didn't say that, and you don't think it. If you did you would be glad you went into the Queensberry trial, glad you were accused, glad you were imprisoned and punished because all these things must bring your vindication more quickly; you are sorry for them all, because in your heart you know you were wrong. This old world in the main is right: it's you who are wrong."

"Of course everything can be argued, Frank; but I hold to my conviction: the best minds even now don't condemn us, and the world is becoming more tolerant.[31] I didn't justify myself in court because I was told I should be punished lightly if I respected the common prejudices, and when I tried to speak afterwards the judge would not let me."

"And I believe," I retorted, "that you were hopelessly beaten and could never have made a fight of it, because you felt the Time-spirit was against you. How else was a silly, narrow judge able to wave you to silence? Do you think he could have silenced me? Not all the judges in Christendom. Let me give you an example. I believe with Voltaire that when modesty goes out of life it goes into the language as prudery. I am quite certain that our present habit of not discussing sexual questions in our books is bound to disappear, and that free and dignified speech will take the place of our present prurient mealy-mouthedness. I have long thought it possible, probable even, in the present state of society in England, where we are still more or less under the heel of the illiterate and prudish Philistinism of our middle class, that I might be had up to answer some charge of publishing an indecent book. The current of the time appears to be against me. In the spacious days of Elizabeth, in the modish time of the

Georges, a freedom of speech was habitual which to-day is tabooed. Our cases, therefore, are somewhat alike. Do you think I should dread the issue or allow myself to be silenced by a judge? I would set forth my defence before the judge and before the jury with the assurance of victory in me! I should not minimise what I had written; I should not try to explain it away; I should seek to make it stronger. I should justify every word, and finally I'd warn both judge and jury that if they condemned and punished me they would only make my ultimate triumph more conspicuous. 'All the great men of the past are with me,' I would cry; 'all the great minds of to-day in other countries, and some of the best in England; condemn me at your peril: you will only condemn yourselves. You are spitting against the wind and the shame will be on your own faces.'

"Do you believe I should be left to suffer? I doubt it even in England to-day. If I'm right, and I'm sure I'm right, then about me there would be an invisible cloud of witnesses. You would see a strange movement of opinion in my favour. The judge would probably lecture me and bind me over to come up for judgment; but if he sentenced me vindictively then the Home Secretary[32] would be petitioned and the movement in my favour would grow, till it swept away opposition. This is the very soul of my faith. If I did not believe with every fibre in me that this poor stupid world is honestly groping its way up the altar stairs to God, and not down, I would not live in it an hour."

"Why do you argue against me, Frank? It is brutal of you."

"To induce you even now to turn and pull yourself out of the mud. You are forty odd years of age, and the keenest sensations of life are over for you. Turn back whilst there's time, get to work, write your ballad and your plays, and not the Alexanders alone, but all the people who really count, the best of all countries—the salt of the earth—will give you another chance. Begin to work and you'll be borne up on all hands: No one sinks to the dregs but by his own weight. If you don't bear fruit why should men care for you?"

He shrugged his shoulders and turned from me with disdainful indifference.

"I've done enough for their respect, Frank, and received nothing but hatred. Every man must dree his own weird. Thank Heaven, life's not without compensations. I'm sorry I cannot please you," and he added carelessly, "M—has asked me to go and spend the summer with him at Gland in Switzerland. *He* does not mind whether I write or not."

"I assure you," I cried, "it is not my pleasure I am thinking about. What can it matter to me whether you write or not? It is your own good I am thinking of."

"Oh, bother good! One's friends like one as one is; the outside public hate one or scoff at one as they please."

"Well, I hope I shall always be your friend," I replied, "but you will yet be forced to see, Oscar, that everyone grows tired of holding up an empty sack."

"Frank, you insult me."

"I don't mean to; I'm sorry; I shall never be so brutally frank again; but you had to hear the truth for once."

"Then, Frank, you only cared for me in so far as I agreed with you?"

"Oh, that's not fair," I replied. "I have tried with all my strength to prevent you committing soul-suicide, but if you are resolved on it, I can't prevent you. I must draw away. I can do no good."

"Then you won't help me for the rest of the winter?"

"Of course I will," I replied, "I shall do all I promised and more; but there's a limit now, and till now the only limit was my power, not my will."

It was at Napoule a few days later that an incident occurred which gave me to a certain extent a new sidelight on Oscar's nature by showing just what he thought of me. I make no scruple of setting forth his opinion here in its entirety, though the confession took place after a futile evening when he had talked to M—of great houses in England and the great people he had met there. The talk had evidently impressed M—as much as it had bored me. I must first say that Oscar's bedroom was separated from mine by a large sitting-room we had in common. As a rule I worked in my bedroom in the mornings and he spent a great deal of time out of doors. On this especial morning, however, I had gone into the sitting-room early to write some letters. I heard him get up and splash about in his bath: shortly afterwards he must have gone into the next room, which was M—'s, for suddenly he began talking to him in a loud voice from one room to the other, as if he were carrying on a conversation already begun, through the open door.

"Of course it's absurd of Frank talking of social position or the great people of English society at all. He never had any social position to be compared with mine!" (The petulant tone made me smile; but what Oscar said was true: nor did I ever pretend to have such a position.)

"He had a house in Park Lane and owned *The Saturday Review* and had a certain power; but I was the centre of every party, the most honoured guest everywhere, at Clieveden and Taplow Court and Clumber. The difference was Frank was proud of meeting Balfour while Balfour was proud of meeting me: d'ye see?" (I was so interested I was unconscious of any indiscretion in listening: it made me smile to hear that I was proud of meeting Arthur Balfour: it would never have occurred to me that I should be proud of that: still no doubt Oscar was right in a general way).

"When Frank talks of literature, he amuses me: he pretends to bring new standards into it; he does: he brings America to judge Oxford and London, much like bringing Macedon or Boeotia to judge Athens—quite ridiculous! What can Americans know about English literature?...

"Yet the curious thing is he has read a lot and has a sort of vision: that Shakespeare stuff of his is extraordinary; but he takes sincerity for style, and poetry as poetry has no appeal for him. You heard him admit that himself last night....

"He's comic, really: curiously provincial like all Americans. Fancy a Jeremiad preached by a man in a fur coat! Frank's comic. But he's really kind and fights for his friends. He helped me in prison greatly: sympathy is a sort of religion to him: that's why we can meet without murder and separate without suicide....

"Talking literature with him is very like playing Rugby football.... I never did play football, you know; but talking literature with Frank must be very like playing Rugby where you end by being kicked violently through your own goal," and he laughed delightedly.

I had listened without thinking as I often listened to his talk for the mere music of the utterance; now, at a break in the monologue, I went into the next room, feeling that to listen consciously would be unworthy. On the whole his view of me was not unkindly: he disliked to hear any opinion that differed from his own and it never came into his head that Oxford was no nearer the meridian of truth than Lawrence, Kansas, and certainly at least as far from Heaven.

Some weeks later I left La Napoule and went on a visit to some friends. He wrote complaining that without me the place was dull. I wired him and went over to Nice to meet him and we lunched together at the Cafe de la Regence. He was terribly downcast, and yet rebellious. He had come over to stay at Nice, and stopped at the Hotel Terminus, a tenth-rate hotel near the station; the proprietor called on him two or three days afterwards and informed him he must leave the hotel, as his room had been let.

"Evidently someone has told him, Frank, who I am. What am I to do?"

I soon found him a better hotel where he was well treated, but the incident coming on top of the Alexander affair seemed to have frightened him.

"There are too many English on this coast," he said to me one day, "and they are all brutal to me. I think I should like to go to Italy if you would not mind."

"The world is all before you," I replied. "I shall only be too glad for you to get a comfortable place," and I gave him the money he wanted. He lingered on at Nice for nearly a week. I saw him several times. He lunched with me at the Reserve once at Beaulieu, and was full of delight at the beauty of the bay and the quiet of it. In the middle of the meal some English people came in and showed their dislike of him rudely. He at once shrank into himself, and as soon as possible made some pretext to leave. Of course I went with him. I was more than sorry for him, but I felt as unable to help him as I should have been unable to hold him back if he had determined to throw himself down a precipice.

FOOTNOTES:

[28] Cfr. Appendix: "Criticisms by Robert Ross."

[29] The incident is worth recording for the honour of human nature. At the moment of Oscar's trial Charles Wyndham had let his theatre, the Criterion, to Lewis Waller and H.H. Morell to produce in it "An Ideal Husband" which had been running for over 100 nights at the Haymarket. When Alexander took Oscar's name off the bill, Wyndham wrote to the young Managers, saying that, if under the altered circumstances they wished to cancel their agreement, he would allow them to do so. But if they "put on" a play of Mr. Wilde's, the author's name must be on all the bills and placards as usual. He could not allow his theatre to be used to insult a man who was on his trial.

[30] Cfr. end of Appendix:—A Last Word.

[31] Cfr. end of Appendix:—A Last Word.

[32] This was written years before a Home Secretary, Mr. Reginald MacKenna, tortured women and girls in prison in England by forcible feeding, because they tried to present petitions in favour of Woman's Suffrage. He afterwards defended himself in Parliament by declaring that "'forcible feeding' was not unpleasant." The torturers of the Inquisition also befouled cruelty with hypocritical falsehood: they would burn their victims; but would not shed blood.

CHAPTER XXV

"The Gods are just and of our pleasant vices
Make instruments to plague us."

It was full summer before I met Oscar again; he had come back to Paris and taken up his old quarters in the mean little hotel in the Rue des Beaux Arts. He lunched and dined with me as usual. His talk was as humorous and charming as ever, and he was just as engaging a companion. For the first time, however, he complained of his health:

"I ate some mussels and oysters in Italy, and they must have poisoned me; for I have come out in great red blotches all over my arms and chest and back, and I don't feel well."

"Have you consulted a doctor?"

"Oh, yes, but doctors are no good: they all advise you differently; the best of it is they all listen to you with an air of intense interest when you are talking about yourself—which is an excellent tonic."

"They sometimes tell one what's the matter; give a name and significance to the unknown," I interjected.

"They bore me by forbidding me to smoke and drink. They

are worse than M—, who grudged me his wine."

"What do you mean?" I asked in wonder.

"A tragi-comic history, Frank. You were so right about M— and I was mistaken in him. You know he wanted me to stay with him at Gland in Switzerland, begged me to come, said he would do everything for me. When the weather got warm at Genoa I went to him. At first he seemed very glad to see me and made me welcome. The food was not very good, the drink anything but good, still I could not complain, and I put up with the discomforts. But in a week or two the wine disappeared, and beer took its place, and I suggested I must be going. He begged me so cordially not to go that I stayed on; but in a little while I noticed that the beer got less and less in quantity, and one day when I ventured to ask for a second bottle at lunch he told me that it cost a great deal and that he could not afford it. Of course I made some decent pretext and left his house as soon as possible. If one has to suffer poverty, one had best suffer alone. But to get discomforts grudgingly and as a charity is the extremity of shame. I prefer to look on it from the other side; M— grudging me his small beer belongs to farce."

He spoke with bitterness and contempt, as he used never to speak of anyone.

I could not help sympathising with him, though visibly the cloth was wearing threadbare. He asked me now at once for money, and a little later again and again. Formerly he had invented pretexts; he had not received his allowance when he expected it, or he was bothered by a bill and so forth; but now he simply begged and begged, railing the while at fortune. It was distressing. He wanted money constantly, and spent it as always like water, without a thought.

I asked him one day whether he had seen much of his soldier boy since he had returned to Paris.

"I have seen him, Frank, but not often," and he laughed gaily. "It's a farce-comedy; sentiment always begins romantically and ends in laughter—*tabulae solvuntur risu.* I taught him so much, Frank, that he was made a corporal and forthwith a nursemaid fell in love with his stripes. He's devoted to her: I suppose he likes to play teacher in his turn."

"And so the great romantic passion comes to this tame conclusion?"

"What would you, Frank? Whatever begins must also end."

"Is there anyone else?" I asked, "or have you learned reason at last?"

"Of course there's always someone else, Frank: change is the essence of passion: the *reason* you talk of is merely another name for impotence."

"Montaigne declares," I said, "that love belongs to early youth, 'the next period after infancy,' is his phrase, but that is at the best a Frenchman's view of it. Sophocles was nearer the truth when he called himself happy in that age had freed him from the whip of passion. When are you going to reach that serenity?"

"Never, Frank, never, I hope: life without desire would not be worth living to me. As one gets older one is more difficult to please: but the sting of pleasure is even keener than in youth and far more egotistic.

"One comes to understand the Marquis de Sade and that strange, scarlet story of de Retz—the pleasure they got from inflicting pain, the curious, intense underworld of cruelty—"

"That's unlike you, Oscar," I broke in. "I thought you shrank from giving pain always: to me it's the unforgivable sin."

"To me, also," he rejoined instantly, "intellectually one may understand it; but in reality it's horrible. I want my pleasure unembittered by any drop of pain. That reminds me: I read a terrible, little book the other day, Octave Mirbeau's 'Le Jardin des Supplices'; it is quite awful, a *sadique* joy in pain pulses through it; but for all that it's wonderful. His soul seems to have wandered in fearsome places. You with your contempt of fear, will face the book with courage—I—"

"I simply couldn't read it," I replied; "it was revolting to me, impossible—"

"A sort of grey adder," he summed up and I nodded in complete agreement.

I passed the next winter on the Riviera. A speculation which I had gone in for there had caused me heavy loss and much anxiety. In the spring I returned to Paris, and of course, asked him to meet me. He was much brighter than he had been for a long time. Lord Alfred Douglas, it appeared, had come in for a large legacy from his father's estate and had given him some money, and he was much more cheerful. We had a great lunch at Durand's and he was at his very best. I asked him about his health.

"I'm all right, Frank, but the rash continually comes back, a ghostly visitant, Frank: I'm afraid the doctors are in league with the devil. It generally returns after a good dinner, a sort of aftermath of champagne. The doctors say I must not drink champagne, and must stop smoking, the silly people, who regard pleasure as their natural enemies; whereas it is our pleasures which provide them with a living!"

He looked fairly well, I thought; he was a little fatter, his skin a little dingier than of old, and he had grown very deaf, but in every other way he seemed at his best, though he was certainly drinking too freely—spirits between times as well as wine at meals.

I had heard on the Riviera during the winter that Smithers had tried to buy a play from him, so one day I brought up the subject.

"By the way, Smithers says that you have been working on your play; you know the one I mean, the one with the great screen scene in it."

"Oh, yes, Frank," he remarked indifferently.

"Won't you tell me what you've done?" I asked. "Have you written any of it?"

"No, Frank," he replied casually, "it's the scenario Smithers talked about."

A little while afterwards he asked me for money. I told him I could not afford any at the moment, and pressed him to write his play.

"I shall never write again, Frank," he said. "I can't, I simply can't face my thoughts. Don't ask me!" Then suddenly: "Why don't you buy the scenario and write the play yourself?"

"I don't care for the stage," I replied; "it's a sort of rude encaustic work I don't like; its effects are theatrical!"

"A play pays far better than a book, you know—"

But I was not interested. That evening thinking over what he had said, I realised all at once that a story I had in mind to write would suit "the screen scene" of Oscar's scenario; why shouldn't I write a play instead of a story? When we met next day I broached the idea to Oscar:

"I have a story in my head," I said, "which would fit into that scenario of yours, so far as you have sketched it to me. I could write it as a play and do the second, third and fourth acts very quickly, as all the personages are alive to me. Could you do the first act?"

"Of course I could, Frank."

"But," I said, "will you?"

"What would be the good, you could not sell it, Frank."

"In any case," I went on, "I could try; but I would infinitely prefer you to write the whole play if you would; then it would sell fast enough."

"Oh, Frank, don't ask me."

The idea of the collaboration was a mistake; but it seemed to me at the moment the best way to get him to do something. Suddenly he asked me to give him L50 for the scenario at once, then I could do what I liked with it.

After a good deal of talk I consented to give him the L50 if he would promise to write the first act; he promised and I gave him the money.[33]

A little later I noticed a certain tension in his relations with Lord Alfred Douglas. One day he told me frankly that Lord Alfred Douglas had come into a fortune of L15,000 or

L20,000, "and," he added, "of course he's always able to get money. He'll marry an American millionairess or some rich widow" (Oscar's ideas of life were nearly all conventional, derived from novels and plays); "and I wanted him to give me enough to make my life comfortable, to settle enough on me to make a decent life possible to me. It would only have cost him two or three thousand pounds, perhaps less. I get L150 a year and I wanted him to make it up to L300.[34] I lost that through going to him at Naples. I think he ought to give me that at the very least, don't you? Won't you speak to him, Frank?"

"I could not possibly interfere," I replied.

"I gave him everything," he went on, in a depressed way. "When I had money, he never had to ask for it; all that was mine was his. And now that he is rich, I have to beg from him, and he gives me small sums and puts me off. It is terrible of him; it is really very, very wrong of him."

I changed the subject as soon as I could; there was a note of bitterness which I did not like, which indeed I had already remarked in him.

I was destined very soon to hear the other side. A day or two later Lord Alfred Douglas told me that he had bought some racehorses and was training them at Chantilly; would I come down and see them?

"I am not much of a judge of racehorses," I replied, "and I don't know much about racing; but I should not mind coming down one evening. I could spend the night at an hotel, and see the horses and your stable in the morning. The life of the English stable lads in France must be rather peculiar."

"It is droll," he said, "a complete English colony in France.

There are practically no French jockeys or trainers worth their salt; it is all English, English slang, English ways, even English food and of course English drinks. No French boy seems to have nerve enough to make a good rider."

I made an arrangement with him and went down. I missed my train and was very late; I found that Lord Alfred Douglas had dined and gone out. I had my dinner, and about midnight went up to my room. Half an hour later there came a knocking at the door. I opened it and found Lord Alfred Douglas.

"May I come in?" he asked. "I'm glad you've not gone to bed yet."

"Of course," I said, "what is it?" He was pale and seemed extraordinarily excited.

"I have had such a row with Oscar," he jerked out, nervously moving about (I noticed the strained white face I had seen before at the Cafe Royal), "such a row, and I wanted to speak to you about it. Of course you know in the old days when his plays were being given in London he was rich and gave me some money, and now he says I ought to settle a large sum on him; I think it ridiculous, don't you?"

"I would rather not say anything about it," I replied; "I don't know enough about the circumstances."

He was too filled with a sense of his own injuries; too excited to catch my tone or understand any reproof in my attitude.

"Oscar is really too dreadful," he went on; "he is quite shameless now; he begs and begs and begs, and of course I have given him money, have given him hundreds, quite as much as he ever gave me: but he is insatiable and recklessly extravagant besides. Of course I want to be quite fair to him: I've already given him back all he gave me. Don't you think that is all anyone can ask of me?"

I looked at him in astonishment.

"That is for you and Oscar," I said, "to decide together. No one else can judge between you."

"Why not?" he snapped out in his irritable way, "you know us both and our relations."

"No," I replied, "I don't know all the obligations and the interwoven services. Besides, I could not judge fairly between you."

He turned on me angrily, though I had spoken with as much kindness as I could.

"He seemed to want to make you judge between us," he cried. "I don't care who's the judge. I think if you give a man back what he has given you, that is all he can ask. It's a d—d lot more than most people get in this world."

After a pause he started off on a new line of thought:

"The first time I ever noticed any fault in Oscar was over that 'Salome' translation. He's appallingly conceited. You know I did the play into English. I found that his choice of words was poor, anything but good; his prose is wooden....

"Of course he's not a poet," he broke off contemptuously, "even you must admit that."

"I know what you mean," I replied; "though I should have to make a vast reservation in favour of the man who wrote 'The

Ballad of Reading Gaol.'"

"One ballad doesn't make a man a poet," he barked; "I mean by poet one to whom verse lends power: in that sense he's not a poet and I am." His tone was that of defiant challenge.

"You are certainly," I replied.

"Well, I did the translation of 'Salome' very carefully, as no one else could have done it," and he flushed angrily, "and all the while Oscar kept on altering it for the worse. At last I had to tell him the truth, and we had a row. He imagines he's the greatest person in the world, and the only person to be considered. His conceit is stupid.... I helped[35] him again and again with that 'Ballad of Reading Gaol' you're always praising: I suppose he'd deny that now.

"He's got his money back; what more can he want? He disgusts me when he begs."

I could not contain myself altogether.

"He seems to blame you," I said quietly, "for egging him on to that insane action against your father which brought him to ruin."

"I've no doubt he'd find some reason to blame me," he whipped out. "How did I know how the case would go?... Why did he take my advice, if he didn't want to? He was surely old enough to know his own interest.... He's simply disgusting now; he's getting fat and bloated, and always demanding money, money, money, like a daughter of the horse-leech—just as if he had a claim to it."

I could not stand it any longer; I had to try to move him to kindness.

"Sometimes one gives willingly to a man one has never had anything from. Misery and want in one we like and admire have a very strong claim."

"I do not see that there is any claim at all," he cried bitterly, as if the very word maddened him, "and I am not going to pamper him any more. He could earn all the money he wants if he would only write; but he won't do anything. He is lazy, and getting lazier and lazier every day; and he drinks far too much. He is intolerable. I thought when he kept asking me for that money to-night, he was like an old prostitute."

"Good God!" I cried. "Good God! Has it come to that between you?"

"Yes," he repeated, not heeding what I said, "he was just like an old fat prostitute," and he gloated over the word, "and I told him so."

I looked at the man but could not speak; indeed there was nothing to be said. Surely at last, I thought, Oscar Wilde has reached the lowest depth. I could think of nothing but Oscar; this hard, small, bitter nature made Oscar's suffering plain to me.

"As I can do no good," I said, "do you mind letting me sleep? I'm simply tired to death."

"I'm sorry," he said, looking for his hat; "will you come out in the morning and see the 'gees'?"

"I don't think so," I replied, "I'm incapable of a resolution now, I'm so tired I would rather sleep. I think I'll go up to Paris in the morning. I have something rather urgent to do."

He said "Good night" and went away.

I lay awake, my eyes prickling with sorrow and sympathy for poor Oscar, insulted in his misery and destitution, outraged and trodden on by the man he had loved, by the man who had thrust him into the Pit....[36]

I made up my mind to go to Oscar at once and try to comfort him a little. After all, I thought, another fifty pounds or so wouldn't make a great deal of difference to me, and I dwelt on the many delightful hours I had passed with him, hours of gay talk and superb intellectual enjoyment.

I went up by the morning train to Paris, and drove across the river to Oscar's hotel.

He had two rooms, a small sitting-room and a still smaller bedroom adjoining. He was lying half-dressed on the bed as I entered. The rooms affected me unpleasantly. They were ordinary, mean little French rooms, furnished without taste; the usual mahogany chairs, gilt clock on the mantelpiece and a preposterous bilious paper on the walls. What struck me was the disorder everywhere; books all over the round table; books on the chairs; books on the floor and higgledy-piggledy, here a pair of socks, there a hat and cane, and on the floor his overcoat. The sense of order and neatness which he used to have in his rooms at Tite Street was utterly lacking. He was not living here, intent on making the best of things; he was merely existing without plan or purpose.

I told him I wanted him to come to lunch. While he was finishing dressing it came to me that his clothes had undergone much the same change as his dwelling. In his golden days in London he had been a good deal of a dandy; he usually wore white waistcoats at night; was particular about the flowers in his buttonhole, his gloves and cane. Now he was decently dressed and that was all; as far below the average as he had been above it. Clearly, he had let go of himself and no longer took pleasure in the vanities: it seemed to me a bad sign.

I had always thought of him as very healthy, likely to live till sixty or seventy; but he had no longer any hold on himself and that depressed me; some spring of life seemed broken in him. Bosie Douglas' second betrayal had been the *coup de grace.*

In the carriage he was preoccupied, out of sorts, and immediately began to apologise.

"I shall be poor company, Frank," he warned me with quivering lips.

The fragrant summer air in the Champs Elysees seemed to revive him a little, but he was evidently lost in bitter reflections and scarcely noticed where he was going. From time to time he sighed heavily as if oppressed. I talked as well as I could of this and that, tried to lure him away from the hateful subject that I knew must be in his mind; but all in vain. Towards the end of the lunch he said gravely:

"I want you to tell me something, Frank; I want you to tell me honestly if you think I am in the wrong. I wish I could think I was.... You know I spoke to you the other day about Bosie; he is rich now and he is throwing his money away with both hands in racing.

"I asked him to settle L1,500 or L2,000 on me to buy me an annuity, or to do something that would give me L150 a year. You said you did not care to ask him, so I did. I told him it was really his duty to do it at once, and he turned round and lashed me savagely with his tongue. He called me dreadful names. Said dreadful things to me, Frank. I did not think it was possible to suffer more than I suffered in prison, but he has left me bleeding ..." and the fine eyes filled with tears. Seeing that I remained silent, he cried out:

"Frank, you must tell me for our friendship's sake. Is it my fault? Was he wrong or was I wrong?"

His weakness was pathetic, or was it that his affection was still so great that he wanted to blame himself rather than his friend?

"Of course he seems to me to be wrong," I said, "utterly wrong." I could not help saying it and I went on:

"But you know his temper is insane; if he even praises himself, as he did to me lately, he gets into a rage in order to do it, and perhaps unwittingly you annoyed him by the way you asked. If you put it to his generosity and vainglory you would get it easier than from his sense of justice and right. He has not much moral sense."

"Oh, Frank," he broke in earnestly, "I put it to him as well as I could, quite quietly and gently. I talked of our old affection, of the good and evil days we had passed together: you know I could never be harsh to him, never.

"There never was," he burst out, in a sort of exaltation, "there never was in the world such a betrayal. Do you remember once telling me that the only flaw you could find in the perfect symbolism of the gospel story was that Jesus was betrayed by Judas, the foreigner from Kerioth, when he should have been betrayed by John, the beloved disciple; for it is only those we love who can betray us? Frank, how true, how tragically true that is! It is those we love who betray us with a kiss."

He was silent for some time and then went on wearily, "I

wish you would speak to him, Frank, and show him how unjust and unkind he is to me."

"I cannot possibly do that, Oscar," I said, "I do not know all the relations between you and the myriad bands that unite you: I should only do harm and not good."

"Frank," he cried, "you do know, you must know that he is responsible for everything, for my downfall and my ruin. It was he who drove me to fight with his father. I begged him not to, but he whipped me to it; asked me what his father could do; pointed out to me contemptuously that he could prove nothing; said he was the most loathsome, hateful creature in the world, and that it was my duty to stop him, and that if I did not, everyone would be laughing at me, and he could never care for a coward. All his family, his brother and his mother, too, begged me to attack Queensberry, all promised me their support and afterwards—

"You know, Frank, in the Cafe Royal before the trial how Bosie spoke to you, when you warned me and implored me to drop the insane suit and go abroad; how angry he got. You were not a friend of mine, he said. You know he drove me to ruin in order to revenge himself on his father, and then left me to suffer.

"And that's not the worst of it, Frank: I came out of prison determined not to see him any more. I promised my poor wife I would not see him again. I had forgiven him; but I did not want to see him. I had suffered too much by him and through him, far too much. And then he wrote and wrote of his love, crying it to me every hour, begging me to come, telling me he only wanted me, in order to be happy, me in the whole world. How could I help believing him, how could I keep away from him? At last I yielded and went to him, and as soon as the difficulties began he turned on me in

Naples like a wild beast, blaming me and insulting me.

"I had to fly to Paris, having lost everything through him—wife and income and self-respect, everything; but I always thought that he was at least generous as a man of his name should be: I had no idea he could be stingy and mean; but now he is comparatively rich, he prefers to squander his money on jockeys and trainers and horses, of which he knows nothing, instead of lifting me out of my misery. Surely it is not too much to ask him to give me a tenth when I gave him all? Won't you ask him?"

"I think he ought to have done what you want, without asking," I admitted, "but I am certain my speaking would not do any good. He shows me hatred already whenever I do not agree with him. Hate is nearer to him always than sympathy: he is his father's son, Oscar, and I can do nothing. I cannot even speak to him about it."

"Oh, Frank, you ought to," said Oscar.

"But suppose he retorted and said you led him astray, what could I answer?"

"Led him astray!" cried Oscar, starting up, "you cannot believe that. You know better than that. It is not true. It is he who always led, always dominated me; he is as imperious as a Caesar. It was he who began our intimacy: he who came to me in London when I did not want to see him, or rather, Frank, I wanted to but I was afraid; at the very beginning I was afraid of what it would all lead to, and I avoided him; the desperate aristocratic pride in him, the dreadful bold, imperious temper in him terrified me. But he came to London and sent for me to come to him, said he would come to my house if I didn't. I went, thinking I could reason with him; but it was impossible. When I told him we must be very careful, for I was afraid of what might happen, he made fun of my fears, and encouraged me. He knew that they'd never dare to punish him; he's allied to half the peerage and he did not care what became of me....

"He led me first to the street, introduced me to the male prostitution in London. From the beginning to the end he has driven me like the Oestrum of which the Greeks wrote, which drove the ill-fated to disaster.

"And now he says he owes me nothing; I have no *claim*, I who gave to him without counting; he says he needs all his money for himself: he wants to win races and to write poetry, Frank, the pretty verses which he thinks poetry.

"He has ruined me, soul and body, and now he puts himself in the balance against me and declares he outweighs me. Yes, Frank, he does; he told me the other day I was not a poet, not a true poet, and he was, Alfred Douglas greater than Oscar Wilde.

"I have not done much in the world," he went on hotly, "I know it better than anyone, not a quarter of what I should have done, but there are some things I have done which the world will not forget, can hardly forget. If all the tribe of Douglas from the beginning and all their achievements were added together and thrown into the balance, they would not weigh as dust in comparison. Yet he reviled me, Frank, whipped me, shamed me.... He has broken me, he has broken me, the man I loved; my very heart is a cold weight in me," ... and he got up and moved aside with the tears pouring down his cheeks.

"Don't take it so much to heart," I said in a minute or two, going after him, "the loss of affection I cannot help, but a hundred or so a year is not much; I will see that you get that every year."

"Oh, Frank, it is not the money; it is his denial, his insults, his hate that kills me; the fact that I have ruined myself for someone who cares nothing; who puts a little money before me; it is as if I were choked with mud....

"Once I thought myself master of my life; lord of my fate, who could do what I pleased and would always succeed. I was as a crowned king till I met him, and now I am an exile and outcast and despised.

"I have lost my way in life; the passers-by all scorn me and the man whom I loved whips me with foul insults and contempt. There is no example in history of such a betrayal, no parallel. I am finished. It is all over with me now—all! I hope the end will come quickly," and he moved away to the window, his tears falling heavily.

FOOTNOTES:

[33] The rest of this story concerns me chiefly and I have therefore relegated it to the Appendix for those who care to read it.

[34] Oscar was already getting L300 a year from his wife and Robert Ross, to say nothing of the hundreds given to him from time to time by other friends.

[35] The truth about this I have already stated.

[36] Though I have reported this conversation as faithfully as I can and have indeed softened the impression Lord Alfred Douglas made upon me at the time; still I am conscious that I may be doing him some injustice. I have never really been in sympathy with him and it may well be that in reporting him

here faithfully I am showing him at his worst. I am aware that the incident does not reveal him at his best. He has proved since in his writings and notably in some superb sonnets that he had a real affection and admiration for Oscar Wilde. If I have been in any degree unfair to him I can best correct it, I think, by reproducing here the noble sonnet he wrote on Oscar after his death: in sheer beauty and sincerity of feeling it ranks with Shelley's lament for Keats:

The Dead Poet[37]

I dreamed of him last night, I saw his face All radiant and unshadowed of distress, And as of old, in music measureless, I heard his golden voice and marked him trace Under the common thing the hidden grace, And conjure wonder out of emptiness, Till mean things put on beauty like a dress And all the world was an enchanted place.

And then methought outside a fast locked gate I mourned the loss of unrecorded words, Forgotten tales and mysteries half said Wonders that might have been articulate, And voiceless thoughts like murdered singing birds And so I woke and knew that he was dead.

[37] In the Appendix I have published the first sketch of this fine sonnet: lovers of poetry will like to compare them.

CHAPTER XXVI

In a day or two, however, the clouds lifted and the sun shone as brilliantly as ever. Oscar's spirits could not be depressed for long: he took a child's joy in living and in every incident of life. When I left him in Paris a week or so later, in mid-summer, he was full of gaiety and humour, talking as delightfully as ever with a touch of cynicism that added piquancy to his wit. Shortly after I arrived in London he wrote saying he was ill, and that I really ought to send him some money. I had already paid him more than the amount we had agreed upon at first for his scenario, and I was hard up and anything but well. I had chronic bronchitis which prostrated me time and again that autumn. Having heard from mutual friends that Oscar's illness did not hinder him from dining out and enjoying himself, I received his plaints and requests with a certain impatience, and replied to him curtly. His illness appeared to me to be merely a pretext. When my play was accepted his demands became as insistent as they were extravagant.

Finally I went back to Paris in September to see him, persuaded that I could settle everything amicably in five minutes' talk: he must remember our agreement.

I found him well in health, but childishly annoyed that my play was going to be produced and resolved to get all the money he could from me by hook or by crook. I never met such persistence in demands. I could only settle with him decently by paying him a further sum, which I did.

In the course of this bargaining and begging I realised that contrary to my previous opinion he was not gifted as a friend, and did not attribute any importance to friendship. His affection for Bosie Douglas even had given place to hatred: indeed his liking for him had never been founded on understanding or admiration; it was almost wholly snobbish: he loved the title, the romantic name—Lord Alfred Douglas. Robert Ross was the only friend of whom he always spoke with liking and appreciation: "One of the wittiest of men," he used to call him and would jest at his handwriting, which was peculiarly bad, but always good-naturedly; "a letter merely shows that Bobbie has something to conceal"; but he would add, "how kind he is, how good," as if Ross's devotion surprised him, as in fact it did. Ross has since told me that Oscar never cared much for him. Indeed Oscar cared so little for anyone that an unselfish affection astonished him beyond measure: he could find in himself no explanation of it. His vanity was always more active than his gratitude, as indeed it is with most of us. Now and then when Ross played mentor or took him to task, he became prickly at once and would retort: "Really, Bobbie, you ride the high horse so well, and so willingly, it seems a pity that you never tried Pegasus"—not a sneer exactly, but a rap on the knuckles to call his monitor to order. Like most men of charming manners, Oscar was selfish and self-centred, too convinced of his own importance to spend much thought on others; yet generous to the needy and kind to all.

After my return to London he kept on begging for money by almost every post. As soon as my play was advertised I found myself dunned and persecuted by a horde of people who declared that Oscar had sold them the scenario he afterwards sold to me.[38] Several of them threatened to get injunctions to prevent me staging my play, "Mr. and Mrs. Daventry," if I did not first settle with them. Naturally, I wrote rather sharply to Oscar for having led me into this hornets' nest.

It was in the midst of all this unpleasantness that I heard from Turner, in October, I believe, that Oscar was seriously ill, and that if I owed him money, as he asserted, it would be a kindness to send it, as he was in great need. The letter found me in bed. I could not say now whether I answered it or not: it made me impatient; his friends must have known that I owed Oscar nothing; but later I received a telegram from Ross saying that Oscar was not expected to live. I was ill and unable to move, or I should have gone at once to Paris. As it was I sent for my friend, Bell, gave him some money and a cheque, and begged him to go across and let me know if Oscar were really in danger, which I could hardly believe. As luck would have it, the next afternoon, when I hoped Bell had started, his wife came to tell me that he had had a severe asthmatic attack, but would cross as soon as he dared.

I was too hard up myself to wire money that might not be needed, and Oscar had cried "wolf" about his health too often to be a credible witness. Yet I was dissatisfied with myself and anxious for Bell to start.

Day after day passed in troubled doubts and fears; but it was not long when a period was put to all my anxiety. A telegram came telling me he was dead. I could hardly believe my eyes: it seemed incredible—the fount of joy and gaiety; the delightful source of intellectual vivacity and interest stilled forever. The world went greyer to me because of Oscar Wilde's death.

Months afterwards Robert Ross gave me the particulars of his last illness.

Ross went to Paris in October: as soon as he saw Oscar, he was shocked by the change in his appearance: he insisted on taking him to a doctor; but to his surprise the doctor saw no ground for immediate alarm: if Oscar would only stop drinking wine and *a fortiori* spirits, he might live for years: absinthe was absolutely forbidden. But Oscar paid no heed to the warning and Ross could only take him for drives whenever the weather permitted and seek to amuse him harmlessly.

The will to live had almost left Oscar: so long as he could live pleasantly and without effort he was content; but as soon as ill-health came, or pain, or even discomfort, he grew impatient for deliverance.

But to the last he kept his joyous humour and charming gaiety. His disease brought with it a certain irritation of the skin, annoying rather than painful. Meeting Ross one morning after a day's separation he apologised for scratching himself:

"Really," he exclaimed, "I'm more like a great ape than ever; but I hope you'll give me a lunch, Bobbie, and not a nut."

On one of the last drives with this friend he asked for champagne and when it was brought declared that he was dying as he had lived, "beyond his means"—his happy humour lighting up even his last hours.

Early in November Ross left Paris to go down to the Riviera with his mother: for Reggie Turner had undertaken to stay with Oscar. Reggie Turner describes how he grew gradually feebler and feebler, though to the end flashes of the old humour would astonish his attendants. He persisted in saying that Reggie, with his perpetual prohibitions, was qualifying for a doctor. "When you can refuse bread to the hungry, Reggie," he would say, "and drink to the thirsty, you can apply for your diploma."

Towards the end of November Reggie wired for Ross and Ross left everything and reached Paris next day.

When all was over he wrote to a friend giving him a very complete account of the last hours of Oscar Wilde; that account he generously allows me to reproduce and it will be found word for word in the Appendix; it is too long and too detailed to be used here.

Ross's letter should be read by the student; but several touches in it are too timid; certain experiences that should be put in high relief are slurred over: in conversation with me he told more and told it better.

For example, when talking of his drives with Oscar, he mentions casually that Oscar "insisted on drinking absinthe," and leaves it at that. The truth is that Oscar stopped the victoria at almost the first cafe, got down and had an absinthe. Two or three hundred yards further on, he stopped the carriage again to have another absinthe: at the next stoppage a few minutes later Ross ventured to remonstrate:

"You'll kill yourself, Oscar," he cried, "you know the doctors said absinthe was poison to you!"

Oscar stopped on the sidewalk:

"And what have I to live for, Bobbie?" he asked gravely. And Ross looking at him and noting the wreck—the symptoms of old age and broken health—could only bow his head and walk on with him in silence. What indeed had he to live for who had abandoned all the fair uses of life?

The second scene is horrible: but is, so to speak, the inevitable resultant of the first, and has its own awful moral. Ross tells how he came one morning to Oscar's death-bed and found him practically insensible: he describes the dreadful loud death-rattle of his breath, and says: "terrible offices had to be carried out."

The truth is still more appalling. Oscar had eaten too much and drunk too much almost habitually ever since the catastrophe in Naples. The dreadful disease from which he was suffering, or from the after effects of which he was suffering, weakens all the tissues of the body, and this weakness is aggravated by drinking wine and still more by drinking spirits. Suddenly, as the two friends sat by the bedside in sorrowful anxiety, there was a loud explosion: mucus poured out of Oscar's mouth and nose, and—

Even the bedding had to be burned.

If it is true that all those who draw the sword shall perish by the sword, it is no less certain that all those who live for the body shall perish by the body, and there is no death more degrading.

* * * * *

One more scene, and this the last, and I shall have done.

When Robert Ross was arranging to bury Oscar at Bagneux he had already made up his mind as soon as he could to transfer his body to Pere Lachaise and erect over his remains some worthy memorial. It became the purpose of his life to pay his friend's debts, annul his bankruptcy, and publish his books in suitable manner; in fine to clear Oscar's memory from obloquy while leaving to his lovable spirit the shining raiment of immortality. In a few years he had accomplished all but one part of his high task. He had not only paid off all Oscar Wilde's debts; but he had managed to remit thousands of pounds yearly to his children, and had established his popularity on the widest and surest foundation.

He crossed to Paris with Oscar's son, Vyvyan, to render the last service to his friend. When preparing the body for the grave years before Ross had taken medical advice as to what should be done to make his purpose possible. The doctors told him to put Wilde's body in quicklime, like the body of the man in "The Ballad of Reading Gaol." The quicklime, they said, would consume the flesh and leave the white bones—the skeleton—intact, which could then be moved easily.

To his horror, when the grave was opened, Ross found that the quicklime, instead of destroying the flesh, had preserved it. Oscar's face was recognisable, only his hair and beard had grown long. At once Ross sent the son away, and when the sextons were about to use their shovels, he ordered them to desist, and descending into the grave, moved the body with his own hands into the new coffin in loving reverence.

Those who hold our mortal vesture in respect for the sake of the spirit will know how to thank Robert Ross for the supreme devotion he showed to his friend's remains: in his case at least love was stronger than death.

One can be sure, too, that the man who won such fervid self-denying tenderness, had deserved it, called it forth by charm of companionship, or magic of loving intercourse.

FOOTNOTES:

[38] See Appendix: p. 589 and especially p. 592.

CHAPTER XXVII

It was the inhumanity of the prison doctor and the English prison system that killed Oscar Wilde. The sore place in his ear caused by the fall when he fainted that Sunday morning in Wandsworth Prison chapel formed into an abscess and was the final cause of his death. The "operation" Ross speaks of in his letter was the excision of this tumour. The imprisonment and starvation, and above all the cruelty of his gaolers, had done their work.

The local malady was inflamed, as I have already said, by a more general and more terrible disease. The doctors attributed the red flush Oscar complained of on his chest and back, which he declared was due to eating mussels, to another and graver cause. They warned him at once to stop drinking and smoking and to live with the greatest abstemiousness, for they recognised in him the tertiary symptoms of that dreadful disease which the brainless prudery in England allows to decimate the flower of English manhood unchecked.

Oscar took no heed of their advice. He had little to live for. The pleasures of eating and drinking in good company were almost the only pleasures left to him. Why should he deny himself the immediate enjoyment for a very vague and questionable future benefit?

He never believed in any form of asceticism or self-denial, and towards the end, feeling that life had nothing more to offer him, the pagan spirit in him refused to prolong an existence that was no longer joyous. "I have lived," he would have said with profound truth.

Much has been made of the fact that Oscar was buried in an out-of-the-way cemetery at Bagneux under depressing circumstances. It rained the day of the funeral, it appears, and a cold wind blew: the way was muddy and long, and only a half-a-dozen friends accompanied the coffin to its resting-place. But after all, such accidents, depressing as they are at the moment, are unimportant. The dead clay knows nothing of our feelings, and whether it is borne to the grave in pompous procession and laid to rest in a great abbey amid the mourning of a nation or tossed as dust to the wind, is a matter of utter indifference.

Heine's verse holds the supreme consolation:

> Immerhin mich wird umgeben
> Gotteshimmel dort wie hier
> Und wie Todtenlampen schweben
> Nachts die Sterne ueber mir.

Oscar Wilde's work was over, his gift to the world completed years before. Even the friends who loved him and delighted in the charm of his talk, in his light-hearted gaiety and humour, would scarcely have kept him longer in the pillory, exposed to the loathing and contempt of this all-hating world.

The good he did lives after him, and is immortal, the evil is buried in his grave. Who would deny to-day that he was a quickening and liberating influence? If his life was given overmuch to self-indulgence, it must be remembered that his writings and conversation were singularly kindly, singularly amiable, singularly pure. No harsh or coarse or bitter word ever passed those eloquent laughing lips. If he served beauty in her myriad forms, he only showed in his works the beauty that was amiable and of good report. If only half-a-dozen men mourned for him, their sorrow was unaffected and intense, and perhaps the greatest of men have not found in their lifetime even half-a-dozen devoted admirers and lovers. It is well with our friend, we say: at any rate, he was not forced to drink the bitter lees of a suffering and dishonourable old age: Death was merciful to him.

My task is finished. I don't think anyone will doubt that I have done it in a reverent spirit, telling the truth as I see it, from the beginning to the end, and hiding or omitting as little as might be of what ought to be told. Yet when I come to the parting I am painfully conscious that I have not done Oscar Wilde justice; that some fault or other in me has led me to dwell too much on his faults and failings and grudged praise to his soul-subduing charm and the incomparable sweetness and gaiety of his nature.

Let me now make amends. When to the sessions of sad memory I summon up the spirits of those whom I have met in the world and loved, men famous and men of unfulfilled renown, I miss no one so much as I miss Oscar Wilde. I would rather spend an evening with him than with Renan or Carlyle, or Verlaine or Dick Burton or Davidson. I would rather have him back now than almost anyone I have ever met. I have known more heroic souls and some deeper souls; souls much more keenly alive to ideas of duty and generosity; but I have known no more charming, no more quickening, no more delightful spirit.

This may be my shortcoming; it may be that I prize humour and good-humour and eloquent or poetic speech, the artist qualities, more than goodness or loyalty or manliness, and so over-estimate things amiable. But the lovable and joyous things are to me the priceless things, and the most charming man I have ever met was assuredly Oscar Wilde. I do not believe that in all the realms of death there is a more fascinating or delightful companion.

One last word on Oscar Wilde's place in English literature. In the course of this narrative I have indicated sufficiently, I think, the value and importance of his work; he will live with Congreve and with Sheridan as the wittiest and most humorous of all our playwrights. "The Importance of Being Earnest" has its own place among the best of English comedies. But Oscar Wilde has done better work than Congreve or Sheridan: he is a master not only of the smiles, but of the tears of men. "The Ballad of Reading Gaol" is the best ballad in English; it is more, it is the noblest utterance that has yet reached us from a modern prison, the only high utterance indeed that has ever come from that underworld of man's hatred and man's inhumanity. In it, and by the spirit of Jesus which breathes through it, Oscar Wilde has done much, not only to reform English prisons, but to abolish them altogether, for they are as degrading to the intelligence as they are harmful to the soul. What gaoler and what gaol could do anything but evil to the author of such a verse as this:

> This too I know—and wise it were
> If each could know the same—
> That every prison that men build
> Is built with bricks of shame,
> And bound with bars, lest Christ should see
> How men their brothers maim.

Indeed, is it not clear that the man who, in his own wretchedness, wrote that letter to the warder which I have reproduced, and was eager to bring about the freeing of the little children at his own cost, is far above the judge who condemned him or the society which sanctions such punishments? "The Ballad of Reading Gaol," I repeat, and some pages of "De Profundis," and, above all, the tragic fate of which these were the outcome, render Oscar Wilde more interesting to men than any of his peers.

He has been indeed well served by the malice and cruelty of his enemies; in this sense his word in "De Profundis" that he stood in symbolic relation to the art and life of his time is justified.

The English drove Byron and Shelley and Keats into exile and allowed Chatterton, Davidson and Middleton to die of misery and destitution; but they treated none of their artists and seers with the malevolent cruelty they showed to Oscar Wilde. His fate in England is symbolic of the fate of all artists; in some degree they will all be punished as he was punished by a grossly materialised people who prefer to go in blinkers and accept idiotic conventions because they distrust the intellect and have no taste for mental virtues.

All English artists will be judged by their inferiors and condemned, as Dante's master was condemned, for their good deeds (*per tuo ben far*): for it must not be thought that Oscar Wilde was punished solely or even chiefly for the evil he wrought: he was punished for his popularity and his preeminence, for the superiority of his mind and wit; he was punished by the envy of journalists, and by the malignant pedantry of half-civilised judges. Envy in his case overleaped itself: the hate of his justicers was so diabolic that they have given him to the pity of mankind forever; they it is who have made him eternally interesting to humanity, a tragic figure of imperishable renown.

APPENDIX

Here are the two poems of Lord Alfred Douglas which were read out in Court, on account of which the prosecution sought to incriminate Oscar Wilde. My readers can judge for themselves the value of any inference to be drawn from such work by another hand. To me, I must confess, the poems themselves seem harmless and pretty—I had almost said, academic and unimportant.

TWO LOVES

TO "THE SPHINX"

> Two loves I have of comfort and despair
> That like two spirits do suggest me still,
> My better angel is a man right fair,
> My worse a woman tempting me to ill.
>
> —*Shakespeare.*

I dreamed I stood upon a little hill,
And at my feet there lay a ground, that seemed
Like a waste garden, flowering at its will
With flowers and blossoms. There were pools that dreamed Black and unruffled; there were white lilies
A few, and crocuses, and violets
Purple or pale, snake-like fritillaries

Scarce seen for the rank grass, and through green nets
Blue eyes of shy pervenche winked in the sun.
And there were curious flowers, before unknown,
Flowers that were stained with moonlight, or with shades
Of Nature's wilful moods; and here a one
That had drunk in the transitory tone
Of one brief moment in a sunset; blades
Of grass that in an hundred springs had been
Slowly but exquisitely nurtured by the stars,
And watered with the scented dew long cupped
In lilies, that for rays of sun had seen
Only God's glory, for never a sunrise mars
The luminous air of heaven. Beyond, abrupt,
A gray stone wall, o'ergrown with velvet moss
Uprose. And gazing I stood long, all mazed
To see a place so strange, so sweet, so fair.
And as I stood and marvelled, lo! across
The garden came a youth, one hand he raised
To shield him from the sun, his wind-tossed hair
Was twined with flowers, and in his hand he bore
A purple bunch of bursting grapes, his eyes
Were clear as crystal, naked all was he,
White as the snow on pathless mountains frore,
Red were his lips as red wine-spilth that dyes
A marble floor, his brow chalcedony.
And he came near me, with his lips uncurled
And kind, and caught my hand and kissed my mouth,
And gave me grapes to eat, and said, "Sweet friend,
Come, I will show thee shadows of the world
And images of life. See, from the south
Comes the pale pageant that hath never an end."
And lo! within the garden of my dream
I saw two walking on a shining plain
Of golden light. The one did joyous seem
And fair and blooming, and a sweet refrain
Came from his lips; he sang of pretty maids

And joyous love of comely girl and boy;
His eyes were bright, and 'mid the dancing blades
Of golden grass his feet did trip for joy.
And in his hands he held an ivory lute,
With strings of gold that were as maidens' hair,
And sang with voice as tuneful as a flute,
And round his neck three chains of roses were.
But he that was his comrade walked aside;
He was full sad and sweet, and his large eyes
Were strange with wondrous brightness, staring wide
With gazing; and he sighed with many sighs
That moved me, and his cheeks were wan and white
Like pallid lilies, and his lips were red
Like poppies, and his hands he clenched tight,
And yet again unclenched, and his head
Was wreathed with moon-flowers pale as lips of death.
A purple robe he wore, o'erwrought in gold
With the device of a great snake, whose breath
Was fiery flame: which when I did behold
I fell a-weeping and I cried, "Sweet youth
Tell me why, sad and sighing, thou dost rove
These pleasant realms? I pray thee speak me sooth
What is thy name?" He said, "My name is Love."
Then straight the first did turn himself to me
And cried, "He lieth, for his name is Shame,
But I am Love, and I was wont to be
Alone in this fair garden, till he came
Unasked by night; I am true Love, I fill
The hearts of boy and girl with mutual flame."
Then sighing said the other, "Have thy will,
I am the Love that dare not speak its name."

LORD ALFRED DOUGLAS.

September, 1892.

IN PRAISE OF SHAME

Unto my bed last night, methought there came
Our lady of strange dreams, and from an urn
She poured live fire, so that mine eyes did burn
At sight of it. Anon the floating flame
Took many shapes, and one cried, "I am Shame
That walks with Love, I am most wise to turn
Cold lips and limbs to fire; therefore discern
And see my loveliness, and praise my name."

And afterward, in radiant garments dressed,
With sound of flutes and laughing of glad lips,
A pomp of all the passions passed along,
All the night through; till the white phantom ships
Of dawn sailed in. Whereat I said this song,
"Of all sweet passions Shame is loveliest."

LORD ALFRED DOUGLAS.

THE UNPUBLISHED PORTION OF "DE PROFUNDIS"

This is not the whole of the unpublished portion of "De Profundis"; but that part only which was read out in Court and used for the purpose of discrediting Lord Alfred Douglas; still, it is more than half of the whole in length and absolutely more than the whole in importance: nothing of any moment is omitted, except the reiteration of accusations and just this repetition weakens the effect of the argument and strengthens the impression of querulous nagging instead of dispassionate statement. If the whole were printed Oscar Wilde would stand worse; somewhat more selfish and more vindictive.

I have commented the document as it stands mainly for the sake of clearness and because it justifies in every particular and almost in every epithet the shadows of the portrait which I have endeavoured to paint in this book. Curiously enough Oscar Wilde depicts himself unconsciously in this part of "De Profundis" in a more unfavourable light than that accorded him in my memory. I believe mine is the more faithful portrait of him, but that is for my readers to determine.

FRANK HARRIS.

NEW YORK, December, 1915.

H.M. Prison, Reading.

DEAR BOSIE,

After long and fruitless waiting I have determined to write to you myself, as much for your sake as for mine, as I would not like to think that I had passed through two long years of imprisonment without ever having received a single line from you, or any news or message even, except such as gave me pain.

Our ill-fated and most lamentable friendship has ended in ruin and public infamy for me, yet the memory of our ancient affection is often with me, and the thought that loathing, bitterness and contempt should for ever take the place in my heart once held by love is very sad to me; and you yourself will, I think, feel in your heart that to write to me as I lie in the loneliness of prison life is better than to publish my letters without my permission, or to dedicate poems to me unasked, though the world will know nothing of whatever words of grief or passion, of remorse or indifference, you may choose to send as your answer or your appeal.

I have no doubt that in this letter which I have to write of your life and mine, of the past and of the future, of sweet things changed to bitterness and of bitter things that may be turned to joy, there will be much that will wound your vanity to the quick. If it prove so, read the letter over and over again till it kills your vanity. If you find in it something of which you feel that you are unjustly accused, remember that one should be thankful that there is any fault of which one can be unjustly accused. If there be in it one single passage that brings tears to your eyes, weep as we weep in prison, where the day no less than the night is set apart for tears. It is the only thing that can save you. If you go complaining to your mother, as you did with reference to the scorn of you I displayed in my letter to Robbie, so that she may flatter and soothe you back into self-complacency or conceit, you will be completely lost. If you find one false excuse for yourself you will soon find a hundred, and be just what you were before. Do you still say, as you said to Robbie in your answer, that I "attribute unworthy motives" to you? Ah! you had no motives in life. You had appetites merely. A motive is an intellectual aim. That you were "very young" when our friendship began? Your defect was not that you knew so little about life, but that you knew so much. The morning dawn of boyhood with its delicate bloom, its clear pure light, its joy of innocence and expectation, you had left far behind you. With very swift and running feet you had passed from Romance to Realism. The gutter and the things that live in it had begun to fascinate you. That was the origin of the trouble[39] in which you sought my aid, and I, unwisely, according to the wisdom of this world, out of pity and kindness, gave it to you. You must read this letter right through, though each word may become to you as the fire or knife of the surgeon that makes the delicate flesh burn or bleed. Remember that the fool to the eyes of the gods and the fool to the eyes of man are very different. One who is entirely ignorant[40] of the modes of Art in its revelation or the moods of thought in its progress, of the pomp of the Latin line or the richer music of the vowelled Greek, of Tuscan sculpture or Elizabethan song, may yet be full of the very sweetest wisdom. The real fool, such as the gods mock or mar, is he who does not know himself. I was such a one too long. You have been such a one too long. Be so no more. Do not be afraid. The supreme vice is shallowness. Everything that is realised is right. Remember also that whatever is misery to you to read, is still greater misery to me to set down. They have permitted you to see the strange and tragic shapes of life as one sees shadows in a crystal. The head of Medusa that turns living men to stone, you have been allowed to look at in a mirror merely. You yourself have walked free among the flowers. From me the beautiful world of colour and motion has been taken away.

I will begin by telling you that I blame myself terribly. As I sit in this dark cell in convict clothes, a disgraced and ruined man, I blame myself. In the perturbed and fitful nights of anguish, in the long monotonous days of pain, it is myself I blame. I blame myself for allowing an intellectual friendship, a friendship whose primary aim was not the creation and contemplation of beautiful things, entirely to dominate my life. From the very first there was too wide a gap between us. You had been idle at your school, worse than idle[41] at your university. You did not realise that an artist, and especially such an artist as I am, one, that is to say, the quality of whose work depends on the intensification of personality, requires an intellectual atmosphere, quiet, peace, and solitude. You admired my work when it was finished: you enjoyed the brilliant successes of my first nights, and the brilliant banquets that followed them: you were proud, and quite naturally so, of being the intimate friend of an artist so distinguished: but you could not understand the conditions requisite for the production of artistic work. I am not speaking in phrases of rhetorical exaggeration, but in terms of absolute truth to actual fact when I remind you that during the whole time we were together I never wrote one single line. Whether at Torquay, Goring, London, Florence, or elsewhere, my life, as long as you were by my side, was entirely sterile and uncreative. And with but few intervals, you were, I regret to say, by my side always.

I remember, for instance, in September, '93, to select merely one instance out of many, taking a set of chambers, purely in order to work undisturbed, as I had broken my contract with John Hare, for whom I had promised to write a play, and who was pressing me on the subject. During the first week you kept away. We had, not unnaturally indeed, differed on the question of the artistic value[42] of your translation of *Salome*. So you contented yourself with sending me foolish letters on the subject. In that week I wrote and completed in every detail, as it was ultimately performed, the first act of an *An Ideal Husband*. The second week you returned, and my work practically had to be given up. I arrived at St. James's Place every morning at 11.30 in order to have the opportunity of thinking and writing without the interruption inseparable from my own household, quiet and peaceful as that household was. But the attempt was vain. At 12 o'clock you drove up and stayed smoking cigarettes and chattering till 1.30, when I had to take you out to luncheon at the Cafe Royal or the Berkeley. Luncheon with its liqueurs lasted usually till 3.30. For an hour you retired to White's. At tea time you appeared again and stayed till it was time to dress for dinner. You dined with me either at the Savoy or at Tite Street. We did not separate as a rule till after midnight, as supper at Willis' had to wind up the entrancing day. That was my life for those three months, every single day, except during the four days when you went abroad. I then, of course, had to go over to Calais to fetch you back. For one of my nature and temperament it was a position at once grotesque and tragic.

You surely must realise that now. You must see now that your incapacity of being alone: your nature so exigent in its persistent claim on the attention and time of others: your lack of any power of sustained intellectual concentration: the unfortunate accident—for I like to think it was no more—that you had not been able to acquire the "Oxford temper" in intellectual matters, never, I mean, been one who could play gracefully with ideas, but had arrived at violence of opinion merely—that all these things, combined with the fact that your desires and your interests were in Life, not in Art, were as destructive to your own progress in culture as they were to my work as an artist. When I compare my friendship with you to my friendship with still younger men, as John Gray and Pierre Louys, I feel ashamed. My real life, my higher life, was with them and such as they.

Of the appalling results of my friendship with you I don't speak at present. I am thinking merely of its quality while it lasted. It was intellectually degrading to me. You had the rudiments[43] of an artistic temperament in its germ. But I met you either too late or too soon. I don't know which. When you were away I was all right. The moment, in the early December of the year to which I have been alluding, I had succeeded in inducing your mother to send you out of England, I collected again the torn and ravelled web of my imagination, got my life back into my own hands, and not merely finished the three remaining acts of the *Ideal Husband*, but conceived and had almost completed two other plays of a completely different type, the *Florentine Tragedy* and *La Sainte Courtesane*, when suddenly, unbidden, unwelcome, and under circumstances fatal to my happiness, you returned. The two works left then imperfect I was unable to take up again. The mood that created them I could never recover. You now, having yourself published a volume of verse, will be able to recognise the truth of everything I have said here. Whether you can or not it remains as a hideous truth in the very heart of our friendship. While you were with me you were the absolute ruin of my art, and in allowing you to stand persistently between Art and myself, I give to myself shame and blame in the fullest degree. You couldn't appreciate, you couldn't know, you couldn't understand. I had no right to expect it of you at all. Your interests were merely in your meals and moods. Your desires were simply for amusements, for ordinary or less ordinary pleasures. They were what your temperament needed, or thought it needed for the moment. I should have forbidden you my house and my chambers except when I specially invited you. I blame myself without reserve for my weakness. It was merely weakness. One half-hour with Art was always more to me than a cycle with you. Nothing really at any period of my life was ever of the smallest importance[44] to me compared with Art. But in the case of an artist, weakness is nothing less than a crime when it is a weakness that paralyses the imagination.

I blame myself for having allowed you to bring me to utter and discreditable financial ruin. I remember one morning in the early October of '92, sitting in the yellowing woods at Bracknell with your mother. At that time I knew very little of your real nature. I had stayed from a Saturday to Monday with you at Oxford. You had stayed with me at Cromer for ten days and played golf. The conversation turned on you, and your mother began to speak to me about your character. She told me of your two chief faults, your vanity, and your being, as she termed it, "all wrong about money." I have a distinct recollection of how I laughed. I had no idea that the first would bring me to prison and the second to bankruptcy.

I thought vanity a sort of graceful flower for a young man to wear, as for extravagance—the virtues of prudence and thrift were not in my own nature or my own race. But before our friendship was one month older I began to see what your mother really meant. Your insistence on a life of reckless profusion: your incessant demands for money: your claim that all your pleasures should be paid for by me, whether I was with you or not, brought me, after some time, into serious monetary difficulties, and what made the extravagance to me, at any rate, so monotonously uninteresting, as your persistent grasp on my life grew stronger and stronger, was that the money was spent on little more than the pleasures of eating, drinking and the like. Now and then it is a joy to have one's table red with wine and roses, but you outstripped all taste and temperance. You demanded without grace and received without thanks. You grew to think that you had a sort of right to live at my expense, and in a profuse luxury to which you had never been accustomed, and which, for that reason, made your appetites all the more keen, and at the end, if you lost money gambling in some Algiers Casino, you simply telegraphed next morning to me in London to lodge the amount of your losses to your account at your bank, and gave the matter no further thought of any kind.

When I tell you that between the autumn of 1892 and the date of my imprisonment, I spent with you and on you, more than L5,000 in actual money, irrespective of the bills I incurred, you will have some idea of the sort of life on which you insisted. Do you think I exaggerate? My ordinary expenses with you for an ordinary day in London—for luncheon, dinner, supper, amusements, hansoms, and the rest of it—ranged from L12 to L20, and the week's expenses were naturally in proportion and ranged from L80 to L130. For our three months at Goring my expenses (rent, of course, included) were L1,340. Step by step with the Bankruptcy Receiver I had to go over every item of my life. It was horrible. "Plain living and high thinking," was, of course, an ideal you could not at that time have appreciated, but such an extravagance was a disgrace to both of us. One of the most delightful dinners I remember ever having had is one Robbie and I had together in a little Soho Cafe, which cost about as many shillings as my dinners to you used to cost pounds. Out of my dinner with Robbie came the first and best of all my dialogues. Idea, title, treatment, mode, everything was struck out at a 3 franc 50c. table d'hote. Out of the reckless dinners with you nothing remains but the memory that too much was eaten and too much was drunk. And my yielding to your demands was bad for you. You know that now. It made you grasping often: at times not a little unscrupulous: ungracious always. There was, on far too many occasions, too little joy or privilege in being your host. You forgot—I will not say the formal courtesy of thanks, for formal courtesies will strain a close friendship—but simply the grace of sweet companionship, the charm of pleasant conversation, and all those gentle humanities that make life lovely, and are an accompaniment to life as music might be, keeping things in tune and filling with melody the harsh or silent places. And though it may seem strange to you that one in the terrible position in which I am situated, should find a difference between one disgrace and another, still I frankly admit that the folly of throwing away all this money on you, and letting you squander my fortune to your own hurt as well as to mine, gives to me and in my eyes a note of common profligacy to my bankruptcy that makes me doubly ashamed of it. I was made for other things.

But most of all I blame myself for the entire ethical degradation I allowed you to bring on me. The basis of character is will power, and my will power became absolutely subject[45] to yours. It sounds a grotesque thing to say, but it is none the less true. Those incessant scenes that seemed to be almost physically necessary to you, and in which your mind and body grew distorted, and you became a thing as terrible to look at as to listen to: that dreadful mania you inherit from your father, the mania for writing revolting and loathsome letters: your entire lack of any control over your emotions as displayed in your long resentful moods of sullen silence, no less than in the sudden fits of almost epileptic rage: all these things in reference to which one of my letters to you, left by you lying about in the Savoy or some other hotel, and so produced in court by your father's counsel, contained an entreaty not devoid of pathos, had you at that time been able to recognise pathos either in its elements or its expression—these, I say, were the origin and causes of my fatal yielding to you in your daily increasing demands. You wore me out. It was the triumph of the smaller over the bigger nature. It was the case of that tyranny of the weak over the strong which somewhere in one of my plays I describe as being "the only tyranny that lasts." And it was inevitable. In every relation of life with others one has to find some *moyen de vivre*.

I had always thought that my giving up to you in small things meant nothing: that when a great moment arrived I could myself re-assert my will power in its natural superiority. It was not so. At the great moment my will power completely failed me. In life there is really no great or small thing. All things are of equal value and of equal size. My habit—due to indifference chiefly at first—of giving up to you in everything had become insensibly a real part of my nature. Without my knowing it, it had stereotyped my temperament to one permanent and fatal mood. That is why, in the subtle epilogue to the first edition of his essays, Pater says that "Failure is to form habits." When he said it the dull Oxford people thought the phrase a mere wilful inversion of the somewhat wearisome text of Aristotelian Ethics, but there is a wonderful, a terrible truth hidden in it. I had allowed you to sap my strength of character, and to me the formation of a habit had proved to be not failure merely, but ruin. Ethically you had been even still more destructive to me than you had been artistically.

The warrant once granted, your will, of course, directed everything. At a time when I should have been in London taking wise counsel and calmly considering the hideous trap in which I had allowed myself to be caught—the booby trap, as your father calls it to the present day—you insisted on my taking you to Monte Carlo, of all revolting places on God's earth, that all day and all night as well, you might gamble as long as the casino remained open. As for me—baccarat[46] having no charms for me—I was left alone outside by myself. You refused to discuss even for five minutes the position to which you and your father had brought me. My business was merely to pay your hotel expenses and your losses. The slightest allusion to the ordeal awaiting me was regarded as a bore. A new brand of champagne that was recommended to us had more interest for you. On our return to London those of my friends who really desired my welfare implored me to retire abroad, and not to face an impossible trial. You imputed mean motives to them for giving such advice and cowardice to me for listening to it. You forced me to stay to brazen it out, if possible, in the box by absurd and silly perjuries. At the end, of course, I was arrested, and your father became the hero of the hour.

As far as I can make out, I ended my friendship with you every three months regularly. And each time that I did so you managed by means of entreaties, telegrams, letters, the interposition of your friends, the interposition of mine, and the like to induce me to allow you back.

But the froth and folly of our life grew often very wearisome to me: it was only in the mire that we met: and fascinating, terribly fascinating though the one[47] topic round which your talk invariably centered was, still at the end it became quite monotonous to me. I was often bored to death by it, and accepted it as I accepted your passion for music halls, or your mania for absurd extravagance in eating and drinking, or any other of your to me less attractive characteristics, as a thing that is to say, that one simply had to put up with, a part of the high price one had to pay for knowing you.

When you came one Monday evening to my rooms, accompanied by two[48] of your friends, I found myself actually flying abroad next morning to escape from you, giving my family some absurd reason for my sudden departure, and leaving a false address with my servant for fear you might follow me by the next train....

Our friendship had always been a source of distress to my wife: not merely because she had never liked you personally, but because she saw how your continual companionship altered me, and not for the better.

You started without delay for Paris, sending me passionate telegrams on the road to beg me to see you once, at any rate. I declined. You arrived in Paris late on a Saturday night and found a brief letter from me waiting for you at your hotel stating that I would not see you. Next morning I received in Tite Street a telegram of some ten or eleven pages in length from you. You stated in it that no matter what you had done to me you could not believe that I would absolutely decline to see you; you reminded me that for the sake of seeing me even for one hour you had travelled six days and six nights across Europe without stopping once on the way; you made what I must admit was a most pathetic appeal, and ended with what seemed to me a threat of suicide and one not thinly veiled. You had yourself often told me how many of your race there had been who had stained their hands in their own blood: your uncle certainly, your grandfather possibly;

many others in the mad bad line from which you come. Pity, my old affection for you, regard for your mother, to whom your death under such dreadful circumstances would have been a blow almost too great for her to bear, the horror of the idea that so young a life, and one that amidst all its ugly faults had still promise of beauty in it, should come to so revolting an end, mere humanity itself—all these, if excuses be necessary, must serve as an excuse for consenting to accord you one last interview. When I arrived in Paris, your tears breaking out again and again all through the evening, and falling over your cheeks like rain as we sat at dinner first at Voisin's, at supper at Paillard's afterwards, the unfeigned joy you evinced at seeing me, holding my hand whenever you could, as though you were a gentle and penitent child; your contrition, so simple and sincere at the moment made me consent to renew our friendship. Two days after we had returned to London, your father saw you having luncheon with me at the Cafe Royal, joined my table, drank of my wine, and that afternoon, through a letter addressed to you, began his first attack on me.... It may be strange, but I had once again, I will not say the chance, but the duty, of separating from you forced on me. I need hardly remind you that I refer to your conduct to me at Brighton from October 10th to 13th, 1894. Three years is a long time for you to go back. But we who live in prison, and in whose lives there is no event but sorrow, have to measure time by throbs of pain, and the record of bitter moments. We have nothing else to think of. Suffering, curious as it may sound to you, is the means by which we exist, because it is the only means by which we become conscious of existing; and the remembrance of suffering in the past is necessary to us as the warrant, the evidence, of our continued identity. Between myself and the memory of joy lies a gulf no less deep than that between myself and joy in its actuality. Had our life together been as the world fancied it to be, one simply of pleasure, profligacies and laughter, I would not be able to recall a single passage in it. It is because it was full of moments and days tragic, bitter, sinister in their warnings, dull or dreadful in their monotonous scenes and unseemly violences, that I can see or hear each separate incident in its detail, can indeed see or hear little else. So much in this place do men live by pain that my friendship with you, in the way through which I am forced to remember it, appears to me always as a prelude consonant with those varying modes of anguish which each day I have to realise, nay more, to necessitate them even; as though my life, whatever it had seemed to myself and others, had all the while been a real symphony of sorrow, passing through its rhythmically linked movements to its certain resolution, with that inevitableness that in Art characterises the treatment of every great theme.... I spoke of your conduct to me on three successive days three years ago, did I not?

I entertained you, of course, I had no option in the matter; but elsewhere, and not in my own home. The next day, Monday, your companion returned to the duties[49] of his profession, and you stayed with me. Bored with Worthing, and still more, I have no doubt, with my fruitless efforts to concentrate my attention on my play, the only thing that really interested me at the moment, you insist on being taken to the Grand Hotel at Brighton.

The night we arrive you fall ill with that dreadful low fever that is foolishly called the influenza, your second, if not your third, attack. I need not remind you how I waited on you, and tended you, not merely with every luxury of fruit, flowers, presents, books and the like that money can procure, but with that affection, tenderness and love that, whatever you may think, is not to be procured for money. Except for an hour's walk in the morning, an hour's drive in the afternoon, I never left the hotel. I got special grapes from London for you as you did not care for those the hotel supplied; invented things to please you; remained either with you or in the room next to yours; sat with you every evening to quiet or amuse you.

After four or five days you recover, and I take lodgings in order to try and finish my play. You, of course, accompany me. The morning after the day on which we were installed I feel extremely ill.

The doctor finds I have caught the influenza from you.

There is no manservant to wait on me, not even any one to send out on a message, or to get what the doctor orders. But you are there. I feel no alarm. The next two days you leave me entirely alone without care, without attendance, without anything. It was not a question of grapes, flowers and charming gifts: it was a question of mere necessities.

And when I was left all day without anything to read, you calmly tell me that you bought the book I wanted, and that they had promised to send it down, a statement which I found by chance afterwards to have been entirely untrue, from beginning to end. All the while you are, of course, living at my expense, driving about, dining at the Grand Hotel, and indeed only appearing in my room for money. On the Saturday night, you having completely left me unattended and alone since the morning, I asked you to come back after dinner, and sit with me for a little. With irritable voice and ungracious manner you promise to do so. I wait till 11 o'clock, and you never appear.

At three in the morning, unable to sleep, and tortured with thirst, I made my way in the dark and cold, down to the sitting-room in the hopes of finding some water there. I found you. You fell on me with every hideous word an intemperate mood, an undisciplined and untutored nature could suggest. By the terrible alchemy of egotism you converted your remorse into rage. You accused me of selfishness in expecting you to be with me when I was ill; of standing between you and your amusements; of trying to deprive you of your pleasures.

You told me, and I know it was quite true, that you had come back at midnight simply in order to change your dress-clothes, and go out again.

I told you at length to leave the room; you pretended to do so, but when I lifted up my head from the pillow in which I had buried it, you were still there, and with brutality of laughter and hysteria of rage you moved suddenly towards me. A sense of horror came over me, for what exact reason I could not make out; but I got out of my bed at once, and bare-footed and just as I was, made my way down the two nights of stairs to the sitting-room.

You returned silently for money; took what you could find on the dressing table, and mantelpiece, and left the house with your luggage. Need I tell you what I thought of you during the two lonely wretched days of illness that followed? Is it necessary for me to state, that I saw clearly that it would be a dishonour to myself to continue even an acquaintance with such a one as you had showed yourself to be? That I recognised that the ultimate moment had come and recognised it as being really a great relief? And that I knew that for the future my art and life would be freer and better and more beautiful in every possible way? Ill as I was, I felt at ease. The fact that the separation was irrevocable gave me peace.

Wednesday was my birthday. Amongst the telegrams and communications on my table was a letter in your handwriting. I opened it with a sense of sadness on me. I knew that the time had gone by when a pretty phrase, an expression of affection, a word of sorrow, would make me take you back. But I was entirely deceived. I had underrated you.

You congratulated me on my prudence in leaving the sick bed, on my sudden flight downstairs. "It was an ugly moment for you," you said, "uglier than you imagine." Ah! I felt it but too well. What it had really meant I do not know; whether you had with you the pistol you had bought to try to frighten your father with, and that thinking it to be unloaded, you had once fired off in a public restaurant in my company; whether your hand was moving towards a common dinner knife that by chance was lying on the table between us; whether forgetting in your rage your low[50] stature and inferior strength, you had thought of some special personal insult, or attack even, as I lay ill there; I could not tell. I do not know to the present moment. All I know is that a feeling of utter horror had come over me, and that I had felt that unless I left the room at once and got away, you would have done or tried to do something that would have been, even to you, a source of lifelong shame....

On your return to town from the actual scene of the tragedy to which you had been summoned, you came at once to me very sweetly and very simply, in your suit of woe, and with your eyes dim with tears. You sought consolation and help, as a child might seek it. I opened to you my house, my home, my heart. I made your sorrow mine also, that you might have help in bearing it. Never even by one word, did I allude to your conduct towards me, to the revolting scenes, and the revolting letter.

The gods are strange. It is not our vices only they make instruments to scourge us. They bring us to ruin through what in us is good, gentle, humane, loving. But for my pity and affection for you and yours, I would not now be weeping in this terrible place.

Of course, I discern in all our relations, not destiny merely, but Doom—Doom that walks always swiftly, because she goes to the shedding of blood. Through your father you come of a race, marriage with whom is horrible, friendship fatal, and that lays violent hands either on its own life, or on the lives of others.

In every little circumstance in which the ways of our lives met, in every point of great or seemingly trivial import in which you came to me for pleasure or help, in the small chances, the slight accidents that look, in their relation to life, to be no more than the dust that dances in a beam, or the leaf that flutters from a tree, ruin followed like the echo of a bitter cry, or the shadow that hunts with the beast of prey.

Our friendship really begins with your begging me, in a most pathetic and charming letter, to assist you in a position appalling to anyone, doubly so to a young man at Oxford. I do so, and ultimately, through your using my name as your friend with Sir George Lewis I begin to lose his esteem and friendship, a friendship of fifteen years' standing. When I was deprived of his advice and help and regard, I was deprived of the one great safeguard of my life. You send me a very nice poem of the undergraduate school of verse for my approval. I reply by a letter of fantastic literary conceits; I compare you to Hylas, or Hyacinth, Jonquil or Narcissus, or some one whom the Great God of Poetry favoured, and honoured with his love. The letter is like a passage from one of Shakespeare's sonnets transposed to a minor key.

It was, let me say frankly, the sort of letter I would, in a happy, if wilful moment, have written to any graceful young man of either university who had sent me a poem of his own making, certain that he would have sufficient wit, or culture, to interpret rightly its fantastic phrases. Look at the history of that letter! It passes from you into the hands of a loathsome companion[51], from him to a gang of blackmailers, copies of it are sent about London to my friends, and to the manager[52] of the theatre where my work is being performed, every construction but the right one is put on it, society is thrilled with the absurd rumours that I have had to pay a high sum of money for having written an infamous letter to you; this forms the basis of your father's worst attack.

I produce the original letter myself in court to show what it really is; it is denounced by your father's counsel as a revolting and insidious attempt to corrupt innocence; ultimately it forms part of a criminal charge; the crown takes it up; the judge sums up on it with little learning and much morality; I go to prison for it at last. That is the result of writing you a charming letter.

It makes me feel sometimes as if you yourself had been merely a puppet worked by some secret and unseen hand to bring terrible events to a terrible issue. But puppets themselves have passions. They will bring a new plot into what they are presenting, and twist the ordered issue of vicissitude to suit some whim or appetite of their own. To be entirely free, and at the same time entirely dominated by law, is the eternal paradox of human life that we realise at every moment; and this, I often think, is the only explanation possible of your nature, if indeed for the profound and terrible mystery of a human soul there is any explanation at all, except one that makes the mystery all the more marvellous still.

I thought life was going to be a brilliant comedy, and that you were to be one of the graceful figures in it. I found it to be a revolting and repellent tragedy, and that the sinister occasion of the great catastrophe, sinister in its concentration of aim and intensity of narrowed will power, was yourself stripped of the mask of joy and pleasure by which you, no less than I, had been deceived and led astray.

The memory of our friendship is the shadow that walks with me here: that seems never to leave me: that wakes me up at night to tell me the same story over and over till its wearisome iteration makes all sleep abandon me till dawn: at dawn it begins again: it follows me into the prison yard and makes me talk to myself as I tramp round: each detail that accompanied each dreadful moment I am forced to recall: there is nothing that happened in those ill-starred years that I cannot recreate in that chamber of the brain which is set apart for grief or for despair; every strained note of your voice, every twitch and gesture of your nervous hands, every bitter word, every poisonous phrase comes back to me: I remember the street or river down which we passed: the wall or woodland that surrounded us; at what figure on the dial stood the hands of the clock; which way went the wings of the wind, the shape and colour of the moon.

There is, I know, one answer to all that I have said to you, and that is that you loved me: that all through those two and a half years during which the fates were weaving into one scarlet pattern the threads of our divided lives you really loved me.

Though I saw quite clearly that my position in the world of art, the interest that my personality had always excited, my money, the luxury in which I lived, the thousand and one things that went to make up a life so charmingly and so wonderfully improbable as mine was, were, each and all of them, elements that fascinated you and made you cling to me; yet besides all this there was something more, some strange attraction for you: you loved me far better than you loved anyone else. But you, like myself, have had a terrible tragedy in your life, though one of an entirely opposite character to mine. Do you want to learn what it was? It was this. In you, hate was always stronger than love. Your hatred[53] of your father was of such stature that it entirely outstripped, overgrew, and overshadowed your love of me. There was no struggle between them at all, or but little; of such dimensions was your hatred and of such monstrous growth. You did not realise that there was no room for both passions in the same soul: they cannot live together in that fair carven house. Love is fed by the imagination, by which we become wiser than we know, better than we feel, nobler than we are; by which we can see life as a whole; by which and by which alone, we can understand others in their real as in their ideal relations. Only what is fine, and finely conceived, can feed love. But anything will feed hate. There was not a glass of champagne that you drank, not a rich dish that you ate of in all those years, that did not feed your hate and make it fat. So to gratify it, you gambled with my life, as you gambled with my money, carelessly, recklessly, indifferent to the consequences. If you lost, the loss would not, you fancied, be yours. If you won, yours, you knew, would be the exultation and the advantages of victory.

Hate blinds people. You were not aware of that. Love can read the writing on the remotest star, but hate so blinded you that you could see no further than the narrow, walled in, and already lust-withered garden of your common desires. Your terrible lack of imagination, the one really fatal defect in your character, was entirely the result of the hate that lived in you. Subtly, silently, and in secret, hate gnawed at your nature, as the lichen bites at the root of some sallow plant, till you grew to see nothing but the most meagre interests and the most petty aims. That faculty in you which love would have fostered, hate poisoned and paralysed.

The idea of your being the object of a terrible quarrel between your father and a man of my position seemed to delight you.

You scented the chance of a public scandal and flew to it. The prospect of a battle in which you would be safe delighted you.

You know what my art was to me, the great primal note by which I had revealed, first myself to myself, and then myself to the world, the great passion of my life, the love to which all other loves were as marsh water to red wine, or the glow worm of the marsh to the magic mirror of the moon.... Don't you understand now that your lack of imagination was the one really fatal defect of your character? What you had to do was quite simple, and quite clear before you; but hate had blinded you, and you could see nothing.

Life is quite lovely to you. And yet, if you are wise, and wish to find life much lovelier still, and in a different manner you will let the reading of this terrible letter—for such I know it is—prove to you as important a crisis and turning point of your life as the writing of it is to me. Your pale face used to flush easily with wine or pleasure. If, as you read what is here written, it from time to time becomes scorched, as though by a furnace blast, with shame, it will be all the better for you. The supreme vice is shallowness. Whatever is realised is right.

How clearly I saw it then, as now, I need not tell you. But I said to myself, "At all costs I must keep love in my heart. If I go into prison without love, what will become of my soul?" The letters I wrote to you at that time from Holloway were my efforts to keep love as the dominant note of my own nature. I could, if I had chosen, have torn you to pieces with bitter reproaches. I could have rent you with maledictions.

The sins of another were being placed to my account. Had I so chosen, I could on either trial have saved myself at his expense, not from shame indeed, but from imprisonment.[54] Had I cared to show that the crown witnesses—the three most important—had been carefully coached by your father and his solicitors, not in reticences merely, but in assertions, in the absolute transference deliberate, plotted, and rehearsed, of the actions and doings of someone else on to me, I could have had each one of them dismissed from the box by the judge, more summarily than even wretched perjured Atkins was. I could have walked out of court with my tongue in my cheek, and my hands in my pockets, a free man. The strongest pressure was put upon me to do so, I was earnestly advised, begged, entreated to do so by people, whose sole interest was my welfare, and the welfare of my house. But I refused. I did not choose to do so. I have never regretted my decision for a single moment, even in the most bitter periods of my imprisonment. Such a course of action would have been beneath me. Sins of the flesh are nothing. They are maladies for physicians to cure, if they should be cured. Sins of the soul alone are shameful. To have secured my acquittal by such means would have been a life-long torture to me. But do you really think that you were worthy of the love I was showing you then, or that for a single moment I thought you were? Do you really think that any period of our friendship you were worthy of the love I showed you, or that for a single moment I thought you were? I knew you were not. But love does not traffic in a market place, nor use a huckster's scales. Its joy, like the joy of the intellect, is to feel itself alive. The aim of love is to love; no more, and no less. You were my enemy; such an enemy as no man ever had. I had given you my life; and to gratify the lowest and most contemptible of all human passions, hatred and vanity and greed, you had thrown it away. In less than three years you had entirely ruined me from every point of view.

After my terrible sentence, when the prison dress was on me, and the prison house closed, I sat amidst the ruins of my wonderful life, crushed by anguish, bewildered with terror, dazed through pain. But I would not hate you. Every day I said to myself, "I must keep love in my heart to-day, else how shall I live through the day?" I reminded myself that you meant no evil to me at any rate....

It all flashed across me, and I remember that for the first and last time in my entire prison life, I laughed. In that laugh was all the scorn of all the world. Prince Fleur de lys! I saw that nothing that had happened had made you realise a single thing. You were, in your own eyes, still the graceful prince of a trivial comedy, not the sombre figure of a tragic show.

Had there been nothing in your heart to cry out against so vulgar a sacrilege, you might at least have remembered the sonnet he wrote who saw with such sorrow and scorn the letters of John Keats sold by public auction in London, and have understood at last the real meaning of my lines:

> "... I think they love not art
> Who break the crystal of a poet's heart
> That small and sickly eyes may glare or gloat."

One cannot always keep an adder in one's breast to feed on one, nor rise up every night to sow thorns in the garden of one's soul.

I cannot allow you to go through life bearing in your heart the burden of having ruined a man like me.

Does it ever occur to you what an awful position I would have been in if, for the last two years, during my appalling sentence, I had been dependent on you as a friend? Do you ever think of that? Do you ever feel any gratitude to those who by kindness without stint, devotion without limit, cheerfulness and joy in giving, have lightened my black burden for me, have arranged my future life for me, have visited me again and again, have written to me beautiful and sympathetic letters, have managed my affairs for me, have stood by me in the teeth of obloquy, taunt, open sneer or insult even? I thank God every day that he gave me friends other than you. I owe everything to them. The very books in my cell are paid for by Robbie out of his pocket money. From the same source[55] are to come clothes for me when I am released. I am not ashamed of taking a thing that is given by love and affection. I am proud of it. But do you ever think of what friends such as More Adey, Robbie, Robert Sherard, Frank Harris, and Arthur Clifton have been to me in giving me comfort, help, affection, sympathy and the like?...

I know that your mother, Lady Queensberry, puts the blame on me. I hear of it, not from people who know you, but from people who do not know you, and do not desire to know you. I hear of it often. She talks of the influence of an elder over a younger man, for instance. It is one of her favourite attitudes towards the question, as it is always a successful appeal to popular prejudice and ignorance. I need not ask you what influence I had over you. You know I had none.

It was one of your frequent boasts that I had none, the only one indeed, that was well founded. What was there, as a mere matter of fact, in you that I could influence? Your brain? It was undeveloped. Your imagination? It was dead. Your heart? It was not yet born. Of all the people who have ever crossed my life, you were the one, and the only one, I was unable in any way to influence in any direction.

I waited month after month to hear from you. Even if I had not been waiting but had shut the doors against you, you should have remembered that no one can possibly shut the doors against love forever. The unjust judge in the gospels rises up at length to give a just decision because justice comes daily knocking at his door: and at night time the friend, in whose heart there is no real friendship, yields at length to his friend "because of his importunity." There is no prison in any world into which love cannot force an entrance. If you did not understand that, you did not understand anything about love at all....

Write to me with full frankness, about yourself: about your life: your friends: your occupations: your books. Whatever you have to say for yourself, say it without fear. Don't write what you don't mean: that is all. If anything in your letter is false or counterfeit I shall detect it by the ring at once. It is not for nothing, or to no purpose that in my lifelong cult of literature, I have made myself,

> "Miser of sound and syllable, no less
> Than Midas of his coinage."

Remember also that I have yet to know you. Perhaps we have yet to know each other. For myself, I have but this last thing to say. Do not be afraid of the past. If people tell you that it is irrevocable, do not believe them. The past, the present and the future are but one moment in the sight of God, in whose sight we should try to live. Time and space, succession and extension, are merely accidental conditions of a thought. The imagination can transcend them and more, in a free sphere of ideal existences. Things, also, are in their essence what we choose to make them. A thing is, according to the mode in which one looks at it. "Where others," says Blake, "see but the dawn coming over the hill, I see the sons of God shouting for joy." What seemed to the world and to myself my future I lost irretrievably when I let myself be taunted into taking the action against your father, had, I daresay, lost in reality long before that. What lies before me is the past. I have got to make myself look on that with different eyes, to make the world look on it with different eyes, to make God look on it with different eyes. This I cannot do by ignoring it, or slighting it, or praising it, or denying it. It is only to be done fully by accepting it as an inevitable part of the evolution of my life and character: by bowing my head to everything that I have suffered.

How far I am away from the true temper of soul, this letter in its changing, uncertain moods, its scorn and bitterness, its aspirations and its failures to realise those aspirations shows you quite clearly. But do not forget in what a terrible school I am setting at my task. And incomplete, imperfect, as I am, yet from me you may have still much to gain. You came to me to learn the pleasure of life and the pleasure of art. Perhaps I am chosen to teach you something much more wonderful, the meaning of sorrow and its beauty.

Your affectionate friend,

OSCAR WILDE.

This letter of Oscar Wilde to Lord Alfred Douglas is curiously self-revealing and characteristic. While reading it one should recall Oscar's provocation. Lord Alfred Douglas had driven him to the prosecution, and then deserted him and left him in prison without using his influence to mitigate his friend's suffering or his pen to console and encourage him. The abandonment was heartless and complete. The letter, however, is vindictive: in spite of its intimate revelations Oscar took care that his indictment should be made public. The flagrant self-deceptions of the plea show its sincerity: Oscar even accuses young Alfred Douglas of having induced him to eat and drink too much.

The tap-root of the letter is a colossal vanity; the bitterness of it, wounded egotism; the falseness of it, a self-righteous pose of ineffable superiority as of a superman. Oscar denies to Alfred Douglas imagination, scholarship, or even a knowledge of poetry: he tells him in so many words:—he is without brain or heart. Then why did he allow himself to be hag-ridden to his ruin by such a creature?

Yet how human the letter is, how pathetic!

OSCAR WILDE'S KINDNESS OF HEART

Here is a note which Oscar Wilde wrote to Warder Martin towards the end of his imprisonment in Reading Gaol. Warder Martin, it will be remembered, was dismissed from his post for having given some sweet biscuits, bought with his own money, to some hungry little children confined in the prison.

Wilde happened to see the children and immediately wrote this note on a scrap of paper and slipped it under his door so that it should catch Warder Martin's eye as he patrolled the corridor.

> Please find out for me the name of A.2.11. Also, the names of the children who are in for the rabbits, and the amount of the fine.
>
> Can I pay this and get them out? If so I will get them out tomorrow. Please, dear friend, do this for me. I must get them out.
>
> Think what a thing for me it would be to be able to help three little children. I would be delighted beyond words: if I can do this by paying the fine tell the children that they are to be released tomorrow by a friend, and ask them to be happy and not to tell anyone.

Here is a second note which shows Oscar's peculiar sensitiveness; what is ugly and terrible cannot, he thinks, furnish even the subject of art; he shrinks from whatever gives pain.

> I hope to write about prison-life and to try and change it for others, but it is too terrible and ugly to make a work of art of. I have suffered too much in it to write plays about it.

A third note simply thanks Warder Martin for all his kindness. It ends with the words:

> ... Everyone tells me I am looking better and happier.
>
> This is because I have a good friend who gives me *The Chronicle* and PROMISES me ginger biscuits. O.W.

MY COLDNESS TOWARDS OSCAR IN 1897

When I talked with Oscar in Reading Gaol, he told me that the only reason he didn't write was that no one would accept his work. I assured him that I would publish it in *The Saturday Review* and would pay for it not only at the rate I paid Bernard Shaw but also if it increased the sale of the journal I'd try to compute its value to the paper and give him that besides. He told me that was too liberal; he would be quite content with what I paid Shaw: he feared that no one else in England would ever publish his work again.

He promised to send me the book "De Profundis" as soon as it was finished. Just before his release his friend, Mr. More Adey, called upon me and wanted to know whether I would publish Oscar's work. I said I would. He then asked me what I would give for it. I told him I didn't want to make anything out of Oscar and would give him as much as I could, rehearsing the proposal I had made to Oscar. Thereupon he told me Oscar would prefer a fixed price. I thought the answer extraordinary and the gentle, urbane manner of Mr. More Adey, whom I hardly knew at that time and misunderstood, got on my nerves. I replied curtly that before I could state a price, I'd have to see the work, adding at the same time that I had wished to do Oscar a good turn, but, if he could find another publisher, I'd be delighted. Mr. More Adey assured me that there was nothing in the book to which any prude even could object, no *arriere pensee* of any kind, and so forth and so on. I answered with a jest, a wretched play on his French phrase.

That night I happened to dine with Whistler and telling him of what had occurred called forth a most stinging gibe at Oscar's expense. Whistler's *mot* cannot be published.

A week or two later Oscar asked me to get him some clothes, which I did and on his release sent them to him, and received in reply a letter thanking me which I reproduce on page 583.

In that same talk with Oscar in Reading Gaol, I was so desirous of helping him that I proposed a driving tour through France. I told him of one I had made a couple of years before which was full of delightful episodes—an entrancing holiday. He jumped at the idea, said nothing would please him better, he would feel safe with me, and so forth. In order to carry out the idea in the best way I ordered an American mail phaeton so that a pair of horses would find the load, even with luggage, ridiculously light. I asked Mr. More Adey whether Oscar had spoken to him of this proposed trip: he told me he had heard nothing of it.

In one letter to me Oscar asked me to postpone the tour; afterwards he never mentioned it. I thought I had been treated rather cavalierly. As I had gone to some expense in getting everything ready and making myself free, I, no doubt, expressed some amazement at Oscar's silence on the matter. At any rate the idea got about that I was angry with him, and Oscar believed it. Nothing could have been further from the truth. What I had done and proposed was simply in his interest: I expected no benefit of any kind and therefore could not be cross; but the belief that I was angry drew this sincere and touching letter from Oscar, which I think shows him almost as perfectly as that still more beautiful letter to Robert Ross which I have inserted in Chapter XIX.

From M. Sebastian Melmoth, Hotel de la Plage, Bernavol-sur-Mer, Dieppe.

June 13, '97

MY DEAR FRANK:

I know you do not like writing letters, but still I think you might have written me a line in answer, or acknowledgment of my letter[56] to you from Dieppe. I am thinking of a story to be called "The Silence of Frank Harris."

I have, however, heard during the last few days that you do not speak of me in the friendly manner I would like. This distresses me very much.

I am told that you are hurt with me because my letter of thanks to you was not sufficiently elaborated in expression. This I can hardly credit. It seems so unworthy of a big strong nature like yours, that knows the realities of life. I told you I was grateful to you for your kindness to me. Words, *now*, to me signify things, actualities, real emotions, realised thoughts. I learnt in prison to be grateful. I used to think gratitude a burden. Now I know that it is something that makes life lighter as well as lovelier for one. I am grateful for a thousand things, from my good friends down to the sun and the sea. But I cannot say more than that I am grateful. I cannot make phrases about it. For *me* to use such a word shows an enormous development in my nature. Two years ago I did not know the feeling the word denotes. Now I know it, and I am thankful that I have learnt that much, at any rate, by having been in prison. But I must say again that I no longer make *roulades* of phrases about the deep things I feel. When I write directly to you, I speak directly: violin variations don't interest me. I am grateful to you. If that does not content you, then you do not understand, what you of all men should understand, how sincerity of feeling expresses itself. But I dare say the story told of you is untrue. It comes from so many quarters that it probably is.

I am told also that you are hurt[57] because I did not go on the driving-tour with you. You should understand, that in telling you that it was impossible for me to do so, I was thinking as much of *you* as of myself. To think of the feelings and happiness of others is not an entirely new emotion in my nature. I would be unjust to myself and my friends, if I said it was. But I think of those things far more than I used to do. If I had gone with you, you would not have been happy, nor enjoyed yourself. Nor would I. You must try to realise what two years cellular confinement is, and what two years of absolute silence means to a man of my intellectual power. To have survived at all—to have come out sane in mind and sound of body—is a thing so marvellous to me, that it seems to me sometimes, not that the age of miracles is over, but that it is just beginning; that there are powers in God, and powers in man, of which the world has up to the present known little. But while I am cheerful, happy, and have sustained to the full that passionate interest in life and art that was the dominant chord of my nature, and made all modes of existence and all forms of expression utterly fascinating to me always—still I need rest, quiet, and often complete solitude. Friends have come to see me here for a day, and have been delighted to find me like my old self, in all intellectual energy and sensitiveness to the play of life, but it has always proved afterwards to have been a strain upon a nervous force, much of which has been destroyed. I have now no *storage*[58] of nervous force. When I expend what I have, in an afternoon, nothing remains. I look to quiet, to a simple mode of existence, to nature in all the infinite meanings of an infinite word, to charge the cells for me. Every day, if I meet a friend, or write a letter longer than a few lines, or even read a book that makes, as all fine books do, a direct claim on me, a direct appeal, an intellectual challenge of any kind, I am utterly exhausted in the evening, and often sleep badly. And yet it is three whole weeks since I was released.

Had I gone with you on the driving tour, where we would have of necessity been in immediate contact with each other from dawn to sunset, I would have certainly broken off the tour the third day, probably broken down the second. You would have then found yourself in a pitiable position: your tour would have been arrested at its outset: your companion would have been ill without doubt: perhaps might have needed care and attendance, in some little remote French village. You would have given it to me, I know. But I felt it would have been wrong, stupid, and thoughtless of me to have started an expedition doomed to swift failure, and perhaps fraught with disaster and distress. You are a man of dominant personality: your intellect is exigent, more so than that of any man I ever knew: your demands on life are enormous: you require response, or you annihilate: the pleasure of being with you is in the clash of personality, the intellectual battle, the war of ideas. To survive you, one must have a strong brain, an assertive ego, a dynamic character. In your luncheon parties, in the old days, the remains of the guests were taken away with the *debris* of the feast. I have often lunched with you in Park Lane and found myself the only survivor. I might have driven on the white roads, or through the leafy lanes, of France, with a fool, or with the wisest of all things, a child: with you, it would have been impossible. You should thank me sincerely for having saved you from an experience that each of us would have always regretted.

Will you ask me why then, when I was in prison, I accepted with grateful thanks your offer? My dear Frank, I don't think you will ask so thoughtless a question. The prisoner looks to liberty as an immediate return to all his ancient energy, quickened into more vital forces by long disuse. When he goes out, he finds he has still to suffer: his punishment, as far as its effects go, lasts intellectually and physically just as it lasts socially: he has still to pay: one gets no receipt for the past when one walks out into the beautiful air....

I have now spent the whole of my Sunday afternoon—the first real day of summer we have had—in writing to you this long letter of explanation.

I have written directly and simply: I need not tell the author of "Elder Conklin" that sweetness and simplicity of expression take more out of one than fiddling harmonics on one string. I felt it my duty to write, but it has been a distressing one. It would have been *better* for me to have lain in the brown grass on the cliff, or to have walked slowly by the sea. It would have been kinder of you to have written to me directly about whatever harsh or hurt feelings you may have about me. It would have saved me an afternoon of strain, and tension.

But I have something more to say. It is pleasanter to me, now, to write about others, than about myself.

The enclosed is from a brother prisoner of mine: released

June 4th: pray read it: you will see his age, offence, and aim in life.

If you can give him a trial, do so. If you see your way to this kind action, and write to him to come and see you, kindly state in your letter that it is about a situation. He may think otherwise that it is about the flogging of A.2.11., a thing that does not interest *you*, and about which *he* is a little afraid to talk.

If the result of this long letter will be that you will help this fellow prisoner of mine to a place in your service, I shall consider my afternoon better spent than any afternoon for the last two years, and three weeks.

In any case I have now written to you fully on all things as reported to me.

I again assure you of my gratitude for your kindness to me during my imprisonment, and on my release.

And am always

Your sincere friend and admirer

OSCAR WILDE.

With regard to Lawley

All soldiers are neat, and smart, and make capital servants. He would be a good *groom*: he is, I believe, a 3rd Hussars man—he was a quiet, well-conducted chap in Reading always.

Naturally I replied to this letter at once, saying that he had been misinformed, that I was not angry and if I could do anything for him I should be delighted: I did my best, too, for Lawley.

Here is his letter of thanks to me for helping him when he came out of prison.

Sandwich Hotel, Dieppe.

MY DEAR FRANK:

Just a line to thank you for your great kindness to me—for the lovely clothes, and for the generous cheque.

You have been a real good friend to me—and I shall never forget your kindness: to remember such a debt as mine to you—a debt of kind fellowship—is a pleasure.

About our tour—later on let us think about it. My friends have been so kind to me here that I am feeling happy already.

Yours,

OSCAR WILDE.

If you write to me please do so under cover to R.B. Ross, who is here with me.

In the next letter of his which I have kept Oscar is perfectly friendly again; he tells me that he is "entirely without money, having received nothing from his Trustees for months," and asks me for even L5, adding, "I drift in ridiculous impecuniosity without a sou."

THE MYSTERY OF PERSONALITY

I transcribe here another letter of Oscar to me from the second year after his release to show his interest in all intellectual things and for a flash of characteristic humour at the expense of the Paris police. The envelope is dated October 13, 1898:—

From M. Sebastian Melmoth, Hotel d'Alsace, Rue des Beaux-arts, Paris.

MY DEAR FRANK:

How are you? I read your appreciation of Rodin's "Balzac" with intensest pleasure, and I am looking forward to more Shakespeare—you will of course put all your Shakespearean essays into a book, and, equally of course, I must have a copy. It is a great era in Shakespearean criticism—the first time that one has looked in the plays not for philosophy, for there is none, but for the wonder of a great personality—something far better, and far more mysterious than any philosophy—it is a great thing that you have done. I remember writing once in "Intentions" that the more objective a work of art is in form, the more subjective it really is in matter—and that it is only when you give the poet a mask that he can tell you the truth. But you have shown it fully in the case of the one artist whose personality was supposed to be a mystery of deep seas, a secret as impenetrable as the secret of the moon.

Paris is terrible in its heat. I walk in streets of brass, and there is no one here. Even the criminal classes have gone to the seaside, and the gendarmes yawn and regret their enforced idleness. Giving wrong directions to the English tourists is the only thing that consoles them.

You were most kind and generous last month in letting me have a cheque—it gives me just the margin to live on and to live by. May I have it again this month? or has gold flown away from you?

Ever yours,

OSCAR.

THE DEDICATION OF "AN IDEAL HUSBAND"

I received the following letter from Oscar early in 1899 I imagine. It was written in the spring after the winter we spent in La Napoule.

From M. Sebastian Melmoth, Gland, Canton Vaud, Switzerland.

MY DEAR FRANK:

I am, as you see from above, in Switzerland with M—: a rather dreadful combination: the villa is pretty, and on the borders of the lake with pretty pines about: on the other side are the mountains of Savoy and Mont Blanc: we are an hour, by a slow train, from Geneva. But M—is tedious, and lacks conversation: also he gives me Swiss wine to drink: it is horrible: he occupies himself with small economies, and mean domestic interests, so I suffer very much. *Ennui* is the enemy.

I want to know if you will allow me to dedicate to you my next play, "The Ideal Husband"—which Smithers is bringing out for me in the same form as the others, of which I hope you received your copy. I should so much like to write your name and a few words on the dedicatory page.

I look back with joy and regret to the lovely sunlight of the Riviera, and the charming winter you so generously and kindly gave me: it was most good of you: how can it ever be forgotten by me.

Next week a petroleum launch is to arrive here, so that will console me a little, as I love to be on the water: and the Savoy side is starred with pretty villages and green valleys.

Of course we won our bet—the phrase on Shelley is in Arnold's preface to Byron: but M—won't pay me! He suffers agony over a franc. It is very annoying as I have had no money since my arrival here. However I regard the place as a Swiss Pension—where there is no weekly bill....

Ever yours,

OSCAR.

I believe I answered; but am not sure. I was naturally delighted to have just "An Ideal Husband" dedicated to me, because I had suggested the plot of it to Oscar—not that the plot was in any true sense mine. An interesting and clever American in Cairo, a Mr. Cope Whitehouse, had given it to me as I tell in this book. The story Whitehouse told may not be true; but my mind jumped at once to the thought of a story where an English Minister would be confronted with some early sin of that sort. I had hardly bettered the story given to me when I related it to Oscar who used it almost immediately with great effect. Dedicatory words are usually as flattering as epitaphs; those of "An Ideal Husband" run:

TO

FRANK HARRIS

A SLIGHT TRIBUTE TO

HIS POWER AND DISTINCTION

AS AN ARTIST

HIS CHIVALRY AND NOBILITY

AS A FRIEND

MRS. WILDE'S EPITAPH

(See page 447)

An evil fate seems to have pursued even Oscar's wife. She died in Genoa and was buried in the corner of the Campo Santo set apart for Protestants. This is what one reads on her tombstone:

CONSTANCE

DAUGHTER OF THE LATE

HORATIO LLOYD, Q.C.

BORN—DIED—

No reference to her marriage or to the famous man who was the father of her two sons.

The irony of chance wills it that the late Horatio Lloyd, Q.C., had been more than suspected of sexual viciousness: cfr. "Criticisms by Robert Ross" at end of Appendix.

SONNET

(See page 517)

TO OSCAR WILDE

I dreamed of you last night, I saw your face
All radiant and unshadowed of distress,
And as of old, in measured tunefulness,
I heard your golden voice and marked you trace
Under the common thing the hidden grace,
And conjure wonder out of emptiness,
Till mean things put on Beauty like a dress,
And all the world was an enchanted place.

And so I knew that it was well with you,
And that unprisoned, gloriously free,
Across the dark you stretched me out your hand.
And all the spite of this besotted crew,
(Scrabbling on pillars of Eternity)
How small it seems! Love made me understand.

ALFRED DOUGLAS.

December 10, 1900.

Whoever chooses to compare this first sketch of the sonnet of 1900 with the sonnet as it was published in 1910 will remark three notable differences.

The first sketch was entitled "To Oscar Wilde," the revision to "The Dead Poet."

In the early draft, the first line:

"I dreamed of you last night, I saw your face," has become less intimate, having been changed into:

"I dreamed of him last night, I saw his face."

Finally the sextet which in the first sketch was very inferior to the rest has now been discarded in favour of six lines which are worthy of the octave. The published sonnet is assuredly superior to the first sketch, superb though that was.

THE STORY OF "MR. AND MRS. DAVENTRY"

(See page 534)

There has been so much discussion about the play entitled "Mr. and Mrs. Daventry," and Oscar Wilde's share in it, that I had better set forth here briefly what happened.

When I returned to London in the summer of 1899 after buying, as I thought, all rights in the sketch of the scenario from Oscar, I wrote at once the second, third and fourth acts of the play, as I had told Oscar I would. I sent him what I had written and asked him to write the first act as he had promised for the L50.

Some time before this I had seen Mr. Forbes Robertson and Mrs. Patrick Campbell in "Hamlet," and Mrs. Patrick Campbell's Ophelia had made a deeper impression on me than even the Hamlet of Forbes Robertson. I wished her to take my play, and as luck would have it, she had just gone into management on her own account and leased the Royalty Theatre.

I read her my play one afternoon, and at once she told me she would take it; but I must write a first act. I told her that I was no good at preliminary scenes and that Oscar Wilde had promised to write a first act, which would, of course, enhance the value of the play enormously.

To my surprise Mrs. Patrick Campbell would not hear of it: "Quite impossible," she said, "a play's not a patchwork quilt; you must write the first act yourself."

"I must write to Oscar then," I replied, "and see whether he has finished it already or not."

Mrs. Campbell insisted that the play, if she was to accept it, must be the work of one hand. I wrote to Oscar at once, asking him whether he had written the first act, adding that if he had not written it and would send me his idea of the scenario, I would write it. I was overjoyed to tell him that Mrs. Patrick Campbell had provisionally accepted the play.

To my astonishment Oscar replied in evident ill-temper to say that he could not write the first act, or the scenario, but at the same time he hoped I would now send him some money for having helped to make my *debut* on the stage.

I returned to tell Mrs. Campbell my disappointment and to see if she had any idea of what she wanted in the first act. She was delighted with my news, and said that all I had to do was to write an act introducing my characters, and that I ought, for the sake of contrast, to give her a mother. Some impish spirit suggested to me the idea of making a mother much younger than her daughter, that is, a very flighty ordinary woman, impulsive and feather-brained, with a mania for attending sales and collecting odds and ends at bargain prices. Full of this idea I wrote the first act off hand.

Mrs. Patrick Campbell did not like it much, and in this, as indeed always, showed excellent judgment and an extraordinary understanding of the requirements of the stage; nevertheless she accepted the play and settled terms. A little later I went to Leeds, where she was playing, and read the play to her and her "Company." We discussed the cast, and I suggested Mr. Kerr to play Mr. Daventry. Mrs. Patrick Campbell jumped at the idea, and everything was settled.

I wrote the good news to Oscar, and back came another letter from him, more ill-tempered than the first, saying he had never thought I would take his scenario; I had no right to touch it; but as I had taken it, I must really pay him something substantial.

The claim was absurd, but I hated to dispute with him or even appear to bargain.

I wrote to him that if I made anything out of the play I would send him some more money. He replied that he was sure my play would be a failure; but I ought to get a good sum down in advance of royalties from Mrs. Patrick Campbell, and at once send him half of it. His letters were childishly ill-conditioned and unreasonable; but, believing him to be in extreme indigence, I felt too sorry for him even to argue the point. Again and again I had helped him, and it seemed sordid and silly to hurt our old friendship for money. I couldn't believe that he would talk of my having done anything that I ought not to have done if we met, so as soon as I could I crossed to Paris to have it out with him.

To my astonishment I found him obdurate in his wrong-headedness. When I asked him what he had sold me for the L50 I paid him, he coolly said he didn't think I was serious, that no man would write a play on another man's scenario; it was absurd, impossible—"*C'est ridicule!*" he repeated again and again. When I reminded him that Shakespeare had done it, he got angry: it was altogether different then—today: "*C'est ridicule!*" Tired of going over and over the old ground I pressed him to tell me what he wanted. For hours he wouldn't say: then at length he declared he ought to have half of all the play fetched, and even that wouldn't be fair to him, as he was a dramatist and I was not, and I ought not to have touched his scenario and so on, over and over again.

I returned to my hotel wearied in heart and head by his ridiculous demands and reiterations. After thrashing the beaten straw to dust on the following day, I agreed at length to give him another L50 down and another L50 later. Even then he pretended to be very sorry indeed that I had taken what he called "his play," and assured me in the same breath that "Mr. and Mrs. Daventry" would be a rank failure: "Plays cannot be written by amateurs; plays require knowledge of the stage. It's quite absurd of you, Frank, who hardly ever go to the theatre, to think you can write a successful play straight off. I always loved the theatre, always went to every first night in London, have the stage in my blood," and so forth and so on. I could not help recalling what he had told me years before, that when he had to write his first play for George Alexander, he shut himself up for a fortnight with the most successful modern French plays, and so learned his *metier*.

Next day I returned to London, understanding now something of the unreasonable persistence in begging which had aroused Lord Alfred Douglas' rage.

As soon as my play was advertised a crowd of people confronted me with claims I had never expected. Mrs. Brown Potter wrote to me saying that some years before she had bought a play from Oscar Wilde which he had not delivered, and as she understood that I was bringing it out, she hoped I would give it to her to stage. I replied saying that Oscar had not written a word of my play. She wrote again, saying that she had paid L100 for the scenario: would I see Mr. Kyrle Bellew on the matter? I saw them both a dozen times; but came to no decision.

While these negotiations were going on, a host of other Richmonds came into the field. Horace Sedger had also bought the same scenario, and then in quick succession it appeared that Tree and Alexander and Ada Rehan had also paid for the same privilege. When I wrote to Oscar about this expressing my surprise he replied coolly that he could have gone on selling the play now to French managers, and later to German managers, if I had not interfered: "You have deprived me of a certain income:" was his argument, "and therefore you owe me more than you will ever get from the play, which is sure to fall flat."

A little later Miss Nethersole presented herself, and when I would not yield to her demands, went to Paris, and Oscar wrote to me saying she ought to stage the piece as she would do it splendidly, or at least I should repay her the money she had advanced to him.

This letter showed me that Oscar had not only deceived me, but, for some cause or other, some pricking of vanity I couldn't understand, was willing to embarrass me as much as possible without any scruple.

Finally Smithers, the publisher of three of Oscar's books, whom I knew to be a real friend of Oscar, came to me with a still more appealing story. When Oscar was in Italy, and in absolute need, Smithers got a man named Roberts to advance L100 on the scenario. I found that Oscar had written out the whole scenario for him and outlined the characters of his drama. This was evidently the completest claim that had yet been brought before me: it was also, Smithers proved, the earliest, and Smithers himself was in dire need. I wrote to Oscar that I thought Smithers had the best claim because he was the first buyer, and certainly ought to have something. Oscar replied, begging me not to be a fool: to send him the money and tell Smithers to go to Sheol. Thereupon I told

Smithers I could not afford to give him any money at the moment; but if the play was a success he should have something out of it.

The play was a success: it was stopped for a week by Queen Victoria's death, in January, and was, I think, the only play that survived that ordeal. Mrs. Patrick Campbell was good enough to allow me to rewrite the first act for the fiftieth performance, and it ran, if I remember rightly, some 130 nights. About the twentieth representation I paid Smithers.

For the first weeks of the run I was bombarded with letters from Oscar, begging money and demanding money in every tone. He made nothing of the fact that I had already paid him three times the price agreed upon, and paid Smithers to boot, and lost through his previous sales of the scenario whatever little repute the success of the piece might have brought me. Nine people out of ten believed that Oscar had written the play and that I had merely lent my name to the production in order to enable him, as a bankrupt, to receive the money from it. Even men of letters deceived themselves in this way. George Moore told Bernard Shaw that he recognised Oscar's hand in the writing again and again, though Shaw himself was far too keen-witted to be so misled. As a matter of fact Oscar did not write a word of the play and the characters he sketched for Smithers and Roberts were altogether different from mine and were not known to me when I wrote my story.

I have set forth the bare facts of the affair here because Oscar managed to half-persuade Ross and Turner and other friends that I owed him money which I would not pay; though Ross had discounted most of his complaints, even before hearing my side.

Oscar got me over to Paris in September under the pretext

that he was ill; but I found him as well as could be, and anxious merely to get more money out of me by any means. I put it all down to his poverty. I did not then know that Ross was giving him L150 a year; that indeed all his friends had helped him and were helping him with singular generosity, and I recalled the fact that when he had had money he never showed any meanness, or any desire to over-reach. Want is a dreadful teacher, and I did not hold Oscar altogether responsible for his weird attitude to me personally.

OSCAR'S LAST DAYS!

LETTER FROM ROBERT ROSS TO—

Dec. 14th, 1900.

On Tuesday, October 9th, I wrote to Oscar, from whom I had not heard for some time, that I would be in Paris on Thursday, October the 18th, for a few days, when I hoped to see him. On Thursday, October 11th, I got a telegram from him as follows:—"Operated on yesterday—come over as soon as possible." I wired that I would endeavour to do so. A wire came in response, "Terribly weak—please come." I started on the evening of Tuesday, October 16th. On Wednesday morning I went to see him about 10.30. He was in very good spirits; and though he assured me his sufferings were dreadful, at the same time he shouted with laughter and told many stories against the doctors and himself. I stayed until 12.30 and returned about 4.30, when Oscar recounted his grievances about the Harris play. Oscar, of course, had deceived Harris about the whole matter—as far as I could make out the story—Harris wrote the play under the impression that only Sedger had to be bought off at L100, which Oscar had received in advance for the commission; whereas Kyrle Bellew, Louis Nethersole, Ada Rehan, and even Smithers, had all given Oscar L100 on different occasions, and all threatened Harris with proceedings—Harris, therefore, only gave Oscar L50 on account,[59] as he was obliged to square these people first—hence Oscar's grievance. When I pointed out to him that he was in a much better position than formerly, because Harris, at any rate, would eventually pay off the people who had advanced money and that Oscar would eventually get something himself, he replied in the characteristic way, "Frank has deprived me of my only source of income by taking a play on which I could always have raised L100."

I continued to see Oscar every day until I left Paris. Reggie and myself sometimes dined or lunched in his bedroom, when he was always very talkative, although he looked very ill. On October 25th, my brother Aleck came to see him, when Oscar was in particularly good form. His sister-in-law, Mrs. Willie, and her husband, Texeira, were then passing through Paris on their honeymoon, and came at the same time. On this occasion he said he was "dying above his means" ... he would never outlive the century ... the English people would not stand him—he was responsible for the failure of the Exhibition, the English having gone away when they saw him there so well-dressed and happy ... all the French people knew this, too, and would not stand him any more.... On October the 29th, Oscar got up for the first time at mid-day, and after dinner in the evening insisted on going out—he assured me that the doctor had said he might do so and would not listen to any protest.

I had urged him to get up some days before as the doctor said he might do so, but he had hitherto refused. We went to a small cafe in the Latin Quartier, where he insisted on drinking absinthe. He walked there and back with some difficulty, but seemed fairly well. Only I thought he had suddenly aged in face, and remarked to Reggie next day how different he looked when up and dressed. He appeared *comparatively* well in bed. (I noticed for the first time that his hair was slightly tinged with grey. I had always remarked that his hair had never altered its colour while he was in Reading;[60] it retained its soft brown tone. You must remember the jests he used to make about it, he always amused the warders by saying that his hair was perfectly white.) Next day I was not surprised to find Oscar suffering with a cold and great pain in his ear; however, Dr. Tucker said he might go out again, and the following afternoon, a very mild day, we drove in the Bois. Oscar was much better, but complained of giddiness; we returned about 4.30. On Saturday morning, November 3rd, I met the Panseur Hennion (Reggie always called him the Libre Penseur), he came every day to dress Oscar's wounds. He asked me if I was a great friend or knew Oscar's relatives. He assured me that Oscar's general condition was very serious—that he could not live more than three or four months unless he altered his way of life—that I ought to speak to Dr. Tucker, who did not realise Oscar's serious state—that the ear trouble was not of much importance in itself, but a grave symptom. On Sunday morning I saw Dr. Tucker—he is a silly, kind, excellent man; he said Oscar ought to write more—that he was much better, and that his condition would only become serious when he got up and went about in the usual way. I begged him to be frank. He promised to ask Oscar if he might talk to me openly on the subject of Oscar's health. I saw him on the Tuesday following by appointment; he was very vague; and though he endorsed Hennion's view to some extent, said that Oscar was getting well now, though he could not live long unless he stopped drinking. On going to see Oscar later in the day I found him very agitated. He said he did not want to know what the doctor had told me. He said he did not care if he had only a short time to live and then went off on to the subject of his debts, which I gather amounted to something over more than L400.[61] He asked me to see that at all events some of them were paid if I was in a position to do so after he was dead; he suffered remorse about some of his creditors. Reggie came in shortly afterwards much to my relief. Oscar told us that he had had a horrible dream the previous night—"that he had been supping with the dead." Reggie made a very typical response, "My dear Oscar, you were probably the life and soul of the party." This delighted Oscar, who became high-spirited again, almost hysterical. I left feeling rather anxious. That night I wrote to Douglas saying that I was compelled to leave Paris—that the doctor thought Oscar very ill—that— ought to pay some of his bills as they worried him very much, and the matter was retarding his recovery—a great point made by Dr. Tucker. On November 2nd, All Souls' Day, I had gone to Pere la Chaise with—. Oscar was much interested and asked me if I had chosen a place for his tomb. He discussed epitaphs in a perfectly light-hearted way, and I never dreamt he was so near death.

On Monday, November 12th, I went to the Hotel d'Alsace with Reggie to say good-bye, as I was leaving for the Riviera next day. It was late in the evening after dinner. Oscar went all over his financial troubles. He had just had a letter from Harris about the Smithers claim, and was much upset; his speech seemed to me a little thick, but he had been given morphia the previous night, and he always drank too much champagne during the day. He knew I was coming to say good-bye, but paid little attention when I entered the room, which at the time I thought rather strange; he addressed all his observations to Reggie. While we were talking, the post arrived with a very nice letter from Alfred Douglas, enclosing a cheque. It was partly in response to my letter I think. Oscar wept a little but soon recovered himself. Then we all had a friendly discussion, during which Oscar walked around the room and declaimed in rather an excited way. About 10.30 I got up to go. Suddenly Oscar asked Reggie and the nurse to leave the room for a minute, as he wanted to say good-bye. He rambled at first about his debts in Paris: and then he implored me not to go away, because he felt that a great change had come over him during the last few days. I adopted a rather stern attitude, as I really thought that Oscar was simply hysterical, though I knew that he was genuinely upset at my departure. Suddenly he broke into a violent sobbing, and said he would never see me again because he felt that everything was at an end—this very painful incident lasted about three-quarters of an hour.

He talked about various things which I can scarcely repeat here. Though it was very harrowing, I really did not attach any importance to my farewell, and I did not respond to poor Oscar's emotion as I ought to have done, especially as he said, when I was going out of the room, "Look out for some little cup in the hills near Nice where I can go when I am better, and where you can come and see me often." Those were the last articulate words he ever spoke to me.

I left for Nice the following evening, November 13th.

During my absence Reggie went every day to see Oscar, and wrote me short bulletins every other day. Oscar went out several times with him driving, and seemed much better. On Tuesday, November 27th, I received the first of Reggie's letters, which I enclose (the others came after I had started), and I started back for Paris; I send them because they will give you a very good idea of how things stood. I had decided that when I had moved my mother to Mentone on the following Friday, I would go to Paris on Saturday, but on the Wednesday evening, at five-thirty, I got a telegram from Reggie saying, "Almost hopeless." I just caught the express and arrived in Paris at 10.20 in the morning. Dr. Tucker and Dr. Kleiss, a specialist called in by Reggie, were there. They informed me that Oscar could not live for more than two days. His appearance was very painful, he had become quite thin, the flesh was livid, his breathing heavy. He was trying to speak. He was conscious that people were in the room, and raised his hand when I asked him whether he understood. He pressed our hands. I then went in search of a priest, and after great difficulty found Father Cuthbert Dunn, of the Passionists, who came with me at once and administered Baptism and Extreme Unction—Oscar could not take the Eucharist. You know I had always promised to bring a priest to Oscar when he was dying, and I felt rather guilty that I had so often dissuaded him from becoming a Catholic, but you know my reasons for doing so. I then sent wires to Frank Harris, to Holman (for communicating with Adrian Hope) and to Douglas. Tucker called again later and said that Oscar might linger a few days. A *garde malade* was requisitioned as the nurse had been rather overworked.

Terrible offices had to be carried out into which I need not enter. Reggie was a perfect wreck.

He and I slept at the Hotel d'Alsace that night in a room upstairs. We were called twice by the nurse, who thought Oscar was actually dying. About 5.30 in the morning a complete change came over him, the lines of the face altered, and I believe what is called the death rattle began, but I had never heard anything like it before; it sounded like the horrible turning of a crank, and it never ceased until the end. His eyes did not respond to the light test any longer. Foam and blood came from his mouth, and had to be wiped away by someone standing by him all the time. At 12 o'clock I went out to get some food, Reggie mounting guard. He went out at 12.30. From 1 o'clock we did not leave the room; the painful noise from the throat became louder and louder. Reggie and myself destroyed letters to keep ourselves from breaking down. The two nurses were out, and the proprietor of the hotel had come up to take their place; at 1.45 the time of his breathing altered. I went to the bedside and held his hand, his pulse began to flutter. He heaved a deep sigh, the only natural one I had heard since I arrived, the limbs seemed to stretch involuntarily, the breathing came fainter; he passed at 10 minutes to 2 p.m. exactly.

After washing and winding the body, and removing the appalling *debris* which had to be burnt, Reggie and myself and the proprietor started for the Maine to make the official declaration. There is no use recounting the tedious experiences which only make me angry to think about. The excellent Dupoirier lost his head and complicated matters by making a mystery over Oscar's name, though there was a difficulty, as Oscar was registered under the name of Melmoth at the hotel, and it is contrary to the French law to be under an assumed name in your hotel. From 3.30 till 5 p.m. we hung about the Maine and the Commissaire de Police offices. I then got angry and insisted on going to Gesling, the undertaker to the English Embassy, to whom Father Cuthbert had recommended me. After settling matters with him I went off to find some nuns to watch the body. I thought that in Paris of all places this would be quite easy, but it was only after incredible difficulties I got two Franciscan sisters.

Gesling was most intelligent and promised to call at the Hotel d'Alsace at 8 o'clock next morning. While Reggie stayed at the hotel interviewing journalists and clamorous creditors, I started with Gesling to see officials. We did not part till 1.30, so you can imagine the formalities and oaths and exclamations and signing of papers. Dying in Paris is really a very difficult and expensive luxury for a foreigner.

It was in the afternoon the District Doctor called and asked if Oscar had committed suicide or was murdered. He would not look at the signed certificates of Kleiss and Tucker. Gesling had warned me the previous evening that owing to the assumed name and Oscar's identity, the authorities might insist on his body being taken to the Morgue. Of course I was appalled at the prospect, it really seemed the final touch of horror. After examining the body, and, indeed, everybody in the hotel, and after a series of drinks and unseasonable jests, and a liberal fee, the District Doctor consented to sign the permission for burial. Then arrived some other revolting official; he asked how many collars Oscar had, and the value of his umbrella. (This is quite true, and not a mere exaggeration of mine.) Then various poets and literary people called, Raymond de la Tailhade, Tardieu, Charles Sibleigh, Jehan Rictus, Robert d'Humieres, George Sinclair, and various English people, who gave assumed names, together with two veiled women. They were all allowed to see the body when they signed their names....

I am glad to say dear Oscar looked calm and dignified, just as he did when he came out of prison, and there was nothing at all horrible about the body after it had been washed. Around his neck was the blessed rosary which you gave me, and on the breast a Franciscan medal given me by one of the nuns, a few flowers placed there by myself and an anonymous friend who had brought some on behalf of the children, though I do not suppose the children know that their father is dead. Of course there was the usual crucifix, candles and holy water.

Gesling had advised me to have the remains placed in the coffin at once, as decomposition would begin very rapidly, and at 8.30 in the evening the men came to screw it down. An unsuccessful photograph of Oscar was taken by Maurice Gilbert at my request, the flashlight did not work properly. Henri Davray came just before they had put on the lid. He was very kind and nice. On Sunday, the next day, Alfred Douglas arrived, and various people whom I do not know called. I expect most of them were journalists. On Monday morning at 9 o'clock, the funeral started from the hotel—we all walked to the Church of St. Germain des Pres behind the hearse—Alfred Douglas, Reggie Turner and myself, Dupoirier, the proprietor of the hotel, Henri the nurse, and Jules, the servant of the hotel, Dr. Hennion and Maurice Gilbert, together with two strangers whom I did not know. After a low mass, said by one of the vicaires at the altar behind the sanctuary, part of the burial office was read by Father Cuthbert. The Suisse told me that there were fifty-six people present—there were five ladies in deep mourning—I had ordered three coaches only, as I had sent out no official notices, being anxious to keep the funeral quiet. The first coach contained Father Cuthbert and the acolyte; the second Alfred Douglas, Turner, the proprietor of the hotel, and myself; the third contained Madame Stuart Merrill, Paul Fort, Henri Davray and Sar Luis; a cab followed containing strangers unknown to me. The drive took one hour and a half; the grave is at Bagneux, in a temporary concession hired in my name—when I am able I shall purchase ground elsewhere at Pere la Chaise for choice. I have not yet decided what to do, or the nature of the monument. There were altogether twenty-four wreaths of flowers; some were sent anonymously. The proprietor of the hotel supplied a pathetic bead trophy, inscribed, "A mon locataire," and there was another of the same kind from "The service de l'Hotel," the remaining twenty-two were, of course, of real flowers. Wreaths came from, or at the request of, the following: Alfred Douglas, More Adey, Reginald Turner, Miss Schuster, Arthur Clifton, the Mercure de France, Louis Wilkinson, Harold Mellor, Mr. and Mrs. Texiera de Mattos, Maurice Gilbert, and Dr. Tucker. At the head of the coffin I placed a wreath of laurels inscribed, "A tribute to his literary achievements and distinction." I tied inside the wreath the following names of those who had shown kindness to him during or after his imprisonment, "Arthur Humphreys, Max Beerbohm, Arthur Clifton, Ricketts, Shannon, Conder,

Rothenstein, Dal Young, Mrs. Leverson, More Adey, Alfred Douglas, Reginald Turner, Frank Harris, Louis Wilkinson, Mellor, Miss Schuster, Rowland Strong," and by special request a friend who wished to be known as "C.B."

I can scarcely speak in moderation of the magnanimity, humanity and charity of John Dupoirier, the proprietor of the Hotel d'Alsace. Just before I left Paris Oscar told me he owed him over L190. From the day Oscar was laid up he never said anything about it. He never mentioned the subject to me until after Oscar's death, and then I started the subject. He was present at Oscar's operation, and attended to him personally every morning. He paid himself for luxuries and necessities ordered by the doctor or by Oscar out of his own pocket. I hope that—or—will at any rate pay him the money still owing. Dr. Tucker is also owed a large sum of money. He was most kind and attentive, although I think he entirely misunderstood Oscar's case.

Reggie Turner had the worst time of all in many ways—he experienced all the horrible uncertainty and the appalling responsibility of which he did not know the extent. It will always be a source of satisfaction to those who were fond of Oscar, that he had someone like Reggie near him during his last days while he was articulate and sensible of kindness and attention....

ROBERT ROSS.

CRITICISMS

BY ROBERT ROSS

Vol. I. Page 80 Line 3. I demur very much to your statement in this paragraph. Wilde was too much of a student of Greek to have learned anything about controversy from Whistler.

No doubt Whistler was more nimble and more naturally gifted with the power of repartee, but when Wilde indulged in controversy with his critics, whether he got the best of it or not, he never borrowed the Whistlerian method. Cf. his controversy with Henley over Dorian Gray.

Then whatever you may think of Ruskin, Wilde learnt a great deal about the History and Philosophy of Art from him. He learned more from Pater and he was the friend and intimate of Burne-Jones long before he knew Whistler. I quite agree with your remark that he had "no joy in conflict" and no doubt he had little or no knowledge of the technique of Art in the modern expert's sense.

[There never was a greater master of controversy than Whistler, and I believe Wilde borrowed his method of making fun of the adversary. Robert Ross's second point is rather controversial. Shaw agrees with me that Wilde never knew anything really of music or of painting and neither the history nor the so-called philosophy of art makes one a connoisseur of contemporary masters. F.H.]

Page 94. Last line. For "happy candle" read "Happy Lamp." It was at the period when oil lamps were put in the middle of the dinner table just before the general introduction of electric light; by putting "candle" you lose the period. Cf. Du Maurier's pictures of dinner parties in *Punch*.

Page 115. I venture to think that you should state that Wilde at the end of his story of 'Mr. W.H.' definitely says that the theory is all nonsense. It always appeared to me a semi-satire of Shakespearean commentary. I remember Wilde saying to me after it was published that his next Shakespearean book would be a discussion as to whether the commentators on Hamlet were mad or only pretending to be. I think you take Wilde's phantasy too seriously but I am not disputing whether you are right or wrong in your opinion of it; but it strikes me as a little solemn when on Page 116 you say that the 'whole theory is completely mistaken'; but you are quite right when you say that it did Wilde a great deal of harm. [Ross does not seem to realise that if the theory were merely fantastic the public might be excused for condemning Oscar for playing with such a subject. As a matter of fact I remember Oscar defending the theory to me years later with all earnestness: that's why I stated my opinion of it. F.H.]

Page 142 Line 19. What Wilde said in front of the curtain was: "I have enjoyed this evening immensely."

[I seem to remember that Wilde said this; my note was written after a dinner a day or two later when Oscar acted the whole scene over again and probably elaborated his effect. I give the elaboration as most characteristic. F.H.]

Vol. II. Page 357 Line 3. Major Nelson was the name of the Governor at Reading prison. He was one of the most charming men I ever came across. I think he was a little hurt by the "Ballad of Reading Gaol," which he fancied rather reflected on him though Major Isaacson was the Governor at the time the soldier was executed. Isaacson was a perfect monster. Wilde sent Nelson copies of his books, "The Ideal Husband" and "The Importance of Being Earnest," which were published as you remember after the release, and Nelson acknowledged them in a most delightful way. He is dead now.

[Major Isaacson was the governor who boasted to me that he was knocking the nonsense out of Wilde; he seemed to me almost inhuman. My report got him relieved and Nelson appointed in his stead. Nelson was an ideal governor. F.H.]

Page 387. In the First Edition of the "Ballad of Reading

Gaol" issued by Methuen I have given the original draft of the poem which was in my hands in September 1897, long before Wilde rejoined Douglas. I will send you a copy of it if you like, but it is much more likely to reach you if you order it through Putnam's in New York as they are Methuen's agents. I would like you to see it because it fortifies your opinion about Douglas' ridiculous contention; though I could explode the whole thing by Wilde's letters to myself from Berneval. Certain verses were indeed added at Naples. I do not know what you will think, but to me they prove the mental decline due to the atmosphere and life that Wilde was leading at the time. Let us be just and say that perhaps Douglas assisted more than he was conscious of in their composition. To me they are terribly poor stuff, but then, unlike yourself, I am a heretic about the Ballad.

Page 411. In fairness to Gide: Gide is describing Wilde after he had come back from Naples in the year 1898, not in 1897, when he had just come out of prison.

Appendix Page 438 Line 20. Forgive me if I say it, but I think your method of sneering at Curzon unworthy of Frank Harris. Sneer by all means; but not in that particular way.

[Robert Ross is mistaken here: no sneer was intended. I added Curzon's title to avoid giving myself the air of an intimate. F.H.]

Page 488 Line 17. You really are wrong about Mellor's admiration for Wilde. He liked his society but loathed his writing. I was quite angry in 1900 when Mellor came to see me at Mentone (after Wilde's death, of course), when he said he could never see any merit whatever in Wilde's plays or books. However the point is a small one.

Page 490 Line 6. The only thing I can claim to have invented in connection with Wilde were the two titles "De Profundis" and "The Ballad of Reading Gaol," for which let me say I can produce documentary evidence. The publication of "De Profundis" was delayed for a month in 1905 because I could not decide on what to call it. It happened to catch on but I do not think it a very good title.

Page 555 Line 18. Do you happen to have compared Douglas' translation of Salome in Lane's First edition (with Beardsley's illustrations) with Lane's Second edition (with Beardsley's illustrations) or Lane's little editions (without Beardsley's illustrations)? Or have you ever compared the aforesaid First edition with the original? Douglas' translation omits a great deal of the text and is actually wrong as a rendering of the text in many cases. I have had this out with a good many people. I believe Douglas is to this day sublimely unconscious that his text, of which there were never more than 500 copies issued in England, has been entirely scrapped; his name at my instance was removed from the current issues for the very good reason that the new translation is not his. But this is merely an observation not a correction.

[I talked this matter over with Douglas more than once. He did not know French well; but he could understand it and he was a rarely good translator as his version of a Baudelaire sonnet shows. In any dispute as to the value of a word or phrase I should prefer his opinion to Oscar's. But Ross is doubtless right on this point. F.H.]

Appendix Page 587. Your memory is at fault here. The charge against Horatio Lloyd was of a normal kind. It was for exposing himself to nursemaids in the gardens of the Temple.

[I have corrected this as indeed I have always used Ross's

corrections on matters of fact. F.H.]

Page 596 Line 13. I think there ought to be a capital "E" in exhibition to emphasise that it is the 1900 Exhibition in Paris.

THE SOUL OF MAN UNDER SOCIALISM

When I was editing "The Fortnightly Review," Oscar Wilde wrote for me "The Soul of Man Under Socialism." On reading it then it seemed to me that he knew very little about Socialism and I disliked his airy way of dealing with a religion he hadn't taken the trouble to fathom. The essay now appears to me in a somewhat different light. Oscar had no deep understanding of Socialism, it is true, much less of the fact that in a healthy body corporate socialism or co-operation would govern all public utilities and public services while the individual would be left in possession of all such industries as his activity can control.

But Oscar's genius was such that as soon as he had stated one side of the problem he felt that the other side had to be considered and so we get from him if not the ideal of an ordered state at least *apercus* of astounding truth and value.

For example he writes: "Socialism ... by converting private property into public wealth, and substituting co-operation for competition, will restore society to its proper condition of a thoroughly healthy organism, and insure the material well-being of each member of the community."

Then comes the return on himself: "But for the full development of Life ... something more is needed. What is needed is Individualism."

And the ideal is always implicit: "Private property has led

Individualism entirely astray. It has made gain not growth its aim."

Humor too is never far away: "Only one class thinks more about money than the rich and that is the poor."

His short stay in the United States also benefited him.... "Democracy means simply the bludgeoning of the people by the people for the people. It has been found out."

Taken all in all a provocative delightful essay which like *Salome* in the aesthetic field marks the end of his *Lehrjahre* and the beginning of his work as a master.

A LAST WORD

In the couple of years that have elapsed since the first edition of this book was published, I have received many letters from readers asking for information about Wilde which I have omitted to give. I have been threatened with prosecution and must not speak plainly; but something may be said in answer to those who contend that Oscar might have brought forward weightier arguments in his defence than are to be found in Chapter XXIV. As a matter of fact I have made him more persuasive than he was. When Oscar declared (as recorded on page 496) that his weakness was "consistent with the highest ideal of humanity if not a characteristic of it," I asked him: "would he make the same defence for the Lesbians?" He turned aside showing the utmost disgust in face and words, thus in my opinion giving his whole case away.

He could have made a better defence. He might have said that as we often eat or drink or smoke for pleasure, so we may indulge in other sensualities. If he had argued that his sin was comparatively venial and so personal-peculiar that it carried with it no temptation to the normal man, I should not have disputed his point.

Moreover, love at its highest is independent of sex and sensuality. Since Luther we have been living in a centrifugal movement, in a wild individualism where all ties of love and affection have been loosened, and now that the centripetal movement has come into power we shall find that in another fifty years or so friendship and love will win again to honor and affinities of all sorts will proclaim themselves without shame and without fear. In this sense Oscar might have regarded himself as a forerunner and not as a survival or "sport." And it may well be that some instinctive feeling of this sort was at the back of his mind though too vague to be formulated in words. For even in our dispute (see Page 500) he pleaded that the world was becoming more tolerant, which, one hopes, is true. To become more tolerant of the faults of others is the first lesson in the religion of Humanity.

The End.

A letter from Lord Alfred Douglas to Oscar Wilde that I reproduce here speaks for itself and settles once for all, I imagine, the question of their relations. Had Lord Alfred Douglas not denied the truth and posed as Oscar Wilde's patron, I should never have published this letter though it was given to me to establish the truth. This letter was written between Oscar's first and second trial; ten days later Oscar Wilde was sentenced to two years imprisonment with hard labor.

FRANK HARRIS.

HOTEL DES DEUX MONDES 22, Avenue de l'Opera, 22 PARIS Wednesday, May 15, 1895.

My darling Oscar:

Have just arrived here.

It seems too dreadful to be here without you, but I hope you will join me next week. Dieppe was too awful for anything; it is the most depressing place in the world, even Petits Chevaux was not to be had as the Casino was closed. They are very nice here, and I can stay as long as I like without paying my bill which is a good thing, as I am quite penniless.

The proprietor is very nice and most sympathetic; he asked after you at once and expressed his regret and indignation at the treatment you had received. I shall have to send this by a cab to the Gare du Nord to catch the post as I want you to get it first post to-morrow.

I am going to see if I can find Robert Sherard to-morrow if he is in Paris.

Charlie is with me and sends you his best love.

I had a long letter from More (Adey) this morning about you. Do keep up your spirits, my dearest darling. I continue to think of you day and night and I send you all my love.

I am always your own loving and devoted boy.

BOSIE.

This letter now published for the first time is the most characteristic I received from Oscar Wilde in the years after his imprisonment. It dates I think from the winter of 1897, say some eight months after his release. F.H.

HOTEL DE NICE Rue des Beaux Arts PARIS

My dear Frank:

I cannot express to you how deeply touched I am by your letter—it is *une vraie poignee de main.* I simply long to see you and to come again in contact with your strong sane wonderful personality.

I cannot understand about the poem (The Ballad of Reading Gaol) my publisher tells me that, as I had begged him to do, he sent the two *first* copies to the "Saturday" and the "Chronicle"—and he also tells me that Arthur Symons told him he had written especially to you to ask you to allow him to do a *signed* article.

I suppose publishers are untrustworthy. They certainly always look it. I hope some notice will appear, as your paper, or rather yourself, is a great force in London and when you speak men listen.

I of course feel that the poem is too autobiographical and that real experience are alien things that should never influence one, but it was wrung out of me, a cry of pain, the cry of Marsyas, not the song of Apollo. Still, there are some good things in it. I feel as if I had made a sonnet out of skilly, and that is something.

When you return from Monte Carlo please let me know. I long to dine with you.

As regards a comedy, my dear Frank, I have lost the mainspring of life and art—*la joie de vivre*—it is dreadful. I have pleasures and passions, but the joy of life is gone. I am going under, the Morgue yawns for me. I go and look at my zinc bed there. After all I had a wonderful life, which is, I fear, over. But I must dine once with you first.

Ever yours,

OSCAR WILDE.

FOOTNOTES:

[39] Oscar told me this story; but as it only concerns Lord Alfred Douglas, and throws no new light on Oscar's character, I don't use it.

[40] This is extravagant condemnation of Lord Alfred Douglas' want of education; for he certainly knew a great deal about the poetic art even then and he has since acquired a very considerable knowledge of "Elizabethan Song."

[41] Whoever wishes to understand this bitter allusion should read his father's letter to Lord Alfred Douglas transcribed in the first volume. The Marquis of Queensberry doesn't hesitate to hint why his son was "sent down" from Oxford.

[42] Cfr. Appendix: "Criticisms by Robert Ross."

[43] Oscar is not flattering his friend in this: Lord Alfred Douglas has written two or three sonnets which rank among the best in the language.

[44] This statement—more than half true—is Oscar Wilde's *Apologia* and justification.

[45] This is, I believe, true and the explanation that follows is probably true also.

[46] Baccarat is not played in the Casino: *roulette* and *trente et quarante* are the games: roulette was Lord Alfred Douglas' favourite.

[47] This is a confession almost as much as an accusation.

[48] Oscar here crosses the *t's* and dots the *i's* of his charge.

[49] The previous accusation repeated, with bitterest sarcasm.

[50] Lord Alfred Douglas is well above the middle height: he holds himself badly but is fully five feet nine inches in height.

[51] The old accusation.

[52] Mr. Beerbohm Tree.

[53] The very truth, it seems to me.

[54] Proving another guilty would not have exculpated Oscar. Readers of my book will remember that I urged Oscar to tell the truth and how he answered me.

[55] As will be seen from a letter of Oscar Wilde which I reproduce later, I supplied the clothes.

[56] His letter was merely an acknowledgment that he had received the clothes and cheque and was grateful. I saw nothing in it to answer as he had not even mentioned the driving tour.

[57] I felt hurt that he dropped the idea without giving me any reason or even letting me know his change of purpose.

[58] I think this was true; though it had never struck me till I read this letter. Later, in order to excuse himself for not working, he magnified the effect on his health of prison life.

A year after his release I think he had as large a reserve of nervous energy as ever.

[59] Fifty pounds was all Oscar asked me: the whole sum agreed upon. As a matter of fact I gave him fifty pounds more before leaving Paris. I didn't then know that he had ever told the scenario to anyone else, much less sold it; though I ought perhaps to have guessed it.—F.H.

[60] I (Frank Harris) noticed at Reading that his hair was getting grey in front and at the sides; but when we met later the grey had disappeared. I thought he used some dye. I only mention this to show how two good witnesses can differ on a plain matter of fact.

[61] Ross found afterwards that they amounted to L620.

MEMORIES OF OSCAR WILDE

BY G. BERNARD SHAW

INTRODUCTION

George Bernard Shaw ordered a special copy of this book of mine: "Oscar Wilde: His Life and Confessions," as soon as it was announced. I sent it to him and asked him to write me his opinion of the book.

In due course I received the following MSS. from him in which he tells me what he thinks of my work:—"the best life of Wilde, ... Wilde's memory will have to stand or fall by it"; and then goes on to relate all his own meetings with Wilde, the impressions they made upon him and his judgment of Wilde as a writer and as a man.

He has given himself this labor, he says, in order that I may publish his views in the Appendix to my book if I think fit—an example, not only of Shaw's sympathy and generosity, but of his light way of treating his own kindness.

I am delighted to be able to put Shaw's considered judgment of Wilde beside my own for the benefit of my readers. For if there had been anything I had misseen or misjudged in Wilde, or any prominent trait of his character I had failed to note, the sin, whether of omission or commission, could scarcely have escaped this other pair of keen eyes. Now indeed this biography of Wilde may be regarded as definitive.

Shaw says his judgment of Wilde is severer than mine—"far sterner," are his words; but I am not sure that this is an exact estimate.

While Shaw accentuates Wilde's snobbishness, he discounts his "Irish charm," and though he praises highly his gifts as dramatist and story-teller he lays little stress on his genuine kindness of nature and the courteous smiling ways which made him so incomparable a companion and intimate.

On the other hand he excuses Wilde's perversion as pathological, as hereditary "giantism," and so lightens the darkest shadows just as he has toned down the lights.

I never saw anything abnormal in Oscar Wilde either in body or soul save an extravagant sensuality and an absolute adoration of beauty and comeliness; and so, with his own confessions and practises before me, I had to block him in, to use painters' jargon, with black shadows, and was delighted to find high lights to balance them—lights of courtesies, graces and unselfish kindness of heart.

On the whole I think our two pictures are very much alike and I am sure a good many readers will be almost as grateful to Shaw for his collaboration and corroboration as I am.

POSTSCRIPT

Since writing this foreword I have received the proof of his contribution which I had sent to Shaw. He has made some slight corrections in the text which, of course, have been carried out, and some comments besides on my notes as Editor. These, too, I have naturally wished to use and so, to avoid confusion, have inserted them in italics and with his initials. I hope the sequence will be clear to the reader.

MY MEMORIES OF OSCAR WILDE

BY BERNARD SHAW

MY DEAR HARRIS:—

"I have an interesting letter of yours to answer; but when you ask me to exchange biographies, you take an unfair advantage of the changes of scene and bustling movement of your own adventures. My autobiography would be like my best plays, fearfully long, and not divided into acts. Just consider this life of Wilde which you have just sent me, and which I finished ten minutes ago after putting aside everything else to read it at one stroke.

"Why was Wilde so good a subject for a biography that none of the previous attempts which you have just wiped out are bad? Just because his stupendous laziness simplified his life almost as if he knew instinctively that there must be no episodes to spoil the great situation at the end of the last act but one. It was a well made life in the Scribe sense. It was as simple as the life of Des Grieux, Manon Lescaut's lover; and it beat that by omitting Manon and making Des Grieux his own lover and his own hero.

"Des Grieux was a worthless rascal by all conventional standards; and we forgive him everything. We think we forgive him because he was unselfish and loved greatly. Oscar seems to have said: 'I will love nobody: I will be utterly selfish; and I will be not merely a rascal but a monster; and you shall forgive me everything. In other words, I will reduce your standards to absurdity, not by writing them down, though I could do that so well—in fact, *have* done it—but by actually living them down and dying them down.'

"However, I mustn't start writing a book to you about Wilde: I must just tumble a few things together and tell you them. To take things in the order of your book, I can remember only one occasion on which I saw Sir William Wilde, who, by the way, operated on my father to correct a squint, and overdid the correction so much that my father squinted the other way all the rest of his life. To this day I never notice a squint: it is as normal to me as a nose or a tall hat.

"I was a boy at a concert in the Antient Concert Rooms in Brunswick Street in Dublin. Everybody was in evening dress; and—unless I am mixing up this concert with another (in which case I doubt if the Wildes would have been present)—the Lord Lieutenant was there with his blue waistcoated courtiers. Wilde was dressed in snuffy brown; and as he had the sort of skin that never looks clean, he produced a dramatic effect beside Lady Wilde (in full fig) of being, like Frederick the Great, Beyond Soap and Water, as his Nietzschean son was beyond Good and Evil. He was currently reported to have a family in every farmhouse; and the wonder was that Lady Wilde didn't mind—evidently a tradition from the Travers case, which I did not know about until I read your account, as I was only eight in 1864.

"Lady Wilde was nice to me in London during the desperate days between my arrival in 1876 and my first earning of an income by my pen in 1885, or rather until, a few years earlier, I threw myself into Socialism and cut myself contemptuously loose from everything of which her at-homes—themselves desperate affairs enough, as you saw for yourself—were part. I was at two or three of them; and I once dined with her in company with an ex-tragedy queen named Miss Glynn, who, having no visible external ears, reared a head like a turnip. Lady Wilde talked about Schopenhauer; and Miss Glynn told me that Gladstone formed his oratorical style on Charles Kean.

"I ask myself where and how I came across Lady Wilde; for we had no social relations in the Dublin days. The explanation must be that my sister, then a very attractive girl who sang beautifully, had met and made some sort of innocent conquest of both Oscar and Willie. I met Oscar once at one of the at-homes; and he came and spoke to me with an evident intention of being specially kind to me. We put each other out frightfully; and this odd difficulty persisted between us to the very last, even when we were no longer mere boyish novices and had become men of the world with plenty of skill in social intercourse. I saw him very seldom, as I avoided literary and artistic society like the plague, and refused the few invitations I received to go into society with burlesque ferocity, so as to keep out of it without offending people past their willingness to indulge me as a privileged lunatic.

"The last time I saw him was at that tragic luncheon of yours at the Cafe Royal; and I am quite sure our total of meetings from first to last did not exceed twelve, and may not have exceeded six.

"I definitely recollect six: (1) At the at-home aforesaid. (2) At Macmurdo's house in Fitzroy Street in the days of the Century Guild and its paper '*The Hobby Horse*.' (3) At a meeting somewhere in Westminster at which I delivered an address on Socialism, and at which Oscar turned up and spoke. Robert Ross surprised me greatly by telling me, long after Oscar's death, that it was this address of mine that moved Oscar to try his hand at a similar feat by writing 'The Soul of Man Under Socialism.' (4) A chance meeting near the stage door of the Haymarket Theatre, at which our queer shyness of one another made our resolutely cordial and appreciative conversation so difficult that our final laugh and shake-hands was almost a reciprocal confession. (5) A really pleasant afternoon we spent together on catching one another in a place where our presence was an absurdity. It was some exhibition in Chelsea: a naval commemoration, where there was a replica of Nelson's Victory and a set of P. & O. cabins which made one seasick by mere association of ideas. I don't know why I went or why Wilde went; but we did; and the question what the devil we were doing in that galley tickled us both. It was my sole experience of Oscar's wonderful gift as a raconteur. I remember particularly an amazingly elaborate story which you have no doubt heard from him: an example of the cumulation of a single effect, as in Mark Twain's story of the man who was persuaded to put lightning conductor after lightning conductor at every possible point on his roof until a thunderstorm came and all the lightning in the heavens went for his house and wiped it out.

"Oscar's much more carefully and elegantly worked out story was of a young man who invented a theatre stall which economized space by ingenious contrivances which were all described. A friend of his invited twenty millionaires to meet him at dinner so that he might interest them in the invention. The young man convinced them completely by his demonstration of the saving in a theatre holding, in ordinary seats, six hundred people, leaving them eager and ready to make his fortune. Unfortunately he went on to calculate the annual saving in all the theatres of the world; then in all the churches of the world; then in all the legislatures; estimating finally the incidental and moral and religious effects of the invention until at the end of an hour he had estimated a profit of several thousand millions: the climax of course being that the millionaires folded their tents and silently stole away, leaving the ruined inventor a marked man for life.

"Wilde and I got on extraordinarily well on this occasion. I had not to talk myself, but to listen to a man telling me stories better than I could have told them. We did not refer to Art, about which, excluding literature from the definition, he knew only what could be picked up by reading about it. He was in a tweed suit and low hat like myself, and had been detected and had detected me in the act of clandestinely spending a happy day at Rosherville Gardens instead of pontificating in his frock coat and so forth. And he had an audience on whom not one of his subtlest effects was lost. And so for once our meeting was a success; and I understood why Morris, when he was dying slowly, enjoyed a visit from Wilde more than from anybody else, as I understand why you say in your book that you would rather have Wilde back than any friend you have ever talked to, even though he was incapable of friendship, though not of the most touching kindness[1] on occasion.

[Footnote 1: Excellent analysis. [Ed.]]

"Our sixth meeting, the only other one I can remember, was the one at the Cafe Royal. On that occasion he was not too preoccupied with his danger to be disgusted with me because I, who had praised his first plays handsomely, had turned traitor over 'The Importance of Being Earnest.' Clever as it was, it was his first really heartless play. In the others the chivalry of the eighteenth century Irishman and the romance of the disciple of Theophile Gautier (Oscar was really old-fashioned in the Irish way, except as a critic of morals) not only gave a certain kindness and gallantry to the serious passages and to the handling of the women, but provided that proximity of emotion without which laughter, however irresistible, is destructive and sinister. In 'The Importance of Being Earnest' this had vanished; and the play, though extremely funny, was essentially hateful. I had no idea that Oscar was going to the dogs, and that this represented a real degeneracy produced by his debaucheries. I thought he was still developing; and I hazarded the unhappy guess that 'The Importance of Being Earnest' was in idea a young work written or projected long before under the influence of Gilbert and furbished up for Alexander as a potboiler. At the Cafe Royal that day I calmly asked him whether I was not right. He indignantly repudiated my guess, and said loftily (the only time he ever tried on me the attitude he took to John Gray and his more abject disciples) that he was disappointed in me. I suppose I said, 'Then what on earth has happened to you?' but I recollect nothing more on that subject except that we did not quarrel over it.

"When he was sentenced I spent a railway journey on a Socialist lecturing excursion to the North drafting a petition for his release. After that I met Willie Wilde at a theatre which I think must have been the Duke of York's, because I connect it vaguely with St. Martin's Lane. I spoke to him about the petition, asking him whether anything of the sort was being done, and warning him that though I and Stewart Headlam would sign it, that would be no use, as we were two notorious cranks, and our names would by themselves reduce the petition to absurdity and do Oscar more harm than good. Willie cordially agreed, and added, with maudlin pathos and an inconceivable want of tact: 'Oscar was NOT a man of bad character: you could have trusted him with a woman anywhere.' He convinced me, as you discovered later, that signatures would not be obtainable; so the petition project dropped; and I don't know what became of my draft.

"When Wilde was in Paris during his last phase I made a point of sending him inscribed copies of all my books as they came out; and he did the same to me.

"In writing about Wilde and Whistler, in the days when they were treated as witty triflers, and called Oscar and Jimmy in print, I always made a point of taking them seriously and with scrupulous good manners. Wilde on his part also made a point of recognizing me as a man of distinction by his manner, and repudiating the current estimate of me as a mere jester. This was not the usual reciprocal-admiration trick: I believe he was sincere, and felt indignant at what he thought was a vulgar underestimate of me; and I had the same feeling about him. My impulse to rally to him in his misfortune, and my disgust at 'the man Wilde' scurrilities of the newspapers, was irresistible: I don't quite know why; for my charity to his perversion, and my recognition of the fact that it does not imply any general depravity or coarseness of character, came to me through reading and observation, not through sympathy.

"I have all the normal violent repugnance to homosexuality —if it is really normal, which nowadays one is sometimes provoked to doubt.

"Also, I was in no way predisposed to like him: he was my fellow-townsman, and a very prime specimen of the sort of fellow-townsman I most loathed: to wit, the Dublin snob. His Irish charm, potent with Englishmen, did not exist for me; and on the whole it may be claimed for him that he got no regard from me that he did not earn.

"What first established a friendly feeling in me was, unexpectedly enough, the affair of the Chicago anarchists, whose Homer you constituted yourself by '*The Bomb*.' I tried to get some literary men in London, all heroic rebels and skeptics on paper, to sign a memorial asking for the reprieve of these unfortunate men. The only signature I got was

Oscar's. It was a completely disinterested act on his part; and it secured my distinguished consideration for him for the rest of his life.

"To return for a moment to Lady Wilde. You know that there is a disease called giantism, caused by 'a certain morbid process in the sphenoid bone of the skull—viz., an excessive development of the anterior lobe of the pituitary body' (this is from the nearest encyclopedia). 'When this condition does not become active until after the age of twenty-five, by which time the long bones are consolidated, the result is acromegaly, which chiefly manifests itself in an enlargement of the hands and feet.' I never saw Lady Wilde's feet; but her hands were enormous, and never went straight to their aim when they grasped anything, but minced about, feeling for it. And the gigantic splaying of her palm was reproduced in her lumbar region.

"Now Oscar was an overgrown man, with something not quite normal about his bigness—something that made Lady Colin Campbell, who hated him, describe him as 'that great white caterpillar.' You yourself describe the disagreeable impression he made on you physically, in spite of his fine eyes and style. Well, I have always maintained that Oscar was a giant in the pathological sense, and that this explains a good deal of his weakness.

"I think you have affectionately underrated his snobbery, mentioning only the pardonable and indeed justifiable side of it; the love of fine names and distinguished associations and luxury and good manners.[2] You say repeatedly, and *on certain planes*, truly, that he was not bitter and did not use his tongue to wound people. But this is not true on the snobbish plane. On one occasion he wrote about T.P. O'Connor with deliberate, studied, wounding insolence, with his Merrion Square Protestant pretentiousness in full cry against the Catholic. He repeatedly declaimed against the vulgarity of the British journalist, not as you or I might, but as an expression of the odious class feeling that is itself the vilest vulgarity. He made the mistake of not knowing his place. He objected to be addressed as Wilde, declaring that he was Oscar to his intimates and Mr. Wilde to others, quite unconscious of the fact that he was imposing on the men with whom, as a critic and journalist, he had to live and work, the alternative of granting him an intimacy he had no right to ask or a deference to which he had no claim. The vulgar hated him for snubbing them; and the valiant men damned his impudence and cut him. Thus he was left with a band of devoted satellites on the one hand, and a dining-out connection on the other, with here and there a man of talent and personality enough to command his respect, but utterly without that fortifying body of acquaintance among plain men in which a man must move as himself a plain man, and be Smith and Jones and Wilde and Shaw and Harris instead of Bosie and Robbie and Oscar and Mister. This is the sort of folly that does not last forever in a man of Wilde's ability; but it lasted long enough to prevent Oscar laying any solid social foundations.[3]

[Footnote 2: I had touched on the evil side of his snobbery, I thought, by saying that it was only famous actresses and great ladies that he ever talked about, and in telling how he loved to speak of the great houses such as Clumber to which he had been invited, and by half a dozen other hints scattered through my book. I had attacked English snobbery so strenuously in my book on "The Man Shakespeare," had resented its influence on the finest English intelligence so bitterly, that I thought if I again laid stress on it in Wilde, people would think I was crazy on the subject. But he was a snob, both by nature and training, and I understand by snob what Shaw evidently understands by it here.]

[Footnote 3: The reason that Oscar, snobbish as he was, and admirer of England and the English as he was, could not lay any solid social foundations in England was, in my opinion, his intellectual interests and his intellectual superiority to the men he met. No one with a fine mind devoted to things of the spirit is capable of laying solid social foundations in England. Shaw, too, has no solid social foundations in that country.

This passing shot at English society serves it right. Yet able men have found niches in London. Where was Oscar's?—G.B.S.]

"Another difficulty I have already hinted at. Wilde started as an apostle of Art; and in that capacity he was a humbug. The notion that a Portora boy, passed on to T.C.D. and thence to Oxford and spending his vacations in Dublin, could without special circumstances have any genuine intimacy with music and painting, is to me ridiculous.[4] When Wilde was at Portora, I was at home in a house where important musical works, including several typical masterpieces, were being rehearsed from the point of blank amateur ignorance up to fitness for public performance. I could whistle them from the first bar to the last as a butcher's boy whistles music hall songs, before I was twelve. The toleration of popular music—Strauss's waltzes, for instance—was to me positively a painful acquirement, a sort of republican duty.

[Footnote 4: I had already marked it down to put in this popular edition of my book that Wilde continually pretended to a knowledge of music which he had not got. He could hardly tell one tune from another, but he loved to talk of that "scarlet thing of Dvorak," hoping in this way to be accepted as a real critic of music, when he knew nothing about it and cared even less. His eulogies of music and painting betrayed him continually though he did not know it.]

"I was so fascinated by painting that I haunted the National Gallery, which Doyle had made perhaps the finest collection of its size in the world; and I longed for money to buy painting materials with. This afterwards saved me from starving: it was as a critic of music and painting in the *World* that I won through my ten years of journalism before I finished up with you on the *Saturday Review*. I could make deaf stockbrokers read my two pages on music, the alleged joke being that I knew nothing about it. The real joke was that I knew all about it.

"Now it was quite evident to me, as it was to Whistler and Beardsley, that Oscar knew no more about pictures[5] than anyone of his general culture and with his opportunities can pick up as he goes along. He could be witty about Art, as I could be witty about engineering; but that is no use when you have to seize and hold the attention and interest of people who really love music and painting. Therefore, Oscar was handicapped by a false start, and got a reputation[6] for shallowness and insincerity which he never retrieved until it was too late.

[Footnote 5: I touched upon Oscar's ignorance of art sufficiently I think, when I said in my book that he had learned all he knew of art and of controversy from Whistler, and that his lectures on the subject, even after sitting at the feet of the Master, were almost worthless.]

[Footnote 6: Perfectly true, and a notable instance of Shaw's insight.]

"Comedy: the criticism of morals and manners *viva voce*, was his real forte. When he settled down to that he was great. But, as you found when you approached Meredith about him, his initial mistake had produced that 'rather low opinion of Wilde's capacities,' that 'deep-rooted contempt for the showman in him,' which persisted as a first impression and will persist until the last man who remembers his esthetic period has perished. The world has been in some ways so unjust to him that one must be careful not to be unjust to the world.

"In the preface on education, called 'Parents and Children,' to my volume of plays beginning with *Misalliance*, there is a section headed 'Artist Idolatry,' which is really about Wilde. Dealing with 'the powers enjoyed by brilliant persons who are also connoisseurs in art,' I say, 'the influence they can exercise on young people who have been brought up in the darkness and wretchedness of a home without art, and in whom a natural bent towards art has always been baffled and snubbed, is incredible to those who have not witnessed and understood it. He (or she) who reveals the world of art to them opens heaven to them. They become satellites, disciples, worshippers of the apostle. Now the apostle may be a voluptuary without much conscience. Nature may have given him enough virtue to suffice in a reasonable environment. But this allowance may not be enough to defend him against the temptation and demoralization of finding himself a little god on the strength of what ought to be a quite ordinary culture. He may find adorers in all directions in our uncultivated society among people of stronger character than himself, not one of whom, if they had been artistically educated, would have had anything to learn from him, or regarded him as in any way extraordinary apart from his actual achievements as an artist. Tartufe is not always a priest. Indeed, he is not always a rascal: he is often a weak man absurdly credited with omniscience and perfection, and taking unfair advantages only because they are offered to him and he is too weak to refuse. Give everyone his culture, and no one will offer him more than his due.'

"That paragraph was the outcome of a walk and talk I had one afternoon at Chartres with Robert Ross.

"You reveal Wilde as a weaker man than I thought him: I still believe that his fierce Irish pride had something to do with his refusal to run away from the trial. But in the main your evidence is conclusive. It was part of his tragedy that people asked more moral strength from him that he could bear the burden of, because they made the very common mistake—of which actors get the benefit—of regarding style as evidence of strength, just as in the case of women they are apt to regard paint as evidence of beauty. Now Wilde was so in love with style that he never realized the danger of biting off more than he could chew: in other words, of putting up more style than his matter would carry. Wise kings wear shabby clothes, and leave the gold lace to the drum major.

"You do not, unless my memory is betraying me as usual, quite recollect the order of events just before the trial. That day at the Cafe Royal, Wilde said he had come to ask you to go into the witness box next day and testify that *Dorian Gray* was a highly moral work. Your answer was something like this: 'For God's sake, man, put everything on that plane out of your head. You don't realize what is going to happen to you. It is not going to be a matter of clever talk about your books. They are going to bring up a string of witnesses that will put art and literature out of the question. Clarke will throw up his brief. He will carry the case to a certain point; and then, when he sees the avalanche coming, he will back out and leave you in the dock. What you have to do is to cross to France to-night. Leave a letter saying that you cannot face the squalor and horror of a law case; that you are an artist and unfitted for such things. Don't stay here clutching at straws like testimonials to *Dorian Gray. I tell you I know*. I know what is going to happen. I know Clarke's sort. I know what evidence they have got. You must go.'

"It was no use. Wilde was in a curious double temper. He made no pretence either of innocence or of questioning the folly of his proceedings against Queensberry. But he had an infatuate haughtiness as to the impossibility of his retreating, and as to his right to dictate your course. Douglas sat in silence, a haughty indignant silence, copying Wilde's attitude as all Wilde's admirers did, but quite probably influencing Wilde as you suggest, by the copy. Oscar finally rose with a mixture of impatience and his grand air, and walked out with the remark that he had now found out who were his real friends; and Douglas followed him, absurdly smaller, and imitating his walk, like a curate following an archbishop.[7] You remember it the other way about; but just consider this. Douglas was in the wretched position of having ruined Wilde merely to annoy his father, and of having attempted it so idiotically that he had actually prepared a triumph for him. He was, besides, much the youngest man present, and looked younger than he was. You did not make him welcome: as far as I recollect you did not greet him by a word or nod. If he had given the smallest provocation or attempted to take the lead in any way, I should not have given twopence for the chance of your keeping your temper. And Wilde, even in his ruin—which, however, he did not yet fully realize—kept his air of authority on questions of taste and conduct. It was practically impossible under such circumstances that Douglas should have taken the stage in any way. Everyone thought him a horrid little brat; but I, not having met him before to my knowledge, and having some sort of flair for his literary talent, was curious to hear what he had to say for himself. But, except to echo Wilde once or twice, he said nothing.[8] You are right in effect, because it was evident that Wilde was in his hands, and was really echoing him. But Wilde automatically kept the prompter off the stage and himself in the middle of it.

[Footnote 7: This is an inimitable picture, but Shaw's fine

sense of comedy has misled him. The scene took place absolutely as I recorded it. Douglas went out first saying—"Your telling him to run away shows that you are no friend of Oscar's." Then Oscar got up to follow him. He said good-bye to Shaw, adding a courteous word or two. As he turned to the door I got up and said:—"I hope you do not doubt my friendship; you have no reason to."

"I do not think this is friendly of you, Frank," he said, and went on out.]

[Footnote 8: I am sure Douglas took the initiative and walked out first.

I have no doubt you are right, and that my vision of the exit is really a reminiscence of the entrance. In fact, now that you prompt my memory, I recall quite distinctly that Douglas, who came in as the follower, went out as the leader, and that the last word was spoken by Wilde after he had gone.—G.B.S.]

"What your book needs to complete it is a portrait of yourself as good as your portrait of Wilde. Oscar was not combative, though he was supercilious in his early pose. When his snobbery was not in action, he liked to make people devoted to him and to flatter them exquisitely with that end. Mrs. Calvert, whose great final period as a stage old woman began with her appearance in my *Arms and the Man*, told me one day, when apologizing for being, as she thought, a bad rehearser, that no author had ever been so nice to her except Mr. Wilde.

"Pugnacious people, if they did not actually terrify Oscar, were at least the sort of people he could not control, and whom he feared as possibly able to coerce him. You suggest that the Queensberry pugnacity was something that Oscar could not deal with successfully. But how in that case could Oscar have felt quite safe with you? You were more pugnacious than six Queensberrys rolled into one. When people asked, 'What has Frank Harris been?' the usual reply was, 'Obviously a pirate from the Spanish Main.'

"Oscar, from the moment he gained your attachment, could never have been afraid of what you might do to him, as he was sufficient of a connoisseur in Blut Bruderschaft to appreciate yours; but he must always have been mortally afraid of what you might do or say to his friends.[9]

[Footnote 9: This insight on Shaw's part makes me smile because it is absolutely true. Oscar commended Bosie Douglas to me again and again and again, begged me to be nice to him if we ever met by chance; but I refused to meet him for months and months.]

"You had quite an infernal scorn for nineteen out of twenty of the men and women you met in the circles he most wished to propitiate; and nothing could induce you to keep your knife in its sheath when they jarred on you. The Spanish Main itself would have blushed rosy red at your language when classical invective did not suffice to express your feelings.

"It may be that if, say, Edmund Gosse had come to Oscar when he was out on bail, with a couple of first class tickets in his pocket, and gently suggested a mild trip to Folkestone, or the Channel Islands, Oscar might have let himself be coaxed away. But to be called on to gallop *ventre a terre* to Erith—it might have been Deal—and hoist the Jolly Roger on board your lugger, was like casting a light comedian and first lover for *Richard III*. Oscar could not see himself in the part.

"I must not press the point too far; but it illustrates, I think, what does not come out at all in your book: that you were a very different person from the submissive and sympathetic disciples to whom he was accustomed. There are things more terrifying to a soul like Oscar's than an as yet unrealized possibility of a sentence of hard labor. A voyage with Captain Kidd may have been one of them. Wilde was a conventional man: his unconventionality was the very pedantry of convention: never was there a man less an outlaw than he. You were a born outlaw, and will never be anything else.

"That is why, in his relations with you, he appears as a man always shirking action—more of a coward (all men are cowards more or less) than so proud a man can have been. Still this does not affect the truth and power of your portrait. Wilde's memory will have to stand or fall by it.

"You will be blamed, I imagine, because you have not written a lying epitaph instead of a faithful chronicle and study of him; but you will not lose your sleep over that. As a matter of fact, you could not have carried kindness further without sentimental folly. I should have made a far sterner summing up. I am sure Oscar has not found the gates of heaven shut against him: he is too good company to be excluded; but he can hardly have been greeted as, 'Thou good and faithful servant.' The first thing we ask a servant for is a testimonial to honesty, sobriety and industry; for we soon find out that these are the scarce things, and that geniuses[10] and clever people are as common as rats. Well, Oscar was not sober, not honest, not industrious. Society praised him for being idle, and persecuted him savagely for an aberration which it had better have left unadvertized, thereby making a hero of him; for it is in the nature of people to worship those who have been made to suffer horribly: indeed I have often said that if the crucifixion could be proved a myth, and Jesus convicted of dying of old age in comfortable circumstances, Christianity would lose ninety-nine per cent. of its devotees.

[Footnote 10: The English paste in Shaw; genius is about the rarest thing on earth whereas the necessary quantum of "honesty, sobriety and industry," is beaten by life into nine humans out of ten.—ED.

If so, it is the tenth who comes my way.—G.B.S.]

"We must try to imagine what judgment we should have passed on Oscar if he had been a normal man, and had dug his grave with his teeth in the ordinary respectable fashion, as his brother Willie did. This brother, by the way, gives us some cue; for Willie, who had exactly the same education and the same chances, must be ruthlessly set aside by literary history as a vulgar journalist of no account. Well, suppose Oscar and Willie had both died the day before Queensberry left that card at the Club! Oscar would still have been remembered as a wit and a dandy, and would have had a niche beside Congreve in the drama. A volume of his aphorisms would have stood creditably on the library shelf with La Rochefoucauld's Maxims. We should have missed the 'Ballad of Reading Gaol' and 'De Profundis'; but he would still have cut a considerable figure in the Dictionary of National Biography, and been read and quoted outside the British Museum reading room.

"As to the 'Ballad' and 'De Profundis,' I think it is greatly to Oscar's credit that, whilst he was sincere and deeply moved when he was protesting against the cruelty of our present system to children and to prisoners generally, he could not write about his own individual share in that suffering with any conviction or sympathy.[11] Except for the passage where he describes his exposure at Clapham Junction, there is hardly a line in 'De Profundis' that he might not have written as a literary feat five years earlier. But in the 'Ballad,' even in borrowing form and melody from Coleridge, he shews that he could pity others when he could not seriously pity himself. And this, I think, may be pleaded against the reproach that he was selfish. Externally, in the ordinary action of life as distinguished from the literary action proper to his genius, he was no doubt sluggish and weak because of his giantism. He ended as an unproductive drunkard and swindler; for the repeated sales of the Daventry plot, in so far as they imposed on the buyers and were not transparent excuses for begging, were undeniably swindles. For all that, he does not appear in his writings a selfish or base-minded man. He is at his worst and weakest in the suppressed[12] part of 'De Profundis'; but in my opinion it had better be published, for several reasons. It explains some of his personal weakness by the stifling narrowness of his daily round, ruinous to a man whose proper place was in a large public life. And its concealment is mischievous because, first, it leads people to imagine all sorts of horrors in a document which contains nothing worse than any record of the squabbles of two touchy idlers; and, second, it is clearly a monstrous thing that Douglas should have a torpedo launched at him and timed to explode after his death. The torpedo is a very harmless squib; for there is nothing in it that cannot be guessed from Douglas's own book; but the public does not know that. By the way, it is rather a humorous stroke of Fate's irony that the son of the Marquis of Queensberry should be forced to expiate his sins by suffering a succession of blows beneath the belt.

[Footnote 11: Superb criticism.]

[Footnote 12: I have said this in my way.]

"Now that you have written the best life of Oscar Wilde, let us have the best life of Frank Harris. Otherwise the man behind your works will go down to posterity[13] as the hero of my very inadequate preface to 'The Dark Lady of the Sonnets.'"

G. BERNARD SHAW.

[Footnote 13: A characteristic flirt of Shaw's humor. He is a great caricaturist and not a portrait-painter.

When he thinks of my Celtic face and aggressive American frankness he talks of me as pugnacious and a pirate: "a Captain Kidd": in his preface to "The Fair Lady of the Sonnets" he praises my "idiosyncratic gift of pity"; says that I am "wise through pity"; then he extols me as a prophet, not seeing that a pitying sage, prophet and pirate constitute an inhuman superman.

I shall do more for Shaw than he has been able to do for me; he is the first figure in my new volume of "Contemporary Portraits." I have portrayed him there at his best, as I love to think of him, and henceforth he'll have to try to live up to my conception and that will keep him, I'm afraid, on strain.

God help me!—G.B.S.]

Friedrich Kerst
Friedrich Nietzsche
Fyodor Dostoyevsky
G.A. Henty
G.K. Chesterton
Gabrielle E. Jackson
Garrett P. Serviss
Gaston Leroux
George A. Warren
George Ade
Geroge Bernard Shaw
George Cary Eggleston
George Durston
George Ebers
George Eliot
George Gissing
George MacDonald
George Meredith
George Orwell
George Sylvester Viereck
George Tucker
George W. Cable
George Wharton James
Gertrude Atherton
Gordon Casserly
Grace E. King
Grace Gallatin
Grace Greenwood
Grant Allen
Guillermo A. Sherwell
Gulielma Zollinger
Gustav Flaubert
H. A. Cody
H. B. Irving
H.C. Bailey
H. G. Wells
H. H. Munro
H. Irving Hancock
H. R. Naylor
H. Rider Haggard
H. W. C. Davis
Haldeman Julius
Hall Caine
Hamilton Wright Mabie
Hans Christian Andersen
Harold Avery
Harold McGrath
Harriet Beecher Stowe
Harry Castlemon
Harry Coghill
Harry Houidini
Hayden Carruth
Helent Hunt Jackson
Helen Nicolay
Hendrik Conscience
Hendy David Thoreau
Henri Barbusse
Henrik Ibsen
Henry Adams
Henry Ford
Henry Frost
Henry James
Henry Jones Ford
Henry Seton Merriman
Henry W Longfellow
Herbert A. Giles
Herbert Carter
Herbert N. Casson
Herman Hesse
Hildegard G. Frey
Homer
Honore De Balzac
Horace B. Day
Horace Walpole
Horatio Alger Jr.
Howard Pyle
Howard R. Garis
Hugh Lofting
Hugh Walpole
Humphry Ward
Ian Maclaren
Inez Haynes Gillmore
Irving Bacheller
Isabel Cecilia Williams
Isabel Hornibrook
Israel Abrahams
Ivan Turgenev
J.G.Austin
J. Henri Fabre
J. M. Barrie
J. M. Walsh
J. Macdonald Oxley
J. R. Miller
J. S. Fletcher
J. S. Knowles
J. Storer Clouston
J. W. Duffield
Jack London
Jacob Abbott
James Allen
James Andrews
James Baldwin
James Branch Cabell
James DeMille
James Joyce
James Lane Allen
James Lane Allen
James Oliver Curwood
James Oppenheim
James Otis
James R. Driscoll
Jane Abbott
Jane Austen
Jane L. Stewart
Janet Aldridge
Jens Peter Jacobsen
Jerome K. Jerome
Jessie Graham Flower
John Buchan
John Burroughs
John Cournos
John F. Kennedy
John Gay
John Glasworthy
John Habberton
John Joy Bell
John Kendrick Bangs
John Milton
John Philip Sousa
John Taintor Foote
Jonas Lauritz Idemil Lie
Jonathan Swift
Joseph A. Altsheler
Joseph Carey
Joseph Conrad
Joseph E. Badger Jr
Joseph Hergesheimer
Joseph Jacobs
Jules Vernes
Julian Hawthrone
Julie A Lippmann
Justin Huntly McCarthy
Kakuzo Okakura
Karle Wilson Baker
Kate Chopin
Kenneth Grahame
Kenneth McGaffey
Kate Langley Bosher
Kate Langley Bosher
Katherine Cecil Thurston
Katherine Stokes
L. A. Abbot
L. T. Meade

L. Frank Baum
Latta Griswold
Laura Dent Crane
Laura Lee Hope
Laurence Housman
Lawrence Beasley
Leo Tolstoy
Leonid Andreyev
Lewis Carroll
Lewis Sperry Chafer
Lilian Bell
Lloyd Osbourne
Louis Hughes
Louis Joseph Vance
Louis Tracy
Louisa May Alcott
Lucy Fitch Perkins
Lucy Maud Montgomery
Luther Benson
Lydia Miller Middleton
Lyndon Orr
M. Corvus
M. H. Adams
Margaret E. Sangster
Margret Howth
Margaret Vandercook
Margaret W. Hungerford
Margret Penrose
Maria Edgeworth
Maria Thompson Daviess
Mariano Azuela
Marion Polk Angellotti
Mark Overton
Mark Twain
Mary Austin
Mary Catherine Crowley
Mary Cole
Mary Hastings Bradley
Mary Roberts Rinehart
Mary Rowlandson
M. Wollstonecraft Shelley
Maud Lindsay
Max Beerbohm
Myra Kelly
Nathaniel Hawthrone
Nicolo Machiavelli
O. F. Walton
Oscar Wilde
Owen Johnson
P.G. Wodehouse
Paul and Mabel Thorne
Paul G. Tomlinson
Paul Severing
Percy Brebner
Percy Keese Fitzhugh
Peter B. Kyne
Plato
Quincy Allen
R. Derby Holmes
R. L. Stevenson
R. S. Ball
Rabindranath Tagore
Rahul Alvares
Ralph Bonehill
Ralph Henry Barbour
Ralph Victor
Ralph Waldo Emmerson
Rene Descartes
Ray Cummings
Rex Beach
Rex E. Beach
Richard Harding Davis
Richard Jefferies
Richard Le Gallienne
Robert Barr
Robert Frost
Robert Gordon Anderson
Robert L. Drake
Robert Lansing
Robert Lynd
Robert Michael Ballantyne
Robert W. Chambers
Rosa Nouchette Carey
Rudyard Kipling
Saint Augustine
Samuel B. Allison
Samuel Hopkins Adams
Sarah Bernhardt
Sarah C. Hallowell
Selma Lagerlof
Sherwood Anderson
Sigmund Freud
Standish O'Grady
Stanley Weyman
Stella Benson
Stella M. Francis
Stephen Crane
Stewart Edward White
Stijn Streuvels
Swami Abhedananda
Swami Parmananda
T. S. Ackland
T. S. Arthur
The Princess Der Ling
Thomas A. Janvier
Thomas A Kempis
Thomas Anderton
Thomas Bailey Aldrich
Thomas Bulfinch
Thomas De Quincey
Thomas Dixon
Thomas H. Huxley
Thomas Hardy
Thomas More
Thornton W. Burgess
U. S. Grant
Upton Sinclair
Valentine Williams
Various Authors
Vaughan Kester
Victor Appleton
Victor G. Durham
Victoria Cross
Virginia Woolf
Wadsworth Camp
Walter Camp
Walter Scott
Washington Irving
Wilbur Lawton
Wilkie Collins
Willa Cather
Willard F. Baker
William Dean Howells
William le Queux
W. Makepeace Thackeray
William W. Walter
William Shakespeare
Winston Churchill
Yei Theodora Ozaki
Yogi Ramacharaka
Young E. Allison
Zane Grey